THE EXECUTIVE GUIDE
TO ASIA-PACIFIC COMMUNICATIONS

ON LINE

ALSO BY DAVID L. JAMES:

Doing Business in Asia:
A Small Business Guide to Success
in the World's Most Dynamic Market

The Executive Guide to Asia-Pacific Communications

DOING BUSINESS ACROSS THE PACIFIC

David L. James

KODANSHA INTERNATIONAL
New York • Tokyo • London

Kodansha America, Inc.
114 Fifth Avenue, New York, New York 10011, U.S.A.

Kodansha International Ltd.
17-14 Otowa 1-chome, Bunkyo-ku, Tokyo 112, Japan

Published in 1995 by Kodansha America, Inc.

LIBRARY OF CONGRESS CATALOGING-IN-PUBLICATION DATA
James, David L., 1933–
    The executive guide to Asia-Pacific communications :
doing business across the Pacific / David L. James.
        p.   cm.
    Includes bibliographical references and index.
    ISBN 1-56836-040-1
    1. Business communication–Asia. 2. Business com-
munication—Pacific Area. 3. Business communication—
Cross-cultural studies.
I. Title.
HF5718.2.A78J36   1995
658.4'5'095—dc20   94-37749

Book design by Laura Lindgren

The text of this book was set in Dante.

Printed in the United States of America

95 96 97 98 99   6 5 4 3 2 1

CONTENTS

1 INTERNATIONAL COMMUNICATIONS DISORDER 5
Coming to terms with the communications barriers that hinder international trade

2 CULTURAL SIGNPOSTS 11
Cultural distinctions that provide the key to successful communications in the Asia-Pacific region

3 BASIC COMMUNICATIONS GUIDELINES 29
Guidelines that will help international businesspeople avoid communications pitfalls in the Asia-Pacific region and build productive relationships there

4 THE COUNTRY CONNECTION 51
Important background facts and characteristics of the fifteen key countries covered by this book

Australia
Canada
China
Hong Kong
Indonesia
Japan
Malaysia
New Zealand

The Philippines
Singapore
South Korea
Taiwan
Thailand
United States
Vietnam

5 LANGUAGE LESSONS 131
Characteristics of the principal languages of the Asia-Pacific region, and ways to lower the language barriers

Acknowledgments

I AM GRATEFUL TO many friends and colleagues who contributed insights, observations, and ideas on Asia-Pacific cultures, communications, and business practices during the writing of this book. I am also grateful to dozens of Asia-Pacific executives and government officials who gave valuable time to be interviewed during my research and to executives throughout the region who completed and returned my survey questionnaire. In particular, I am grateful to the executives who gave permission for their letterheads and business cards to be used as illustrations. Names of other persons and companies are mentioned with express permission or are derived from publicly reported accounts believed to be accurate.

Special thanks go to my wife, Sheila, for an unceasing stream of thoughtful ideas and constructive suggestions in the course of my writing, and to my business colleague, Robert B. Hewett, a longtime "Asia hand" with a distinguished career in journalism and education in the region, whose review of the manuscript produced many contributions that helped to assure the book's accuracy. Special thanks also go to Gordon Wise, my editor at Kodansha America, who encouraged me to write this book and contributed many ideas that sharpened its focus and broadened its potential interest and usefulness for Asia-Pacific executives and others. Notwithstanding such fine help, any errors in the book are my own.

Thanks also go to the following individuals, who provided information or thoughts that were especially helpful: Will Bailey, Lt. Col. Jo Ann Ball, Jim Becker, Pam Becker, Cao Thi Bích Vân, Dave Erdman, David Heenan, Consul-General of Japan Kensaku Hogen, Adam James, Brian James, Paul Lenihan, Win Lenihan, Victor Hao Li, Reed Maurer, Leonard Pearlin, John Reed, Russell Woo, Sharon Woo, Scott Young, and Zhu Lanye.

THE EXECUTIVE GUIDE
TO ASIA-PACIFIC COMMUNICATIONS

INTRODUCTION

A TIMELY TOPIC

This world does not need more statements, and it does not need more communications that travel in only one direction. Rather, the world needs communications that are received, understood, and returned with goodwill and the promise of continued interaction. It needs communications that will build enduring relationships. These communications must reach the mind, and sometimes the heart, of the receiver. Words are not enough. The sender must communicate in a way that strikes a responsive chord in the receiver and gains the receiver's attention.

As the world grapples with the reality of a global marketplace, governments are giving abundant attention to the structural impediments to international trade and investment. The trading nations struggled for years to reduce tariffs and duties on goods and services through the mechanism of the General Agreement on Tariffs and Trade (GATT), first implemented in 1962 and concluded in 1993. The European Economic Community is breaking down centuries-old trading barriers. China and the countries of the former Soviet Union are rapidly adopting economic reforms that promote international trade and investment. Canada and the United States have reduced trade barriers with their Free Trade Agreement; Canada, the United States, and Mexico have signed a similar agreement, the North American Free Trade Agreement (NAFTA). The Association of Southeast Asian Nations (ASEAN)—Brunei, Indonesia, Malaysia, the Philippines, Singapore, and Thailand—works to reduce barriers among its members. And there are efforts to create a broader Asian trade bloc.

However, while governments labor to reduce tariffs, duties, and other structural barriers to the improvement of trade, they give little official attention to reducing the most pervasive barriers of all: communication obstacles that inhibit the formation and efficiency of international transactions.

This book is about communications in the Asia-Pacific region. It is for international businesspeople—executives, managers, administrators, professionals, and their assistants and executive secretaries. It is for travelers on international airlines or the Internet. It is for everyone who wants to participate in the dynamism of the world's fastest-growing economies and who recognizes that the ability to communicate effectively in the Asia-Pacific region is the key to success there.

Here are some of the questions that international businesspeople ask most often about Asia-Pacific communications:

▲ How do you start off on the right track with someone from a different culture in the region, or a different country?
▲ How can your communications help build a solid business relationship with people from another culture?
▲ Once you have an established relationship, what are the most efficient ways to communicate in the region?
▲ Should brochures and marketing materials be translated into another language?
▲ How do you maintain efficient communications during an overseas trip in the region? Should you take a notebook computer? Can a modem or a cellular phone be used overseas?

This book answers these questions and many more. It examines the cultural and national makeup of the principal countries of the region and gives the reader the substantive knowledge needed to understand how people communicate in each country. Cultural issues are explored to give insight into the reasons behind differing communications practices. Practical tips are set forth in boxes throughout the book to highlight and further illustrate points covered in the text. And the Resource Files toward the end of the book contain more detailed information to aid Asia-Pacific communications.

I worked in the Asia-Pacific region for over twenty years as an executive of multinational corporations that have diverse activities there. I served on a team of advisers to one Southeast Asian country and as a diplomatic representative of another. I was also the director of business programs at the East-West Center, a research and education institution in Honolulu established by the U.S. Congress in 1960 to promote better relations between the United States and Asia-Pacific countries.

In preparing this book, I interviewed dozens of Asia-Pacific business executives. In addition, I conducted a survey of Asia-Pacific business communications practices with a questionnaire sent to over 400 executives in the region. This book is the result of my experience and research.

I

INTERNATIONAL COMMUNICATIONS DISORDER

On any given day, countless business executives sit behind their desks around the world planning business strategies, lining up sales calls, and designing products and services. Too many of them concentrate on markets that are familiar and comfortable—their own domestic markets. When they do target international markets, they usually go only for ones of a common culture and language. These executives do not know how to go about communicating with potential customers, clients, and partners in "foreign" countries. They suffer from what I call ICD—International Communications Disorder.

Business executives throughout the world suffer from ICD, but there is no trading area on earth in which the ailment is more prevalent than in the Asia-Pacific region. Here is a snapshot of some typical questions and comments of ICD sufferers in the Asia-Pacific region:

▲ "How do I phrase a letter to someone in China? Do I send it by fax? Mail? Courier? Do I need to get it translated into Chinese? Should I just pick up the phone?"

▲ "I met that guy at a trade show in Tokyo. He was very friendly. Should I address my letter to him as 'Dear Hiroshi' or 'Dear Mr. Morito'?"

▲ "I'm from Bangkok, and I just do not understand those Americans. What do I have to do to get the attention of their top officers?"

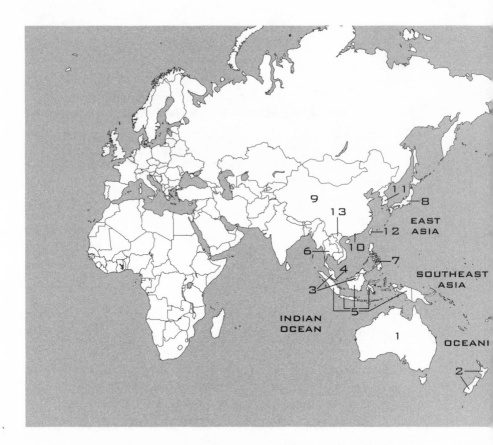

- ▲ "How do I arrange to see the people I need to see on my trip next month to Sydney, Singapore, Seoul, and Tokyo? Do I need introductions? Do I send letters? How much notice do they need?"
- ▲ An American: "Those Koreans. They're just like the Japanese, aren't they?"
- ▲ A Chinese: "Those Australians. They're just like the Americans, aren't they?"

International Communications Disorder is a serious business problem in a world that is now a global marketplace. With trade barriers coming down and market demand stimulated by an "information explosion" that puts current world events and lifestyles on television screens in even the most remote village, ICD amounts to lost business. Modern communications technology is actually several steps ahead of international business. Technology has provided sophisticated tools of

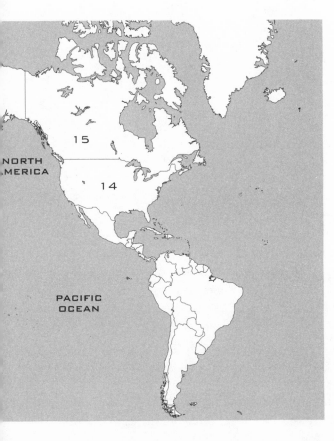

Countries featured in
this book:

1. Australia
2. New Zealand
3. Malaysia
4. Singapore
5. Indonesia
6. Thailand
7. The Philippines
8. Japan
9. China
10. Hong Kong
11. South Korea
12. Taiwan
13. Vietnam
14. United States
15. Canada

communication: telephones and fax machines are available almost everywhere; cellular phones add communications capability outside the office in most cities; and computers and modems can transmit complex data over the Internet, the "information highway." But international business struggles to build effective cross-cultural business relationships; it struggles to connect seller and buyer.

ICD IN THE ASIA-PACIFIC REGION

Let's take a closer look at the Asia-Pacific region. It is characterized by vast distances, a diversity of languages and cultures, and in many areas an inadequate infrastructure—poor roads, inferior telecommunications, and deficient government services. Its principal countries include those of Oceania (Australia and New Zealand), Southeast Asia (Malaysia, Singapore, Indonesia, Thailand, the Philippines), East Asia (Japan, China, Hong Kong, South Korea, Taiwan), and North

America (the United States and Canada). Others play a small but growing role in the region's trade: Mexico, Peru, Chile, Russia, Vietnam, Papua New Guinea, and various Pacific island nations. There is also the small but oil-rich nation of Brunei in Southeast Asia. In all, these countries span two-thirds of the earth's surface and are home to half of its people. China alone, with 1.2 billion inhabitants, is home to one-fifth of the world's population.

The terms *East* and *West,* and *Asians, Easterners,* and *Westerners* can be misleading in this diverse mix of nations and cultures. They originated in Europe from a geographic perspective but are now used largely in cultural and political contexts. Today, the related terms *Easterners* and *Far East* are seldom used, and the geographic location of Australia and New Zealand (culturally "Western" nations) in the "East" seems anomalous. This book primarily uses only two of these terms, *Asians* and *Westerners,* and uses them in a cultural, not geographic, context. Indeed, many "Asians" live in "Western" countries, and many "Westerners" live in "Asian" countries. And although there are geographic references in the book to two of the three major segments of Asia (Southeast Asia and East Asia), there is no mention of the important third segment: South Asia, consisting of India, Bangladesh, Pakistan, and Sri Lanka. South Asia, although one of the world's most important regions, is not yet a major participant in the Asia-Pacific economic region.

In geographic terms, the Asia-Pacific region is so vast that getting from one location to another presents enormous logistical and time problems under the best of circumstances. A nonstop flight from Sydney to Tokyo takes eleven hours; one from Hong Kong to Los Angeles takes fourteen hours. Telephone connections are often excellent, but east-west time zones can be an inconvenience. When it's 2:00 P.M. in Vancouver, it's 5:00 A.M. the next day in Bangkok. When it's noon in Jakarta, it's 9:00 P.M. the preceding day in San Francisco.

Despite geographic challenge and cultural diversity, the economies of the Asia-Pacific region have grown at twice the rate of those of the rest of the world in recent years. Growth rates in Southeast Asia, with the exception of the Philippines, have exceeded 6 percent per annum for several years running. China's overall growth has exceeded 10 percent, and in the industrial sector has been over 20 percent. Japan's mature economy has grown at around 3 percent in recent years, but its external trade and investment have fueled more rapid growth throughout the region. Japan and China are now the second and third largest economies in the world, after the United States.

Moreover, growth in the region might be even stronger if communications were less difficult. Compare the Asia-Pacific region with the European region. Distances are often double, as are time zone differences to North America. A nonstop flight from Tokyo to Kuala Lumpur is about nine hours, whereas one from Rome to Paris is only two hours. The time zone difference between New York City and London is five hours; between Los Angeles and Bangkok, it is nine hours.

The languages and cultures of the Asia-Pacific region are not necessarily more diverse than those of the European region, but they are less commonly understood. Most European businesspeople speak at least two other languages. Most Asia-Pacific businesspeople speak only one other language. And most Americans speak no language other than English. Moreover, Europeans are relatively comfortable in their international communications despite a long history of wars, confrontations, and competition. The reason is that Europeans have been interacting with one another for much longer. Their civilizations are not older (China claims to have the oldest continuing civilization on earth), but they were more adventurous. Over the centuries they were the source of more exploration, conquering, and trading than any other region on earth. In contrast, most of the nations of the Asia-Pacific region were isolated or insular, leading to the development of independent and unique cultures and traditions.

If business communications in the Asia-Pacific region are more difficult than in the European region, why are Asia-Pacific economies growing more rapidly? In part it is because European economies are more mature. It is also because the economies of Eastern Europe and the former Soviet Union were fettered until recently by bureaucratic central planning and impractical ideological goals. However, with the European Economic Community now a reality, and with the Soviet system now adopting market-oriented economic reforms, the region has the potential to improve its performance.

HELP FOR ICD SUFFERERS

This book is designed to help businesspeople in the Asia-Pacific region overcome ICD—those lapses in communications between businesspeople operating in the region that hamper successful performance. International Communications Disorder is found in all forms of communication—letters and faxes, face-to-face meetings, telephone conversations, and sales promotion efforts. It can be active or passive, arising from action or inaction. It can be an offensive statement made in a letter or over the telephone, or it can be the failure to observe a common courtesy or protocol. It can be a simple and forgivable matter, such as failure to use the correct honorific in addressing a letter, or a complex and subtle matter, such as belittling the status of a senior official, a slight that will never be forgotten.

This book provides insight and practical guidance that will help you identify and prevent instances of International Communications Disorder. It will help you understand the cultural distinctions of different countries around the region and know how to deal with them. The book describes the communicating practices of individual countries. It reviews the various methods and techniques of communicating today and in the future—by mail, fax, courier, e-mail, telephone, and face to face. And it gives practical advice on how to make your communications more effective: what works for others, what to do or not do, how to avoid mistakes and gaffes that lose business, and how to communicate in ways that get, maintain, and expand business.

The fourteen principal trading countries of the Asia-Pacific region are covered, plus one that is just emerging, Vietnam. In all, they are as follows:

Australia	The Philippines
Canada	Singapore
China	South Korea
Hong Kong	Taiwan
Indonesia	Thailand
Japan	United States
Malaysia	Vietnam
New Zealand	

In acquiring the skills and knowledge for successful communicating in the Asia-Pacific region, it is best to start with the basics: the most substantive cultural characteristics of the people who make up the region.

2

CULTURAL SIGNPOSTS

Case One

The vice president, marketing, of a medium-sized American manufacturer wrote to three South Korean wholesale distributors, attention "President." He had obtained the names of the distributors from a reliable American colleague who had done business in Asia for a long time. He explained in each letter what a terrific product his company made, how it was better than any similar product on the market, and how he himself was dedicated to developing a substantial market presence for the product in South Korea. He went on for three pages and enclosed colorful brochures. At the end of the letter, he asked if the distributor would be interested in handling the product.

Three weeks went by without a word from any of the distributors. He sent a copy of the letter to each of them with a short cover letter asking for a response. None ever came.

Case Two

A Japanese business executive, head of the Chicago office of a Japanese bank, met with an executive of a small American telephone equipment company that had developed a new communications technology and was looking for major financing of several million dollars. The American followed up by providing substantial details on the company's prod-

11

ucts, financial condition, and the new technology. The Japanese responded that several departments of the bank's Tokyo office would need to examine the information.

After several weeks, having heard nothing from the Japanese, the American went elsewhere for the financing. The company thrived, and its new financial backer had an important new client. The Japanese and the American went their separate ways.

Case Three

On their first meeting in Jakarta to discuss a proposed joint venture, the president of an Indonesian company and his counterpart, the president of an Australian company, exchanged business cards. The Indonesian's card was edged in gold and listed three academic degrees after his name. The Australian's card simply stated his name, title, company, address, and telephone number. Thinking the Indonesian was pretentious, the Australian cut straight to the point, asking for direct comments on the terms of the proposed deal. The Indonesian ignored the question and asked if he was enjoying his visit to Jakarta.

The meeting soon adjourned, and the joint venture never got off the ground.

Examples of International Communications Disorder are prevalent in each of these cases. In Case One, the American failed to use the names of the people he wrote to. His letter was too long. He used too much immodest puffery. He came to the point of his letter only at the end. He made no attempt to establish a common relationship by reference to, or introduction by, someone known to the addressee. To make matters worse, he was a vice president presuming to speak directly to a president. All of this might have been overlooked by another American but not by a South Korean.

In Case Two, the Japanese indicated to the American that a decision on financing could not be made until a number of corporate bureaucracies at the Tokyo head office reviewed the proposal. After the meeting the Japanese let several weeks go by without communicating with the American. To an entrepreneurial American from a small company, typically impatient, the delay indicated that the bank was unable to make decisions quickly enough to meet his company's needs.

In Case Three, the Australian took offense at the Indonesian's business card, which appeared to flaunt his academic achievements. He reacted by demanding an immediate discussion of the business at hand. The Indonesian was offended by the Australian's unwillingness to establish a social relationship before discussing business.

It is impossible to catalogue all the situations in which an international business executive can stumble in his or her communications. The best way to lay a foundation that will help avoid mistakes and gaffes in the Asia-Pacific region, and to achieve successful communications there, is to understand the region's cultural signposts. This chapter addresses those signposts.

INDIVIDUALISM AND COLLECTIVISM

While it is dangerous to stereotype people or groups of people, it remains true that there are two principal culture groupings in the world, individualist cultures and collectivist cultures. Asians tend to be collectivists. Westerners tend to be individualists. Comparing the two helps us to recognize this cultural signpost.

Individualist cultures predominate in the United States, Australia, Canada, New Zealand, and parts of Western Europe. In these cultures group goals are usually subordinated to personal goals; independence and personal achievement are valued highly; discipline is often loose. The individual is the core of the social unit. People in these cultures cherish their freedoms—the right to free speech, the right to protest. They value candor and directness. They are accustomed to making independent decisions and taking independent action. They strive for personal accomplishment, and they are eager to stand out from the crowd.

Collectivist cultures predominate in Asia, Eastern Europe, Africa, and Latin America, where personal goals are often subordinated to group goals. The family and the employment organization are the core social units; duty, harmony, politeness, and modesty are very important; discipline is high. Individuals are not encouraged to stand out from the crowd. As Confucius taught, "The nail that protrudes is hammered down."

Consistent with these broad characteristics, individualists tend to be the ones who excel in inventing things, and collectivists tend to be the ones who excel in activities that call for group effort, such as manufacturing and servicing. On the psychological level, the emphasis on harmony in collectivist cultures may make Asians tend to be more intuitive and subtle in their thoughts and actions than Westerners, who often seem to be more logical and linear in their responses and reasoning. Asians, for example, pay more attention to relationships than to contracts, while Westerners pay more attention to schedules than to social protocol.

The most significant feature of collectivist cultures for international businesspeople is the emphasis on family and group ties. This feature largely accounts for the close and often exclusive affiliations of local businesses in Asia. Take for example the Japanese *keiretsu,* groups of corporations such as Mitsubishi or Sumitomo that are bound together by cross-stockholdings and do significant amounts of business chiefly with their corporate siblings, exchanging information and cooperating in joint ventures. Or *chaebols,* the large conglomerates of South Korea. Similarly, vast networks of Chinese family-owned businesses operate in Taiwan, Hong Kong, and elsewhere in Asia.

This emphasis on family and group ties also accounts for the importance to Asians of long-term personal relationships. Whereas Westerners, especially Americans, are often compulsive about getting down to business right away, sealing a deal with a written contract, and riding off in a cloud of dust to confront the next challenge, most Asians will want to develop a personal relationship with a business partner before making an agreement of any significance. Even then it can take years before they will feel that a solid business relationship exists.

An American export-import executive from Seattle who had done business in Asia for more than twenty years once arranged for a Japanese friend—with whom he had had a successful business relationship for a long time—to send a letter of introduction to another Japanese, with whom the American also hoped to do business. His Japanese friend wrote, "Although we have known Mr. Smith *only seven years,* we have found him to be an honorable and trustworthy person."

Recognizing cultural signposts is one thing, but it often can be difficult in practice for a member of another cultural group to take those signposts as guides.

Westerners who acknowledge a collectivist signpost often have difficulty heeding it when it conflicts with an individualist value. For example, an American might know that he is breaching the harmony of his relationship with an Asian by criticizing the Asian's performance in a letter that will be read by others, but the American will believe that it is more important to be open and forthright in his business dealings.

> ### ICD Prevention Tip—Executive Secretaries and Assistants
>
> *Secretaries and assistants can help avert cultural conflict, whether you are Western or Asian. In addition to alerting you to cultural differences, they can maintain up-to-date files of important information about your business contacts—not only addresses and telephone and fax numbers but other information that will help build strong business relationships: a contact's corporate connections, names of family members, personal interests, dates of personal or business anniversaries, and significant social or business events involving you and a contact.*

HIERARCHY

A second important cultural signpost in the Asia-Pacific region is hierarchy in business relationships. Here there are significant Asian-Western distinctions, with people from collectivist cultures tending to respect authority and status more than people from individualist cultures. There are also important distinctions based on national cultures, with some nations, such as Japan and South Korea, tending to emphasize discipline and rank to a greater degree than personal freedoms. Confucius and other Asian philosophers whose views have come to be accepted in Asia, and especially East Asia, taught that people are *unequal*. Consequently, in contrast to Western cultures, people in Asia are often willing to accept their fate and their status in society. They are also often less inclined to seek personal recognition or reach for higher status. These attitudes, coupled with emphasis on the recognition of elders and authority figures in a family or group, result in Asians giving greater weight to hierarchy in their business dealings than Westerners normally do. For example, Asians will want Westerners to establish clearly the titles and positions they hold in their organizations. Asians need to understand these matters before any business can be done.

Accordingly, business cards are always exchanged in the Asia-Pacific region, because they establish group identity and status. It is also customary, and a sign of respect, for a business executive to have one side of his or her business card printed in the language of the country visited. An executive might therefore have several cards made up before traveling, in the language of each of the countries being visited. For the same reasons, letters of introduction from someone who knows both parties (such as a banker, consultant, or business associate) are important; proper introductions are needed to establish identity and status. When Westerners request appointments by writing or faxing an Asian who does not already know them, they often receive no response because the Asian considers them outsiders. To an Asian, no obligation is owed an outsider.

Finally, Westerners need to be sensitive to the relative status of people. If a Westerner accidentally gives equal or greater deference to an Asian executive's underling, the executive will be offended. Also, Westerners will find that Asians work within well-defined roles. If a Westerner asks an Asian engineer to comment on a marketing plan, the engineer will probably not respond or will be uncomfortable in doing so.

> **ICD Prevention Tip—
> Business Cards**
>
> *Although cards can be printed for you in the local language on short notice after your arrival in most Asia-Pacific destination cities, it is best to have them printed before departing on your trip to be certain that the translation is correct and the printing well done.*

DISCIPLINE

Asians are often appalled at the dissension and lack of conformity that can be displayed by Westerners. Westerners talk back, protest, and openly disagree with political leaders, colleagues, and even their employers. Western management theories even commend contention in the workplace, while Asian practice, especially when influenced by Confucian principles of duty, respect, and loyalty, is to carry out orders without question. By Western standards, Asians appear to be wonderful citizens and employees. They are law-abiding and supportive. Asian workers often line up in perfectly ordered ranks each morning to sing a company song, recite a statement of commitment, or receive the day's orders, and their activities are characterized by military precision.

Indeed, military discipline is seen as a strong characteristic of Asia-Pacific business. In recent years military theories have been successfully applied by Asians and others to business management and negotiations. *A Book of Five Rings,* written in the early 1600s by a Japanese samurai named Miyamoto Musashi, recently enjoyed renewed popularity as a metaphor for business success in both Japan and the West. The book is a collection of instructions in the use of the sword in combat, but it is also seen as a thoughtful strategic analysis of the struggles that underlie every level of human interaction.

In communications and business dealings, Asians can expect to find Westerners spontaneous and contentious, sometimes apparently thoughtless or inconsiderate, and often lacking a strategic approach to the business at hand. Westerners can expect to find Asians reticent until an official position is approved by their superiors, hesitant to make decisions on their own, and often obsessed with long-term strategic planning.

DECISION MAKING

A fourth important cultural signpost lies in how decisions are made by businesspeople in the Asia-Pacific region. In keeping with collectivism, decision making in Asian cultures is much more consultative than in Western cultures. Typically, any major decision in an Asian family or group is made only after wide review and discussion by all persons concerned.

This pattern has major implications for Westerners who communicate with Asians. It means that a written response from an Asian, if a decision is required, will take longer than a Westerner would think necessary. Before responding, the Asian will review the issues and cor-

> ### ICD Prevention Tip for Westerners— Response Time
>
> *Don't press for an early response from an Asian. Expect that response time will expand significantly in relation to the size of his or her organization and the complexity of the issues you raise. Also, don't try to get a decision over the telephone. Even if adequate time has passed and a decision has been reached, an Asian will normally want to communicate the decision in writing (to avoid any misunderstanding), and at a time agreed on by others within the organization.*

respondence with various interested colleagues and departments in his organization.

During negotiation meetings between Asians and Westerners, the Westerners should not be surprised if their Asian counterparts call for frequent recesses to consult privately or to contact colleagues outside the room or at headquarters. Asians often take copious notes in meetings so that the progress of discussions can be reviewed with colleagues. Sometimes meetings will break off for days on end while Asians consult and Westerners cool their heels. Westerners may find this decision-making process protracted, but it tends to produce sound and easily executed decisions. All implications and repercussions will have been carefully considered, and the means of implementing the decisions will have been well thought out.

> ### ICD Prevention Tip—Negotiations
>
> *Asians should make their review process as efficient as possible. At meetings away from home, each side should arrange for a separate meeting room to which they can adjourn. Westerners should prepare for a long stay. Take reading materials, audiotapes, and at least one change of clothing.*

THE ROLE OF EDUCATION AND EDUCATORS

In Case Three at the beginning of this chapter, the Indonesian's distinguished academic credentials not only came across as pretentious to his Australian counterpart but also failed to impress him. It would probably have been the same if the Australian had been an American or another Westerner. Westerners respect education, but they simply do not place as high a value on it as do Asians.

There are two reasons why Asians value academic accomplishment so greatly. First, in economically undeveloped countries (which still constitute much of Asia), academic success is seen as high achievement. There is often little else to value. In communities that are small and poor, few people attain much economic power. Gifted people excel primarily through academic achievement. Second, academics are considered an important resource for self-improvement. Professors, teachers, and other intellectual leaders are revered for the hope they hold for future generations. This is especially true in countries where Confucian philosophies prevail—that is, in most of East Asia. (See "Religion and Philosophy.")

Many Asians spend extraordinary amounts of time and effort in schools. South Korea leads the pack. Its children spend 240 days in school every year, attending six days a week and eight hours a day—compare this with the United States's averages of 180 days per year,

five days a week, and six hours a day. However, the style of education in Asia is different from that in the West. Because of the cultural importance of hard work, duty, obedience, and group connections, the Asian educational process is highly diligent but somewhat methodical. Students are encouraged to learn by rote. The assertions of professors and teachers are seldom questioned, and imaginative thinking is often discouraged. As a consequence, Asians are often knowledgeable on many subjects, and eager to take that learning further, but are sometimes resistant to new ideas. At college and graduate school levels, students who get into the better schools by dint of talent, hard work, or connections often relax their efforts after admission.

In the West, where freedom of expression rides high and the thinking of philosophers such as John Stuart Mill (who taught that excellence emerges in a free marketplace of ideas) persists, students are encouraged to challenge their professors and their professors' doctrines. The Western style seems to favor the student who is naturally excellent and diligent, but students with less ability can fall to the side and probably not gain as much from their education as their Asian counterparts.

THE ROLE OF GOVERNMENT

In keeping with their collectivist cultures, the governments of Asian countries play a supportive and developmental role for their people, not just a regulatory or supervisory one. Accordingly, Asian governments are highly active in the economic and private sectors of their countries. In contrast to most Western governments, they are hands-on in their dealings with business, and relations between government and business tend to be closer. It is this collaborative role that contributed to Japan's rapid economic growth and led to the label "Japan Inc." The governments of Singapore, South Korea, and Indonesia play similar collaborative roles with business, strongly influencing the economic success of their countries.

Of course, Western governments also involve themselves extensively in the regulation of business, but deep suspicion and resentment underlie the relations between business and government. A favorite oxymoron in the United States, and one that can be counted on to bring a laugh among American businesspeople at an appropriate moment, is the parodied comment, "I am from the government, and I am here to help you!"

Individualism is the root of Western businesspeople's antipathy toward government. By and large Westerners do not want government help, and they certainly do not want government interference. Western business interests normally resist strongly any efforts by legislators, bureaucrats, and courts to inhibit their activities, and they accept help only grudgingly. An example of their resistance is found in the recent efforts of the U.S. telecommunications industry to elude government regulation in the course of developing "communications superhighways." A comprehensive battle is being waged to put together massive mergers and strategic alliances in an industry that has long been highly regulated, and in the face of antitrust laws that not so many years ago resulted in the breakup of the American Telephone and

> **ICD Prevention Tip—Introductions**
>
> *In arranging letters of introduction for a trip to an Asian country, a Western businessperson can look to the government trade offices of the country visited and to the trade offices there of his government. Also, letters of introduction from highly placed government officials in his own country will carry considerable weight in the Asian country, perhaps even more than those from business executives.*

Telegraph Company (AT&T) into nine separate corporations. By contrast, in Singapore, Japan, and other Asian countries, governments are valued, active participants in the race to establish leading positions in the "Information Age."

One consequence of the closer relationship between government and business in Asian countries is that Asian government trade offices can be of more service to foreign businesspeople than Western government trade offices. For example, an American businessperson can establish more valuable contacts with Japanese firms through an office of the Japan External Trade Organization (JETRO) than a Japanese can establish with American firms through an office of the U.S. Department of Commerce. Another consequence is that Asian bureaucrats will be involved in business transactions in their countries at an earlier stage than Western bureaucrats. It is therefore often necessary for Western business executives to meet directly with Asian bureaucrats in connection with a business transaction (for example, to obtain government clearances and approvals), usually in the company of an Asian partner. Westerners are often surprised by the extent of this bureaucratic involvement but are also often pleased to discover a positive, cooperative attitude on the part of government officials. When doing business in Western countries, Asians will probably have much less to do with government officials.

> **ICD Prevention Tip— Government Contacts**
>
> *When dealing with government officials in another country, Asian or Western, the best strategy is to leave all direct communications to your local partners and representatives. They will have invaluable knowledge of the formalities and political traditions involved.*

ETHNIC AND NATIONAL IDENTITIES

Despite the rapid emergence of the "Global Village," where satellite television and international trade bring each of us into daily contact with peoples and cultures all over the world, we live in an age in which ethnic and national identity is strongly felt. There is a shocking dark side to this. While one would now think that people understand and get along with one another better, there are seemingly mindless, and often bloody, confrontations all around the world. Serbs, Croats, and Muslims fight to control territory in Bosnia, Catholic republicans and

Protestant loyalists struggle against each other in Northern Ireland, Arabs and Jews confront one another in the Middle East, Hindus and Muslims fight in various places in South Asia, and ethnic and tribal warfare persists in Africa. Newly independent nations in Eastern Europe and the former Soviet Union squabble domestically and among themselves, competing for resources and influence, and struggling to adopt economic and political reforms. Separatist movements resurface, as in Quebec Province, Canada. Ultraconservative groups, such as the neo-Nazis in Germany, appear to be gaining strength.

It is interesting that few of the globe's current trouble spots are in the Asia-Pacific region. This may be because strong economic growth serves as a palliative. For example, the Chinese community in Malaysia, which rioted in the 1960s over government measures designed to transfer some of the economic power held by Chinese-Malaysians over to native Malays, is going about business as usual—and did so throughout the 1970s and 1980s—notwithstanding the continuance of pro-Malay measures. With Malaysia's strong overall economic growth, it seems there is plenty of prosperity for everyone.

However, the signpost to be noted here is that ethnic and national identity cannot be ignored in international business communications. Rather, it is more important than ever. Everyone seeks recognition—his or her own place in the sun. Perhaps this is because there is now no place to hide in this shrinking world laid increasingly bare under the microscope of the international news media.

Ethnic identity is a complicated issue. While Koreans and Japanese are each quite homogeneous, Chinese and Malays consist of many subgroups. In Indonesia there are over 300 identifiable ethnic groups, virtually all of Malay stock but many of them strikingly different by nature. For example, the Batak people of north-central Sumatra tend to be intellectual and proud, sometimes with volatile tempers. They are normally more direct and open than most Indonesians. The Javanese people of central Java are more indirect and deferential. They excel in entertaining and serving, and many are professional servants.

But such differences are not entirely geographic. The Chinese, for example, have one of the most extensive ethnic networks in the world. Held together by a collectivist nature, a strong resistance to absorption by other cultures, and a common written language (albeit with many spoken dialects, some of which may not be easily understood by a speaker of another dialect), these linkages have endured for centuries. Not only are there communities outside mainland China—such as Taiwan, Hong Kong, and Singapore—that are predominantly Chinese but there are also substantial Chinese communities in, to name a few places, Malaysia, Indonesia, Thailand, Vietnam, and the major cities of North America. Moreover, overseas Chinese control significant segments of business in Indonesia, Malaysia, and elsewhere where they are an ethnic minority. Owing to these ethnic linkages, Chinese from different countries who otherwise have no direct relationship nevertheless communicate well with one another. This is especially evident in international business, and they certainly maintain the most far-reaching and cohesive network in the Asia-Pacific region.

> **ICD Prevention Tip—Connections**
>
> *If you are ethnic Chinese, look for opportunities to communicate with Chinese businesspeople in other countries. If not, while you will never become a full-fledged member of the clan, you will still tap into an important network. Be sure to ask your Chinese colleagues to introduce you to other Chinese businesspeople.*

Ethnic identity is also particularly important to the Japanese and Koreans. Their overseas networks are not as extensive as those of the Chinese, but they are just as cohesive, possibly even more so because they have not been overseas as long.

When it comes to national identity, an international businessperson needs to know that a letter to a South Korean in Seoul goes to the Republic of Korea (the ROK), not the Democratic People's Republic of Korea (which is North Korea), and that a letter to a person in Taipei goes to the Republic of China (the ROC), not the People's Republic of China (which is mainland China). Feelings of nationalism are intense in these countries. A mistake here can be a

> **ICD Prevention Tip—Ethnic Sensitivities**
>
> *Do not assume that an association with an ethnic Chinese will carry weight in non-Chinese circles. Caution: In Indonesia and Thailand, it is common for ethnic Chinese to have names in the language of their adopted country; it is not always easy for a foreigner to know if a person is an ethnic Chinese.*

serious insult. Likewise, a New Zealander hates to be confused with an Australian, and vice versa. And a Canadian certainly does not want to be taken for an American; the Yanks are OK, but living next door to them is like living in the shadow of a rich relative.

There are also important regional identities within larger countries. While a foreigner will be forgiven for overlooking them, points can be made in demonstrating a sensitivity to them. In the United States, people who live in the middle of the country—the Midwest—are considered more conservative and protectionist, less interested in international affairs, than those who live in the large metropolitan areas of the east and west coasts. In Australia people from Melbourne are considered to be conservative, those from Sydney to be liberal. In the Philippines people from Cebu are thought to be better at business pursuits than people from Manila. These differentiations obtain in various ways and to various degrees throughout the Asia-Pacific region.

Another side to ethnic and national identity—sometimes negative, sometimes positive—is that memories often persist. For example, deep resentments are held toward the Japanese throughout the Asia-Pacific region as a result of atrocities committed during World War II. This is especially true in Korea, China, and Southeast Asia. Fortunately, however, the passage of time and Japan's own economic strength (despite recent reversals) have erased much of this stigma. Americans, on the other hand, are quite popular as a result of their intervention in the war, even among the Japanese, who believe they were well treated following Japan's surrender. There are also deep resentments held against the Chinese in a number of countries, because of the economic power and influence they wield. This is especially true in Indonesia, Malaysia, and Thailand, where ethnic Chinese control large corporations and have extensive holdings of property and other assets.

RELIGION AND PHILOSOPHY

Finally, there are the cultural signposts of religion and philosophy. These do not help you much to distinguish collectivists and individualists or to identify specific ethnic groups and nationalities. Religions and philosophies are too diverse and ubiquitous for that. For example, in South Korea about 20 percent of the population are Buddhist, 21 percent are of various denominations of Christianity, and another 5 percent are Taoist and Confucian. In the United States, although more than 80 percent of the population are Christian, there are over 200 religious denominations. Roman Catholics constitute the largest single denomination, with over 58 million members. Protestants of various denominations number over 86 million. Among non-Christians, there are about 6 million Jews. Nonetheless, the broad signposts of religion and philosophy help to clarify or reinforce your observations of other cultural signposts, and heeding them broadens your understanding of people in another country.

Confucian philosophy helps to explain the strong work ethic and collectivist traditions of East Asia. Confucius lived in China in the sixth century B.C. and founded a body of

> **ICD Prevention Tip—
> Religious Sensitivities**
>
> *Westerners tend to view religion as a matter of personal belief; Asians tend to view it as one of individual identity. In much of Asia one of the first questions that a visitor might be asked by a new acquaintance is what his or her religion is. A Westerner might consider this to be prying, but to an Asian it is simply a collectivist's need to identify people in terms of their relationships within society.*

philosophy that spread throughout Asia, being incorporated into the fabric of life of East Asia and into many of its religions. More of an ethical theorist than a spiritual leader, Confucius discerned a pattern of relationships between ruler and subject, parents and children, husband and wife, and student and teacher. He was not interested in life after death or in mystical beliefs. His theories focused on social order and were based on notions of compassion, etiquette, duty, loyalty, and trust.

Confucianism holds that the family unit is the root of social stability and political order. It teaches that a person's identity is that of his or her family or group. In addition, it teaches that one's quest in life is to improve the human condition through hard work and self-cultivation for the benefit of one's family or group. It is in this connection that education is viewed as the key to human development.

There is much evidence of Confucian philosophy in Asian business practices. The training and education of employees, for example, is continual. Also, employers and employees tend to accept a strong commitment to each other, many people working for only one employer for their entire careers. Japanese employers are famous for retaining their employees through thick and thin, although recent tough economic times have forced many employers to lay off workers.

One reason that East Asians are so comfortable and successful in the business world may be that Confucianism also teaches that the ultimate meaning of life is realized through ordinary, practical living. Hence, there is no guilt or shame attached to being a workaholic, for there is no appeal to placing oneself above material pursuits.

Islam is the major religion in Indonesia, Malaysia, and parts of Thailand and the Philippines. It too

> **ICD Prevention Tip— Religious Sensitivities**
>
> *Religion and philosophy play an important part in the lives of people throughout the Asia-Pacific region, but it is difficult to know how they may apply to any one individual. An international businessperson is well advised to maintain a high regard for the beliefs of others and to avoid proselytizing. A Christmas card, for example, will not be welcomed by a Muslim, but a card with warm wishes for Ramadan, a Muslim religious observance similar to a Christian's Lent, will be much appreciated.*

teaches values that are relevant to commerce. Islam stresses the virtues of collective commitment and hard work and the benefits of material prosperity. It also emphasizes the importance of initiative and freedom of action. Like Confucianism, it does not exclude commercial activities from a religious life. Indeed, Islam is often referred to as the religion of traders because it is accommodating to the lives of people in commerce and has been widely spread by people from trading nations.

Buddhism, the major religion of Thailand and with a strong following in Japan, Korea, and elsewhere in Asia, is a contrast to Confucianism and Islam. Instead of playing an interactive role in the commercial lives of its followers, it teaches that material wealth and personal achievement do not matter much. One must follow a middle path, avoid extremes, and be tolerant of others. Indeed, it teaches that there is little one can do to change one's fate. Work is a means to an end, not an end in itself. The goal of life is to endure.

Other religions with followings in Asia are Shintoism, Taoism, and Hinduism. Also, ancestor worship often has a following alone or in connection with a more recognized religion. Shintoism is the principal religion of Japan. It is a loosely organized religion, without an authoritative creed or scripture, that expresses gratitude to the beneficent forces of nature and appeasement of malevolent forces. Divinities are found in numerous animate and inanimate objects. Its central concepts are harmony, purity, and truthfulness. An ancient Japanese poem perhaps expresses its nebulous but genuine religious sentiment: "Unknown to me who resides here; tears flow from a sense of unworthiness and gratitude."

Taoism is a philosophy as well as a religion. The two are not related, and Taoist philosophy (which advocates individuality, spiritual freedom, naturalism, simplicity, religious mysticism, governmental restraint, and the transcendental ideal in art) has a greater following than the religion. Religious Taoism is primarily a system of ethics, stressing piety, devotion, and various earthly objectives: happiness, health, wealth, begetting children, and longevity.

Hinduism is the principal religion of India, but its followers are in the minority in other countries. Various gods and images (the principal gods being Vishnu, Krishna, and Shiva) are seen as manifestations of a single divinity. The principal aims of the religion are preservation of social order (with stratified social classes, called castes) and preservation of the family, with utmost respect for elders.

In Australia, Canada, New Zealand, the Philippines, and the United States (as well as most nations of Europe and Latin America), Christianity is the dominant religion. Rather than collectivist values, Christianity—especially Protestantism—focuses on the individual. It teaches charity, love of neighbor, and repentance, with a promise of salvation to believers. Those who are morally good will be rewarded in an afterlife; those who are wicked will be punished. The individual is responsible for his or her acts. Correspondingly, Christianity stresses independence and self-reliance.

3

Basic Communications Guidelines

One of the serious afflictions of International Communications Disorder is loss of business. And complications from ICD include the loss of valuable time and goodwill in building productive business relationships. In a book about business communications in an area as large and diverse as the Asia-Pacific region, it is not always possible to prescribe specific cures for every instance of ICD—circumstances vary too widely. However, it is possible to lay out some basic guidelines, which, in combination with an understanding of the region's cultural signposts and individual countries, will serve the international businessperson well.

ASSESS THE FORMALITY FACTOR

One thing is certain: stereotypes don't work. Everybody is different, even in homogeneous, collectivist societies such as Japan and South Korea. People within a family or an organization are different. Organizations are different from one another. Nations are different. However, before a relationship is established, a communicator needs to make some assumptions about the person to whom a communication is addressed.

One basic assumption involves the Formality Factor. Before embarking on communications to a person or organization you do not know, assess the probable Formality Factor. That is, take a guess at the degree of formality the person or organization will expect from you. Bear the following in mind as you make your assessment:

▲ Asians are more formal than Westerners.
▲ Older people are more formal than younger people.
▲ People in larger organizations are more formal than people in smaller organizations.
▲ People in older, established organizations are more formal than people in younger, entrepreneurial organizations.
▲ People in older industries (for example, mining) are more formal than people in newer industries (for example, computer technology).

Here is a general formality ranking for the countries discussed in this book:

COUNTRY	RANKING	FORMALITY FACTOR
Japan	Most formal	very high
South Korea		high to very high
Indonesia		high
Malaysia		high
China		moderately high
Vietnam		moderately high
Thailand		moderate
Singapore		moderate
Taiwan		moderate
Hong Kong		moderate
The Philippines		moderate
New Zealand		moderately low
Canada		moderately low
United States		low
Australia	Least formal	very low

Chapter 4 identifies the Formality Factor of each country discussed. However, that *country* Formality Factor is only a starting point. More important is the Formality Factor in terms of the *organization* and *person* with whom you are dealing.

Let assessment of the Formality Factor be your first communications guideline.

IN THE BEGINNING

Arrange an introduction. Unless you are a famous person, or represent a well-known company that almost anyone would love to do business with, it will help immensely if you are first introduced to the person with whom you intend to communicate. Introductions are especially important if a high Formality Factor is involved. To give a clear example, an introduction is especially important if you want to communicate with an older, senior executive at a large Japanese organization.

An introduction need not be a big deal. Government trade offices (see Resource File, "Useful Contacts and Sources of Information"), banks, accounting firms, law firms, and consultants often provide this service at little or no cost. An introduction also need not be made by someone known to the person to whom you are introduced, although that is the best circumstance. It is enough that there is a relationship between the introducer and the person to whom you are introduced, or between their organizations. Even if there is no relationship between the introducer and the person or organization to whom you are introduced, it is sometimes enough if the introducer is a person of high status, such as an official of your own government or an executive of a well-known corporation.

The introduction can be for purposes of arranging a personal meeting or for commencing a written correspondence. For more on introductions, see Chapter 14.

If the Formality Factor for your initial communication is low, you may choose to forgo an introduction and try to communicate directly from the start. The risks are that you might fail and may also spoil chances of arranging an introduction later. But these risks will be reduced if you follow the other guidelines of this section.

Set up a personal meeting if possible. Time and time again Asia-Pacific executives whom I interviewed for this book or who answered the book's survey questionnaire emphasized the importance of beginning a business relationship with a face-to-face meeting. They said that this is especially important for Westerners seeking relationships with Asians. It is helpful, but not as important, for Asians seeking relationships with Westerners or for Westerners seeking relationships with Westerners. The difference is that Asians, being from collectivist cultures, place a high value on the personal side of a relationship and tend to discount people who are not members of their family, clan, organization, or nation. Westerners, being individualists, are more focused on the potential material outcome of a relationship and tend to overlook its societal aspects. The advantages of a personal visit are that it enables both parties to gain a better understanding of each other, to communicate their messages better, and to garner information that will assist in building a continuing relationship.

After a relationship is established, communications often become informal and very efficient. Some years ago a senior executive of Cleveland Cliffs Iron Ore Company negotiated substantial long-term "take or pay" contracts with Mitsui & Co. to supply iron ore to Japanese steel mills from Cleveland Cliffs' Robe River mine in Western Australia. The relationship began with a formal introduction of the Cleveland Cliffs executive to Mitsui through Mitsui's bank, followed by several social visits. Detailed contracts were eventually concluded, and Cleveland Cliffs began supplying the ore on a regular basis. Production and contract problems sometimes occurred, and the Cleveland Cliffs executive would visit Mitsui in Tokyo to discuss them. "The formal introduction and those early personal visits were crucial," says the Cleveland Cliffs executive. "And after a few years our relationship was so good that all I had to do was pick up the telephone or send a telex to Mitsui to resolve a production or contract problem."

Connect with the *right* person. A communication addressed merely to an organization, or to a nameless department head or officer of an organization, will probably be delivered directly to the janitor—for disposal. Furthermore, a great amount of time, expense, and energy can be wasted if your communication is directed to the wrong person. That person will probably sit on your communication and ultimately deliver it to someone with even less interest in it.

You should carefully identify the name, title, and address of the person who is most likely to give appropriate attention to your communication. Sometimes the person or firm who introduced you to the organization can identify the right person to contact, although this introducer will need to know from you what you hope to gain from the encounter in order to send you in the right direction. Also, sometimes a letter or fax to the organization itself, asking for the name and title of the proper person to contact on a certain subject, will elicit the desired information. A telephone call is another way to identify the right person, but it carries a risk of obtaining inaccurate, extemporaneous information. There is also a risk of being misunderstood, if your language or accent is different from that of the person with whom you speak. (For more on names, titles, and addresses, see Chapter 6.)

> **ICD Prevention Tip—Names**
>
> *To track down the correct name, title, and address of a person you want to contact, see if the person's organization has a representative office in your city or in another city in your country. That office might be able to help. If this fails, try the nearest trade or consular office of the person's country.*

Observe rank. Many Asians and some Westerners are highly sensitive to status and rank. That means that you should not only use a person's correct title in your communication but also acknowledge the high position of a senior official. The latter can often be accomplished by a reference to the person's "busy schedule" or "extensive responsibilities." Conversely, you should avoid communications that purport to pair a junior executive with a senior executive.

An American consultant recently complained that he was having difficulty getting several Japanese-American joint ventures off the ground because the CEOs of the American companies kept sending junior executives to Japan to meet with the CEOs of the Japanese companies. This was insulting to the Japanese, who responded by sending their own junior executives to the meetings, and nothing was getting achieved.

In correspondence to an executive whose relative rank in his organization is higher than your own, you should get one of your high-ranking officials into the act, at least to sign the letter. This is useful even if the other executive's organization is much smaller than yours. If it is not practical to do this, your communication should acknowledge in some way the high rank of the other executive (for example, by indicating that the CEO of your firm sends greetings and asked you to contact the executive on his or her behalf).

Do not use first names at first, possibly ever. One of the most difficult things for Westerners, especially Americans and Australians, to accept is that Asians (except Thais and Vietnamese) normally prefer to be addressed by their family names, even by their friends. Westerners, after only a brief association with an Asian, will want to address an Asian by his or her first name.

Westerners are best advised to address Asians by their family names until invited to do otherwise. Using family names is not an unfriendly formality in the eyes of Asians. It is part of their collectivist traditions that the family name is the most important part of their identity, contrary to individualist traditions.

Put your best foot forward. Just as a salesperson should never make a call in a rumpled suit and scuffed shoes, your initial communications should make a good impression. They should be tailored with your best guess on the Formality Factor, leaning on the formal side at the outset.

A letter, delivered by mail or courier, should be your first communication, even if only to confirm a meeting arranged by an introducer. A fax is not appropriate unless there is an unavoidable time constraint. Your stationery should be of high quality. The letterhead and typing should be clean and crisp. (For more on letters and faxes, see Chapters 7 and 8.)

Be clear and concise. Another point repeatedly made by executives interviewed for this book and in responses to the survey questionnaire is that communications should be explicit and to the point. Few executives, even Asian executives, have the patience to spend more than a couple of moments deciphering the purpose of a written communication. Once the purpose of a communication is understood, the executive can *be* an executive, that is, can start making decisions. If the communication presents an issue of interest to the executive, further communications can result.

In a face-to-face meeting the person who sought the meeting will have already communicated its purpose in the process of setting it up, and the person granting the meeting will have agreed to a discussion on the matter. At the beginning of the meeting, there will be some socializing, but the person who sought the meeting should come quickly to the point and be clear about what he or she seeks to accomplish by the meeting. (For more on face-to-face meetings, see Chapter 14.)

Whether your initial communications are in writing or face to face, take special care to write or speak clearly and concisely. This is especially important if you are writing or speaking to someone whose first language is not your own. If this is the case, use short, declarative sentences when writing, and avoid jargon, difficult words, and idioms. In face-to-face meetings do the same, and also speak deliberately and enunciate clearly. (For more on letter writing, see Chapter 7.)

Avoid surprises, and follow up promptly and precisely. Your initial communications should result in no surprises for the people with whom you communicate. If a face-to-face meeting is arranged, its purpose should be communicated in advance, you should appear on time, and the discussion (apart from social pleasantries) should not stray from the meeting's purpose. After the meeting a thank-you letter should be sent immediately, and you should do promptly anything you committed to do during the meeting.

If your initial communications are by correspondence, you should be precise about what you will do next, and then do it. If you say that you will correspond or telephone on a certain day, do so. If you say you will send samples or brochures, make certain that they are sent without delay.

> **ICD Prevention Tip— First Impressions**
>
> *If your first communication will be a letter enclosing your brochure or other marketing materials, consider sending it by courier. Courier delivery, though expensive, makes an excellent first impression.*

CONTINUING COMMUNICATIONS

Dave Erdman, president of PacRim Marketing Group Inc., a direct marketing and sales promotion firm based in Honolulu, Hawaii, that assists clients with market entry in Japan and the United States, says that successful communications in the Asia-Pacific region are primarily a matter of frequent, thoughtful correspondence. Face-to-face visits are important, but between visits frequent written communications are needed to keep a relationship alive and well.

Don't be a stranger. In the course of a business relationship, there is often more that you will want to conceal from your counterpart than you will want to reveal. You do not want to reveal negative matters, such as production problems that could delay delivery dates. You do not want to communicate matters unrelated to your business relationship; they might raise unnecessary questions. You do not want to disclose minor developments that would be more meaningful at a later time, when you might be able to announce a major breakthrough or success. However, this does not mean that you should not remain in touch.

You might say to yourself that you don't have time to write a lot of letters, faxes, and reports, even if you wanted to. But in international business there is more to be gained from communicating a lot than from communicating a little. This is because differences in cultural and national backgrounds sow seeds of suspicion that can normally be dispelled with frequent communication. Accordingly, you should work hard at staying in frequent touch with an international counterpart. Arrange face-to-face meetings. Send interim status reports. Advise the counterpart of industry developments that are relevant

> **ICD Prevention Tip—Keeping In Touch**
>
> *Your communications need not relate strictly to active business projects. If you are visiting a counterpart's city on other business, you can arrange a meeting to give a short status report. At other times you can send magazine articles of interest, reports about your company's activities, your observations on economic or industry developments, congratulations on a counterpart's own successes, or simply holiday greetings. If a personal relationship has developed, you can inquire about your counterpart's health and family.*

to your activities. Even after a project with the counterpart is concluded, maintain an active correspondence.

Don't be a phony. A Japanese executive once told me that the criticism of Americans most often voiced by Japanese was that Americans are "insincere." He explained that many Japanese perceive Americans as saying one thing and doing another. They also view Americans as patronizing and condescending. And he added, "Americans aren't the only ones!"

No doubt Americans and others, including Japanese, come across to their international counterparts as insincere from time to time. Sometimes they *are* insincere, but sometimes they only give an impression of insincerity in trying to be someone they are not, often in an effort to please. They will promise more than they can deliver; they will exaggerate their capability or their authority; they will attempt to flatter their counterpart and their counterpart's culture and traditions, and in their flattery will seem to patronize or mock them. For example, Westerners sometimes attempt to mimic Asian mannerisms in the hope of flattering their counterparts but with the result of embarrassing them.

The best advice here is to be yourself. This is all that is expected of you. You can use a few phrases of your counterpart's language if it is not yours, and you can use the greetings and gestures of your counterpart's culture, but to do more is to risk coming across as patronizing and condescending unless you are known to be accomplished in your counterpart's language and culture.

Play it straight. In letters, telephone conversations, and face-to-face meetings, unless you are communicating with someone whose culture and first language are the same as yours, avoid subtle or double meanings,

> ### ICD Prevention Tip—Genuine Interest
>
> *One way to form a strong bond with your overseas counterpart, and avoid conduct or comments that might appear insincere or patronizing, is to deepen your knowledge of his or her country and culture. Do more than read a tourist guidebook. Read up on the history of the country and the arts and activities in which its people take pride. Sometimes a well-written novel set in the country reveals much about its people. Whether your approach is fact or fiction, you will find that greater knowledge will expand your level of genuine interest.*

irony, puns, and humor. Otherwise, the risk is high that you will be misunderstood or offend others. Also make it a standard communications rule that there is no such thing as a "dumb question," a question with an answer that should be obvious to the person who asks it. If your counterpart asks a question that seems to you to have an obvious answer, do not treat it in an offhand manner or as if it had been made in jest. Answer it fully and thoughtfully.

Lay foundations that will demonstrate your reliability and then build upon them. In your communications make commitments that you can fulfill and then fulfill them faithfully. For example, if you are planning a trip to Singapore and want to visit a colleague there, do not merely telephone for an appointment. Instead, send the colleague a fax with your itinerary and say that you will telephone on a certain date at a certain time to arrange an appointment. Then do just that. If you expect to send merchandise samples to a counterpart in Seoul next month, do not merely wait until next month and send them. Instead, write now and say that the samples will be sent on a certain date. Then send them on that date.

In other words, signal what you will do and then do it. From small matters to big ones, demonstrate that you honor your commitments, that you are reliable in all things, and that you keep your colleagues closely informed. As you did in the beginning, avoid surprises and follow up promptly and precisely. (See the "In the Beginning" section of this chapter.)

Westerners: Tone down your individualism. Asians are uncomfortable with people who "toot their own horns." For most Asians the family and the group or organization come first. Confucius taught that one should be modest. Bragging and self-promotion are never appropriate.

Westerners should use modest phrases in describing their capabilities and those of their companies. At the simplest level, use the word *we* more often and the word *I* less.

But don't be a mystery person. While no one—Asian or Western—likes a braggart, everyone likes to know with whom he or she is dealing. You can be sure that international businesspeople have more than a passing interest in those with whom they are associated. Find opportunities to communicate all the good things you would like a counterpart to know about you, your company, and its products and services.

A bit of name-dropping is always acceptable, if it is truthful and not overdone. Asians especially are impressed by your associations with people and organizations of status. But boastful conduct is ill-advised, especially in the company of Asians, who disapprove of displays of self-importance.

Be personable and considerate. Most businesspeople in the Asia-Pacific region highly value the personal side of their business relationships. This is especially true of Asians. But wherever you are in the world, personal relationships are the foundations of sound business relationships.

The communications opportunities here are double what you might first think. They are present not only when you can do something considerate for your counterpart but also when you can thank the counterpart for something done for you. Never miss an opportunity to write a thank-you note—for a luncheon, a dinner, a meeting, an unsolicited communication, or whatever. When writing for other reasons, say something pleasant about the last contact you had—a productive meeting or an enjoyable social event, or a suggestion by the counterpart that proved useful to you. Even negative events, such as earthquakes, floods, or other tragic occurrences (including illnesses or death in a counterpart's family), can be mentioned—with appropriate concern and empathy—when you communicate.

> **ICD Prevention Tip— Self-Promotion**
>
> *One way of communicating your achievements without bragging about them is to let others sing your praises. When arranging an introduction to a person with whom you hope to do business, make certain that your introducer is well briefed on the accomplishments of you and your organization. Also, supply copies of favorable news articles and commentaries about you and your organization.*

In your communications, take a moment to inject something personal. Set business thoughts aside for that moment, visualize your counterpart as a person, and say something considerate.

Asians: be more informal. There are many opportunities for Asians to improve their communications with Westerners by being more informal. One of the comments that endeared Henry Kissinger to the Washington press corps, after he became U.S. secretary of state, occurred when he was asked how he preferred to be addressed—as Mr. Secretary, Dr. Kissinger, or what? Kissinger replied, "'Your Excellency' will do." With that ironically humorous response, lampooning a title for his position with a pompous exaggeration, he established an informal camaraderie with the press corps that did not lessen his stature.

Asians can establish a similar informality with the "first name thing" that is such a cultural characteristic of Westerners. Early in a relationship with a Westerner, an Asian who is normally addressed only by family name can say to the Westerner, "Please call me by my first name." Another tactic is to place less stress on protocol and rank in communications with Westerners. If a Westerner has inappropriately addressed a letter to a person of higher rank than himself, let the response come from that person, personally acknowledging the letter and referring the matter to the appropriate executive, "who will be able to give it immediate attention."

Avoid form presentations and overused expressions. All international executives need to avoid the cobwebs of presentation and language that obscure their message. Any alert executive can immediately tell when a communication is a form letter. Even with word processing that can embed a reference to the addressee in the body of the letter (e.g., "Therefore, Mr. Smith, we hope . . ."), a form letter will give itself away. The purpose of the communication is irretrievably undermined, for the executive will feel slighted that you do not regard him or her as worthy of truly personal correspondence.

The same goes for overused expressions, trite and hackneyed phrases, and platitudes. (A few examples: "that's what it's all about," "conspicuous by his absence," "explored every avenue," "her own worst enemy," "leave no stone unturned," "powers that be," "through thick and thin.") They come across as full of air, like balloons, and they burst in the face of the writer or speaker.

Again, be clear and concise. Use short, declarative sentences and avoid jargon, difficult words, subtle meanings, and humor. (See the "In the Beginning" section of this chapter.)

Westerners: Emphasize the positive and avoid criticism. Not long ago, in a meeting between Indonesian officials and a group of American advisers who were working on a project sponsored in part by the United States, an American government official openly and severely criticized the advisers for various perceived failings. Although the official intended to show his support for the Indonesian side, the Indonesians fell silent and were clearly embarrassed. In Indonesia, as in other Asian societies, it is poor form to express negative feelings. This is especially true in Japan, where people find it difficult to say a simple no. This aversion made headlines in 1993 when U.S. president Bill Clinton remarked to Russia's president Boris Yeltsin that "sometimes when the Japanese say yes, they mean no." In response, Japan's then prime minister Kiichi Miyazawa quipped that Clinton's statement reminded him of the old American song "Yes! We have no bananas."

Although Japan presents the clearest example, negative expressions in Asia-Pacific communications are generally unwelcome. Therefore, when writing to an Asia-Pacific colleague, put yourself in a positive frame of mind and think of ways that you can express your thoughts positively. When speaking face to face, control any anger or annoyance and phrase statements in a positive way. Avoid criticism if you possibly can, especially of Asians, for whom criticism entails loss of face.

Loss of face for Asians is similar to embarrassment for Westerners, but for Asians it is a much more personal and intense feeling. In collectivist cultures, to make a mistake or show a weakness is to bring shame to oneself and to one's family, organization, or group as well. The offender loses status and power. In individualist cultures embarrassment is a more temporary thing.

If criticism and negative issues cannot be avoided, as when there are business problems that must be corrected, a face-to-face meeting is often essential. To deal with such

---

ICD Prevention Tip—Loss of Face

In addition to avoiding conduct that causes a counterpart to lose face, you should do what you can to extricate the counterpart from a potential loss of face. For example, if you discover that the counterpart made a mistake in calculating his company's fee in a contract proposal made to you, quietly bring this to his attention and give him an opportunity to correct the mistake before you respond formally.

issues by correspondence or telephone is to risk substantial damage to a relationship.

Don't put an Asian on the spot. No one wants to be put on the spot if there is a risk of embarrassment or loss of face, but this is especially true of Asians.

On a recent visit to Tokyo, an American called on a Japanese executive to whom he had been introduced on an earlier visit. At the meeting the American presented a small gift to the Japanese. Although the meeting had been arranged in advance, the Japanese was not prepared for an exchange of gifts. His face flushed a bright red, and the remainder of the meeting was a shambles of lost face. In Japan gift giving is a social ritual of great importance, but it is not always observed for casual office visits, even visits by overseas businesspeople. The lesson for the American was that in arranging the meeting he should have mentioned that he would be "bringing a small gift." (See Chapter 14 for more about gift giving.)

In another incident, a hands-on Canadian executive, steeped in the technical details of how a proposed joint venture product would be manufactured in South Korea, repeatedly questioned his Korean counterpart on the fine points of the manufacturing process. Suddenly the Korean stood up and left the room. He did not return. It is not the normal management style for senior Korean executives to be well informed about product manufacturing, and this executive would have lost face if his inability to respond to the Canadian's pointed questions had become apparent. Similarly, correspondence that requires specific responses, especially when the responses must be negative, will often never be answered by Asians.

Westerners need to communicate with Asians in ways that enable Asians to avoid potential loss of face. This can be done by Westerners asking themselves, before sending a communication or attending a meeting, "Would I myself be comfortable in responding openly on this subject?"

Beware political subjects relating to another's country. Discussion of politics is a great temptation for international businesspeople. They have a keen interest in domestic political events and are well read on international political subjects. However, they do not value highly the opinions of outsiders about the politics of their own countries. This is especially true of people from collectivist societies. These societies tend to be highly nationalistic and supportive of their governments.

In your communications, you may refer to the politics of your own country all you like. Others will be interested in and entertained by your comments. But do not let the references reflect negatively on others (for example, do not praise the human rights record of your country, whether or not addressing someone from a country where human rights violations are thought to occur). And try to keep the references positive rather than critical. This is especially important when addressing Asians, who might find it odd for you to be overly critical—i.e., disrespectful—of your own government.

Treat women well. Some years ago the Sulphur Export Corporation, a U.S. company, arranged a luncheon meeting at New York City's University Club for a visiting delegation of high-level government officials from another country. At that time the University Club did not admit women, even as luncheon guests. Unhappily for executives of the Sulphur Export Corporation, the head of the visiting delegation was a woman. They had not recognized her name as a woman's name, and no one had thought to check. It was an embarrassing incident for everyone. Since then the status and prerogatives of women have changed dramatically in the United States and elsewhere in the world. Women hold senior positions in business and government, and women's groups and others continue to combat discriminatory practices. Moreover, women in senior positions expect to receive recognition commensurate with their status.

International executives, especially ones from organizations and countries that are highly male-oriented, such as Japan and South Korea, need to be alert to the possibility that a counterpart is a woman, and, if so, they need to treat her in accordance with her status in her organization. If a counterpart's gender is not clear (as, for example, if only first initials are used with a family name), it is acceptable for you to inquire before communicating further or before meeting for the first time.

Asians: Be more open and literal. An American executive who had worked in Jakarta for several years was describing an Indonesian official to me not long ago. The executive said that the official seems competent and is very pleasant. "Of course," he added, "you never know what he's thinking."

Westerners are culturally more direct and explicit than Asians. Consequently, they often feel that Asians are not clear in their communications. They complain that they frequently do not know what an Asian is thinking. They say that Asians are "inscrutable," even secretive. This perception sometimes leads to misunderstandings and distrust. To avoid this, when communicating with Westerners, Asians should try to be more open, literal, explicit, direct, frank, forthright, and candid. This can often be accomplished by adding explanations and examples to one's communications that might seem wholly unnecessary.

Westerners: Allow adequate response time. Businesspeople in Hong Kong and Taiwan are known for prompt decision making. Conversely, their counterparts in Japan and South Korea are known for deliberate decision making. Decision making generally takes longer in Asian societies because collectivist traditions seek a consensus. Typically, proposals are reviewed from bottom to top, with final decisions made at the top. This is not unlike the process in Western societies, except that the Asian process is more thorough and time-consuming. Westerners should therefore anticipate that responses from Asians might take longer than responses from other Westerners.

> **ICD Prevention Tip—Response Time**
>
> *Be explicit about when you expect a response. If there are reasons why a response is needed by a certain date, politely explain them and convey your appreciation for your counterpart's gracious understanding.*

Asians: Speed up your response time. One of the famous tactics used by Asians in business negotiations with Westerners is to remain silent for long periods. The Westerners, having little patience, will repeatedly cave in on negotiating points in order to make progress in the discussions or to meet some self-imposed deadline. Asians might not wish to relinquish this negotiating tactic, but in other circumstances they can often improve their communications with Westerners if they speed up their responses. Lengthy periods of silence not only severely test Westerners' patience, but also intensify suspicion and distrust.

If an adequate response cannot be prepared within the time that a Westerner might expect to receive it, send a letter or fax stating that the matter is under consideration and you will respond by a specific date. Then make certain that your response is sent by that date.

Be sensitive to communications expenses of others. One international executive interviewed for this book remarked that, despite the many telecommunications bargains and discounts that exist today, the costs of communicating seem to grow and grow. She asked, "How do you tell a counterpart that you prefer not to respond by fax or return an overseas telephone call because you need to control expenses?" The answer obviously depends on the relationship with the counterpart, but in your own communications to others you need to be sensitive to the expense they will incur in responding to you. Think twice before you say, "Please respond by fax" or "Please telephone me at your early convenience" or "Please send the materials by courier."

Watch the numbers. There are lucky and unlucky numbers in every society. In most cultures, Western and Asian included, the number 3 tends to be highly significant and often lucky. However, the number 13 is considered so unlucky that architects of high-rise office buildings and apartments often omit the thirteenth floor, designating that floor number fourteen. (People seem willing to overlook that the renumbered floor is still actually the thirteenth.)

Asians tend to be more superstitious about numbers than Westerners. The number 4 is unlucky in Japan and in Chinese societies, in part because the word for "four" sounds like the word for "death." Japanese and Chinese will go to great lengths to avoid using or giving items that are four in number or that add up to four, such as two pairs of socks. It is bad luck in these societies to have the number 4 in one's street address or telephone number. Four is also unlucky in Korea. In addition, 6 is unlucky in Thailand, and 9 in Japan. In Vietnam, 10 and 13 are unlucky, as are combinations of numbers that add up to 10 or 13.

In Chinese cultures the numbers 3, 6, and 8 are thought to bring good fortune. Three represents life, and 8 represents prosperity. Two 6s or three 8s, as in the numbers 66 and 888, are especially lucky. August 8, 1988, was a very lucky day. Both 7 and 8 are lucky numbers in Japan, and 5, 7, and 9 are lucky in Korea. In the Philippines any number that is round in shape or has the shape of money (like a coin or like a dollar sign, $), such as 0 or 8, is considered lucky. In Vietnam 8 and 9 are lucky numbers.

Sometimes, however, there is little one can do to avoid unlucky numbers. My business address is 44 Montgomery Street in San Francisco, but in this case many positive factors, such as location, outweigh the disadvantage of having an address with a number (44) that is considered by some to be unlucky. (See the accompanying table for a summary of Asia-Pacific numbers that are lucky or unlucky, popular or unpopular.)

ICD Prevention Tip—Numbers

Asia-Pacific businesspeople should become number conscious. They should determine which numbers are favored or disfavored by their counterparts from other cultures. When planning significant actions that will involve a counterpart from another culture, such as setting the dates for a contract signing and a celebration dinner, it is a good idea to ask the counterpart if the proposed dates—or any other numbers associated with the plans, including the number of guests invited to the dinner—appear favorable.

Be color conscious. Colors also often hold a greater significance for Asians than they do for Westerners. Some colors signify good fortune; others signify bad luck. Accordingly, Asia-Pacific businesspeople need to be aware of the meanings of certain colors used in their companies' stationery, packaging, and promotional materials. They also may need to be aware of the significance of colors they use in wrapping gifts given to Asians and in clothing worn when meeting Asians.

Black is avoided in virtually all Asia-Pacific countries because of its association with death. In particular it should never be used as the border of a page or card, because this is the way death notices normally appear. However, black is generally preferred as the color for printing ink and pen ink.

White is also avoided in Japan, and sometimes in Chinese cultures, because of an association with death. Funeral envelopes and wreath ribbons are white. One should therefore avoid white gift wrapping, white flowers, and predominantly white clothing, but white stationery and plain white dress shirts for men are standard. In Vietnam a combination of predominantly black and white clothing is to be carefully avoided. In Korea and Thailand, however, there are no negative associations for the color white.

Red is the color of good fortune, life, and happiness in Chinese cultures and in Vietnam, Thailand, and the Philippines. It is often displayed and worn on holidays and festive occasions. Money gifts are presented in red envelopes, and red ribbons are used on congratulatory and wedding wreaths. However, the Chinese, Koreans, and Japanese associate red ink with the severance of relationships because it is often used for death notices. Generally, a red ink pen should never be used to sign one's name, especially in Korea, where a person's death is indicated by marking across the name with a red ink pen. However, underlining words in red for emphasis does not have a negative connotation.

Blue is a popular color with Koreans, but it is sometimes associated with mourning in Chinese cultures.

Gold is very popular in most Asian cultures because it signifies wealth and money. However, in Japan, leaves that are painted gold or made of gold signify bad luck, indicating the death of a living thing.

Green is generally popular, especially in the Philippines and Vietnam, because of an association with money. However, it is considered unlucky in Japan.

Yellow is generally a popular color, but it is avoided in Malaysia in personal wear or commercial use because it is the color of royalty. It is considered presumptuous and offensive to use a color preferred by the sultans and their families.

Purple is avoided in Chinese cultures because it is considered the color of barbarians. Purple is also avoided at weddings in Japan because it is thought to fade easily and might signify the fading of marital happiness. (See the accompanying table for a summary of Asia-Pacific colors that are lucky or unlucky, popular or unpopular.)

ICD Prevention Tip—Colors

Westerners should consult their Asian friends and colleagues as to the significance of colors in their marketing and presentation materials, in gift wrapping, and even in the clothing they intend to wear to important meetings and on social occasions.

Let harmony be your guide. One of the most interesting beliefs originating in the region, held by many across China and beyond, is that the design of homes and offices, their color schemes, and the placement of doors, windows, and furniture, can

ASIA-PACIFIC NUMBERS AND COLORS
ICD LUCKY LIST

NUMBER	WHERE LUCKY OR POPULAR	WHERE UNLUCKY OR UNPOPULAR
0	Philippines	—
3	All Asia-Pacific countries	—
4	—	Chinese cultures, Japan, South Korea
5	South Korea	—
6	Chinese cultures	Thailand, Vietnam
7	Western countries, Japan, South Korea	—
8	Chinese cultures, Japan, Philippines, Vietnam	—
9	South Korea, Vietnam	—
10	—	Vietnam
13	—	All Asia-Pacific countries

▲ ▲ ▲

COLOR	WHERE LUCKY OR POPULAR	WHERE UNLUCKY OR UNPOPULAR
Black	—	All Asia-Pacific cultures
White	—	Chinese cultures, Japan, Vietnam
Red	Chinese cultures, Japan, Philippines, South Korea, Thailand, Vietnam	Names and red ink: Chinese cultures, Japan, South Korea
Blue	South Korea	Chinese cultures
Gold	Asian cultures generally	On leaves: Japan
Green	Philippines, Vietnam	Japan
Yellow	All Asia-Pacific cultures	In personal wear or commercially: Malaysia
Purple	—	Chinese cultures

have a profound effect on the inhabitants' well-being and fortune. This is the philosophy of *feng shui*, (pronounced "fung shway," literally "wind and water" in Chinese), an intricate blend of pragmatism, aesthetics, and superstition that has its origins in the Yellow River Valley region of China thousands of years ago. Stories abound of cases in which a company's or household's ill fortune persisted until changes were made on the advice of a *feng shui* diviner, or goemancer. Good fortune returns after furniture

> **ICD Prevention Tip—Harmony**
>
> *A basic concept of feng shui, that order and harmony in one's life affects one's fortunes, is especially applicable to business communications and relationships in Asia. Orchestrate and design your communications with a consistent approach. For example, have a clear message, follow up on a routine basis, and use uncomplicated language.*

blocking doorways is moved to encourage the approach of opportunities, clutter is disposed of to promote a feeling of order and control, outside noise is reduced to minimize alien influences, or desks are shifted to give a wide view of an entrance to provide a sense of security.

4

THE COUNTRY CONNECTION

THE PREVIOUS CHAPTERS OFFERED CULTURAL SIGNPOSTS and communications guidelines that will help the international executive navigate the diverse crosscurrents of the Asia-Pacific region. This chapter goes a step further. It sets forth information about individual countries in the region, and their general characteristics, that someone from another country needs to know in order to be an effective Asia-Pacific communicator. This chapter supplies the country connection.

AUSTRALIA

On Top Down Under

Bill Fisher, a career diplomat and recently Australia's ambassador to Israel, has a large globe of the world in his office. A visitor will sometimes comment that the globe is turned upside down, and Fisher will say, "Not at all. Australia is always on top." This remark says a lot about the ebullient Australians, those fun-loving, competitive, and often raucous "blokes" who live in "the Land of Wonder, the Land Down Under," as Australia is described in its tourist advertising.

Australians are proud and sensitive people. Strongly aware of Australia's achievements, yet also conscious of not always being taken seriously by their counterparts in the Northern Hemisphere, they often feel slighted by ill-considered comments or what they perceive as cavalier treatment more readily than most Westerners.

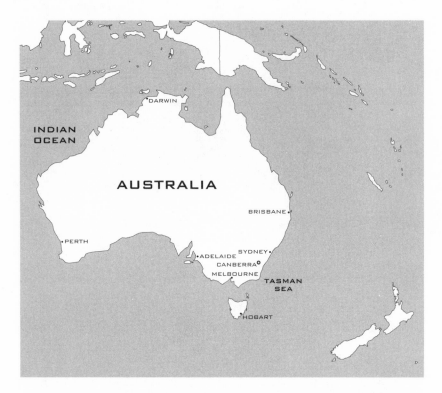

Australians' sensitivities are caused in part by the uniqueness of their political and physical positions in the world. They are linked by their early national history to England, Ireland, Scotland, and Europe, yet they are situated on the other side of the world from these origins. They inhabit a land full of unusual creatures and resources: uncommon flora and fauna, vast mineral wealth. The indigenous Aborigines are unlike any other native groups on earth.

Some say that the sensitivities of many Australians are also the result of the country's national beginnings as an English penal colony. In 1788, after the American Revolution eliminated North America as a destination for unwanted convicts, England began sending prisoners to its settlement at Sydney Cove and nearby Botany Bay. Over the following eighty years, some 157,000 convicts were sent to Australia. Most of these were eventually released and made their homes in Australia, some becoming leading citizens. But resentment toward England lives on: one Australian likes to tell the story that when his grandmother sent his father to mail letters at the post office near their home she insisted that he buy penny stamps. His father, then a small boy, would have to lick and paste large numbers of stamps on each letter. The reason for the penny stamps was that stamps of larger denominations bore portraits of Queen Victoria, and his mother was "damned if she'd have anyone in her family licking the backside of a British queen."

Apart from convicts, many free settlers came to Australia beginning in the late 1700s. Many came

ICD Prevention Tip—Conversation

Although the penal colony beginnings of Australia are part of history, many contemporary Australians are descendants of the early convicts. In the past this was a source of embarrassment to many. Today some Australians find it fashionable to boast of convict forebears. To be safe, people from other countries who communicate with Australians should look to other topics of conversation.

from Ireland and Scotland in the 1800s, and none of these groups held warm feelings toward England. As newer generations of immigrants have tended to be from the surrounding Asian region, feelings toward England are increasingly ambivalent among Australians today. Although their country remains a part of the British Commonwealth (and the British monarch is independently sovereign of Australia), Australians maintain a strong independence from Britain and perhaps today feel instead a greater kinship toward Americans.

It is probably in part because of this national history of contentious beginnings and British dominance that Australians are typically averse to class distinctions and the exercise of authority. They seem to love a classless camaraderie, resenting anyone who acts

ICD Prevention Tip— National Identity

In communicating with Australians, go easy on references to the country's ties to England. For example, avoid references that might imply that Australia follows British government policies or that Australians emulate British tastes.

"upper teeth" or "puts on airs." Taxi drivers have been known to feel insulted if a lone male passenger rides in the backseat rather than up front with them. Australians want to be on a first name basis with new acquaintances almost from the start. In business there is a restless tension between management and workers—trade unions are exceptionally strong in Australia—and foreign multinationals that own businesses in Australia find that the local management strongly resists direction from headquarters.

Although English is Australia's official language, Australian slang, called "Strine" by some, and the Australian accent constitute a formidable challenge for non-Australians —even those whose first language *is* English. On average, Australians employ more slang than any other English-language speakers,

and English words sound quite different in the mouth of an Australian. For example, the word *mate*—meaning close friend, not spouse—is often pronounced "mite."

Australian slang could be the subject of a whole book. Here are just a few examples of slang words that can be heard even in business conversation:

WORD OR PHRASE	MEANING
Aussie	Australian
Bloody	All-purpose adjective; not necessarily profane
Bush	Countryside; rustic
Cuppa	Cup of tea
Dinkum	Fair, honest
Fair go	A fair, reasonable chance
Good on ya!	An expression of approval, sometimes ironic
No worries! She'll be right.	Everything will come out fine
Ta	Thank you
Tall poppy	High achiever
Tucker	Food

In business, slang phrases often come from the sporting or gaming world. For example, Australians will say, "Let that one go through to the keeper," a reference to cricket, meaning, "Don't bother with it, don't pursue the point." They will also say, "Take a punt" (a punt is a bet), meaning "Go with it, bet on that." Australians also often add an *s* to a word for a short-form reference, for example, calling Dillingham Corporation "Dillingham's." They also like to use diminutives; for instance, they will refer to a biscuit (cookie) as a "bickie" and a man named David as "Davey."

In international communications, some Australians tend to be too informal, especially in observing hierarchical protocol when dealing with Asians. Some also tend to be too casual in responding to communications from business correspondents whose Formality Factor is higher.

Once known for its white-only immigration policies and anti-Asian attitudes, Australia is rapidly adjusting to the realities of its proximity to Asia. Fully 60 percent of its international trade is now with Asia, and Asian immigrants, now more than 4 percent of the population, make up the largest annual proportion of immigrants. Thousands of Asian students graduate from Australian universities each year; Japanese are heavily invested in Australian industry; Vietnamese refugees from the 1970s are now valued members of the workforce. The traditional image—and outlook—of Australia is swiftly changing.

▲ ▲

COUNTRY DATA: AUSTRALIA

FORMALITY FACTOR • Very low
POPULATION • 17.3 million
GROSS DOMESTIC PRODUCT • $288.6 billion*

---

* Economic data in this chapter are based on purchasing power parity estimates set forth in the *World Development Report 1993* (published for the World Bank by Oxford University Press, 1993), data from *The World Bank Atlas 1994*, and other sources available from the *Far Eastern Economic Review* and *EIU World Outlook*. Monetary amounts are stated in U.S. dollars.

INCOME PER CAPITA • $16,680

AVERAGE GROWTH RATE, 1985–1992 • 0.7 percent

GOVERNMENT • Parliamentary state

ETHNIC GROUPS • European 95%, Asian 4%, Aboriginal and other 1%

RELIGION* • Anglican 24%, Roman Catholic 26%, other Christian 23%

BUSINESS HOURS • Normal business hours are Monday through Friday, 9:00 A.M. to 5:00 P.M., with an hour and a half taken off at noon.

LITERACY • 100%

LANGUAGE • English is spoken throughout Australia.

TELECOMMUNICATIONS • International direct dialing is available throughout Australia. Locally purchased phone cards are in common use.

SPORTS • Tennis, sailing, golf, and various water sports are the most popular participating sports. The most popular spectator sports are Australian Rules football, cricket, soccer, and horse racing.

MONEY • Australian currency is denominated as the dollar, expressed internationally as "A$." The exchange rate of the Australian dollar is presently about US$0.74.[†] International banking transactions are sophisticated. Major international credit cards are accepted throughout the country.

MAJOR HOLIDAYS

New Year's Day	January 1
Australia Day	Last Monday of January
Good Friday, Easter	March or April, four days including the following Monday
Anzac Day	April 25
Queen's Birthday	A Monday in early June
Melbourne Cup Day (official only in Victoria but observed everywhere)	First Tuesday in November
Christmas Day	December 25
Boxing Day	December 26

▼ ▼

---

* Estimated percentages of population indicating a religious affiliation.

† Exchange rates quoted throughout this book are based on averages at the time of writing. For up-to-date rates, consult your bank or the financial pages of a current newspaper.

CANADA

Sleeping with the Elephant

The greatest offense one can commit in communicating with a Canadian is to confuse him or her with an American. Canadians do actually like Americans, but they dislike the incessant, pervasive influences that emanate from their neighbor to the south. Former Canadian Prime Minister Pierre Trudeau once said, "Living next to the United States is like sleeping with an elephant. No matter how friendly and even-tempered the beast, one is affected by every twitch and grunt." American culture and events fill Canadian airwaves; acid rain from American industrial centers pollutes Canadian forests; American products dominate Canadian shelf space.

André Gide, the French novelist, once observed that Canadians like Americans but not the United States, whereas they like England but not the English. The issue here is one of Canadian "integrity," as Canadians like to put it. Canadians feel somewhat threatened by their proximity to the United States; indeed, 90 percent of Canada's population live within 100 miles of the U.S. border. On the other hand, Canadian attitudes toward others, such as the British, can be more objective. As Canada is a member of the British Commonwealth, there are many historical and ancestral ties with Britain; nonetheless, Canadians still judge British people on their own merits, and normally find themselves more in tune with Americans.

Perhaps Canadians' concern for their "integrity" has as much to do with the diversity of their background—a diversity that often undermines their sense of national identity—as with anything else. Like those of Australia, New Zealand, and the United States, the vast majority of Canada's population settled there in the last two centuries, pushing aside native groups. Settlers of various ethnic origins from England and across Europe established areas that maintain distinct identities to this day, such as the Scots in Nova Scotia and the French in Québec. In recent decades immigrants have come from other British Commonwealth nations, including India and countries in Africa. Large numbers came recently from Hong Kong and Vietnam, many settling in British Columbia, where the population of Vancouver is now more than 50 percent Asian.

However, unlike Australia, New Zealand, and the United States, Canada nurtures its diversity as much as its shared interests. Regional and ethnic differences are not only recognized but encouraged. From the 1950s the French-speaking eastern province of Québec, with about 25 percent of Canada's population, has sought various forms of recognition and independence from the larger nation, the most apparent being the federal legal requirement that public signs and notices be written in both French and English. Separatists in Québec continue to work for complete withdrawal from Canada; meanwhile, the western Canadian provinces, complaining that the taxes they pay support the more populous eastern provinces, often speak of independence for themselves too. The people of the First Nations (Native Americans belonging to several groups, including the Inuit) constitute about 3 percent of the Canadian population, and many live on lands reserved by the Canadian government. Self-government for these groups, too, is a subject of current debate.

> **ICD Prevention Tip—**
> **National and Regional Identity**
>
> *In communicating with Canadians, be especially sensitive to their national and regional identities. Above all, avoid comparisons to the United States. Also, where you can, recognize the unique characteristics of their respective provinces, such as the maritime and forest products industries of British Columbia, the beauty of Alberta's Banff National Park, and the French cuisine and culture of Québec. To many Canadians regional identity is more important than national identity.*

Another aspect of national "integrity," especially in the western provinces, is a concern over foreign exploitation of Canada's resources. For this reason many Canadians object to the export of unfinished products from their country's forests and mines, and to foreign ownership of their industries. In the 1970s there was a strong Buy Back Canada movement, during which government corporations were formed to acquire American-owned Canadian industries, and laws were enacted to review and control new foreign investment.

Despite this strong desire for self-protection, Canada is very much a member of the international community. Its diplomatic relations are superb around the globe, and Canadians often enjoy international positions of trust and influence. In business and government circles alike, Canada is viewed as a country without an ideological ax to grind. Despite early European connections, Canada is now fully oriented to the Asia-Pacific region, which borders its western shores. Canadians are especially liked in China, where Canadian doctor Norman Bethune is remembered for his sacrifices in the Chinese Revolution during and following World War II. He attached himself to the ill-equipped forces of Mao Ze-dong's Eighth Route Army and worked tirelessly, trekking long distances through the mountains, treating the wounded, and training doctors. An ardent communist, he chose to participate in history rather than observe it from afar.

Notwithstanding Canada's dual recognition of English and French, English remains the accepted international business language throughout the country, even in Québec. Canadians' accents in speaking English are not especially strong unless English is their second language, and only a few English words are distinctively Canadian in accent, such as words with the syllable *out* as in *about,* which is often pronounced "aboot." Slang expressions, other than American ones, are not as prevalent as in many other English-speaking countries. Here are a few that an international businessperson might encounter:

WORD OR PHRASE	MEANING
Eh?	Don't you agree? (as in "It's good, eh?") Or an interlocution added for emphasis (as in "He's ready to sign the contract, eh, and a telephone call comes in from the home office, eh, and suddenly the deal is off.")
Gearing ratio	Ratio between equity and debt (financial term)
Riding (n.)	Political constituency
Shout (n.)	Call (as in "Give me a shout on the telephone.")

▲ ▲

COUNTRY DATA: CANADA

FORMALITY FACTOR • Moderately low

POPULATION • 27.3 million

GROSS DOMESTIC PRODUCT • $527.4 billion

INCOME PER CAPITA • $19,320

AVERAGE GROWTH RATE, 1985–1992 • 0.3 percent

GOVERNMENT • Parliamentary state

ETHNIC GROUPS • British origin 40%, French origin 27%, other European 23%, native Canadians 3%

RELIGION • Roman Catholic 47%, United Church 16%, Anglican 10%

BUSINESS HOURS • Normal business hours are Monday through Friday, 9:00 A.M. to 5:00 P.M., with an hour and a half taken off at noon.

LITERACY • 99%

LANGUAGES • English and French are the two official languages. About 24 percent of the population speak French.

TELECOMMUNICATIONS • Canada has international direct dialing in all cities and has sophisticated telecommunications services.

SPORTS • Ice hockey is Canada's most popular spectator sport, and one in which Canadians have long excelled. North American football, on a field somewhat larger and with slightly different rules than in the United States, is also popular. Other major sports activities include skiing, golf, hiking, and various water sports.

MONEY • Canadian currency is denominated as the dollar, expressed internationally as "C$." The exchange rate of the Canadian dollar is presently about US$0.74. International banking transactions are sophisticated. Major international credit cards are accepted throughout the country.

MAJOR HOLIDAYS

New Year's Day	January 1
Good Friday, Easter	March or April, four days including the following Monday
Victoria Day	May 18
Canada Day	July 1
Labour Day	September 7
Thanksgiving Day	October 12
Remembrance Day	November 11
Christmas Day	December 25
Boxing Day	December 26

▼ ▼

CHINA

Developing Giant

What developing country also has the world's third largest economy (after the United States and Japan)? The People's Republic of China. Yet China today is something of an adolescent as a world economy: oversized and exuberant, in many areas underdeveloped, but also growing faster than its motor skills can quite control.

Less than two decades ago, in 1976, when Mao Ze-dong and Zhou En-lai died and the Cultural Revolution came to an end, China was in economic terms a backward-looking recluse. Now, as a result of economic reforms introduced in 1978, and "faster, bolder" economic growth endorsed by the Chinese leadership in 1992, China has burst on the global economic scene with lightning speed and vitality. The country's annual economic growth has averaged over 10 percent in the

last decade. Economic growth of the city of Guangzhou (formerly called Canton), north of Hong Kong, alone averaged greater than 20 percent in the last few years. The most striking statistic is that China's private sector has strongly outpaced growth in the state-owned and collective sectors. In 1990, for example, output of the private sector grew by 21.6 percent compared with the others' 2.9 percent and 9.1 percent.

Growth in China has been sparked in part by a number of economic zones, called Special Economic Zones, Development Zones, and Open Economic Zones, established in the 1980s to promote trade and foreign investment. These zones, situated in the coastal and southern provinces, now play an important role in China's economic growth. They provide tax incentives, tariff concessions, and reduced costs of land and labor. They also facilitate technology transfer, joint ventures, and research projects.

Growth is all around. In Shanghai new buildings are going up everywhere you look, and roads are under construction at every turn. In 1976 China essentially had only one major television station, controlled by the central government, and few people owned television sets. Today there are about 600 television stations and over 250 million sets.

It is a wonder that such a large country is growing so rapidly. In land area, China is massive, the third largest country in the world (after Russia and Canada) and slightly larger than the United States. In terms of population—close to 1.2 billion people—China is huge, with one-fifth of the world's people. Such size clearly presents enormous logistical and governmental problems. Indeed, China appears "out of control" from time to time. Steps taken in 1988 to cool an overheated economy resulted in a recession in 1988–89. A more recent overheating and double-digit inflation brought harsh monetary restrictions in 1993. Corruption is also a problem in some sectors, with advantages being taken by those in positions to grant governmental approvals or provide access to materials and markets. Leadership succession is another problem, as power is still exercised by a small group of elderly politicians in Beijing.

Another problem has surfaced as a result of China's economic success: there is a growing disparity between the income of the average Chinese and that of some individuals, who are profiting immensely in China's emerging market economy. Upscale imported products are selling well in the larger cities. Even a showroom for expensive Ferrari automobiles recently opened in Beijing, with price tags and massive import and luxury taxes for a single automobile that would take the average Chinese some fifty years of savings to afford. Such imbalances in personal wealth may become a political problem for the Chinese leadership.

China's Premier Li Peng, in a speech at the opening of the National People's Congress in Beijing in March 1994, called for a balance between growth and reform on the one hand and stability on the other. He also called for a sharp reduction in China's growth rate, and cited a need to oppose "money-worship, ultra-individualism, and decadent lifestyles" and to continue the crackdown on corruption and crime.

Although China is still a developing country in an economic sense, it is one of the greatest civilizations of all time, having contributed significantly to art, science, and philosophy over the centuries, and with a recorded history beginning over 3,000 years ago. Even during its Cultural Revolution and the isolation of recent decades, it has maintained technological progress. In sports, its athletes have continued to win Olympic medals.

> **ICD Prevention Tip—Business Style**
>
> *Although China is now an important player in international trade, it was "out of the loop" for several decades as a result of the Cultural Revolution. Do not expect high levels of business sophistication and efficiency in most of your dealings with the Chinese. Be explicit and patient in your communications.*

Feudal dynasties and an imperial system prevailed in China until 1911, when the Manchu Dynasty was overthrown by forces led by Dr. Sun Yat-sen and a republican system began to develop. Political and military factions contended for power from the early 1920s (the Chinese Communist Party was founded in Shanghai in 1921), and Japan began to exert economic and soon military control over much of the country. In the 1930s Japanese policy toward China became increasingly aggressive. Japan occupied Manchuria and attacked or invaded other parts of the country during this period. In 1937 the Sino-Japanese War broke out, uniting diverse Chinese factions against Japan and continuing to the end of World War II. The Japanese occupation of China eventually collapsed as World War II entered its final phase, but a united China was not the result. Civil war erupted in 1945 between the Nationalist Party under Chiang Kai-shek and the Communist Party under Mao Ze-dong. The Communists won that war, and the Nationalists moved their government to Taiwan.

> **ICD Prevention Tip— Small Talk**
>
> *For small talk in correspondence or conversation with Chinese, good topics include Chinese culture and history, China's economic progress, and the excellence of its athletes.*

The military forces led by Mao were fueled by revolutionary zeal and a deprived population that had suffered from twelve years of warfare. Following the Communists' victory in 1949, a period of agrarian reform and social restructuring substantially changed the economy and political organization of the country. A centrally planned socialist government and economy prevailed for the following two decades. A strong industrial base, following the Soviet Union's model, was developed during this time. Then a period of isolation and anti-intellectualism, dubbed the Cultural Revolution, brought on the disintegration and stagnation of China's social and produc-

> **ICD Prevention Tip— National Loyalty**
>
> *The Chinese, like others from collectivist cultures, are loyal citizens. In communications with them it is best to avoid political discussions and any criticism of government leadership and policies. Correspondingly, it will not reflect well on you if you criticize your own government.*

> ## ICD Prevention Tip—National Sensitivities
>
> *In correspondence or other communications with Chinese, you should refer to China as "China" or "the People's Republic of China," not "Mainland China." Hong Kong and Taiwan should not be mentioned as separate countries. Taiwan should be referred to as the "Province of Taiwan" not (as Taiwan calls itself) "the Republic of China." If you use a map with any of your communications, be certain that Hong Kong and Taiwan are not labeled on it as independent countries.*

tive systems from 1966 to 1976. Following this, China entered its present period of modernization, economic reform, and gradual opening to international trade.

Although Westerners and Western influences were present in China from the early 1800s, and Western religious missionaries have been persistent in their efforts to serve and proselytize the Chinese, China tends to remain aloof from foreign influences. And it is well to remember that China remains a communist country, despite its recent capitalistic leanings. Although a private sector is emerging, businesspeople from "free world" countries will encounter attitudes and practices markedly different from their own. Moreover, many of the Chinese with whom they will deal, even in business, are essentially government bureaucrats.

China also adamantly claims sovereignty over Hong Kong and Taiwan. Hong Kong will revert to China in 1997 as the result of a Joint Declaration of China and Great Britain made in 1984. No such plans are in the works for Taiwan; Beijing simply does not recognize Taiwan's assertions of independence.

There are four principal problems facing international businesspeople who would trade with China. First, China has a low per capita income. Although there is strong pent-up demand, the great majority of China's people do not have much money to spend. Second, China's infrastructure is poor. Getting goods into the distribution system is an immense task. Transportation systems and telecommunications are still poor in many areas. Third, China is not a homogeneous market; its provinces differ in many ways. Therefore, marketing strategies cannot be applied across the board. Fourth, foreign exchange restrictions inhibit the free transfer of currency from China. Foreigners cannot easily get their profits and capital investments out of the country.

▲ ▲

COUNTRY DATA: CHINA

FORMALITY FACTOR • Moderately high

POPULATION • 1.2 billion

GROSS DOMESTIC PRODUCT • $1.9 trillion

INCOME PER CAPITA • $1,680

AVERAGE GROWTH RATE, 1985–1992 • 6.2 percent

GOVERNMENT • Socialist republic

ETHNIC GROUPS • Han Chinese 93%, Zhuang, Hui, Uygur, Yi, Miao, Manchu, Tibetan, others

RELIGION • China is officially atheist, but its constitution allows freedom of religious belief, and there are Buddhists, Taoists, Confucians, Muslims, and others. There are also a few Christian churches and Islamic mosques in the major cities. Percentages for religious affiliations are not available.

BUSINESS HOURS • Normal business hours are Monday through Saturday, 8:00 A.M. to 6:00 P.M., with an hour and a half to two hours taken off at noon.

LITERACY • 73%

LANGUAGES • Mandarin is the official language of China, but there are many dialects, the principal ones being Cantonese, Wu (Shanghai), Fukinese, and Hakka. The written language consists of ideographic characters and is uniform throughout China. English is spoken by some but not many.

TELECOMMUNICATIONS • Telephones are not as prevalent in China as in more developed countries, nor do they work very well. However, hotels and many offices have modern telephone equipment and fax machines.

SPORTS • Gymnastics, Ping-Pong, riflery, and weight lifting are a few of the more popular sports.

MONEY • "People's currency" is issued by the People's Bank of China. The principal denomination is the yuan, and prices are expressed in yuan. The currency itself is known as Renminbi, or RMB. The two words—*yuan* and *Renminbi*—are often used interchangeably, with *yuan* used to express amounts of currency. Accordingly, an item might be priced as "100 yuan in RMB."

One U.S. dollar is equal to about eight and a half yuan.

MAJOR HOLIDAYS

New Year's Day	January 1
Chinese New Year	Late January or early February*
Labor Day	May 1
National Day	October 1

USEFUL PHRASES

English	Mandarin[†]	Phonetic Pronunciation[††]
Hello	Ni hao	Knee how
Good morning	Zao shang hao	Tzaow shang how
Good evening	Wan shang hao	Wahn shang how
Good night	Wan an	Wahn ahn
Good-bye	Zai jian	Dzye jee-en
Yes	Dui	Doo-ee
No	Bu dui	Boo doo-ee
Please	Qing	Ching
How much?	Duo shao?	Doo-oh shah-oh?
Thank you	Xie xie	Shee-yeh shee-yeh
You're welcome	Bu xie	Boo shee-yeh
Cheers	Gan bei	Kahm pie
I don't understand	Wo bu dong	Wah boo dong

▼ ▼

HONG KONG

Reemergent Business Center

A few years ago many in Hong Kong and elsewhere wondered whether this center of Asia-Pacific business communications, deal making, and finance had any future at all. In 1984 the governments of the People's Republic of China and Great Britain signed a Joint Declaration for the return of Hong Kong to China on July 1, 1997. Hong Kong, together with Kowloon Peninsula and the New Territories, will

---

*   Date varies

†   Pinyin romanization

††   Rough phonetic guidelines are based on American pronunciation.

CHINA

NEW TERRITORIES

KOWLOON

VICTORIA

LANTAU ISLAND   HONG KONG ISLAND

HONG KONG

then become a Special Administrative Region within China with a high degree of autonomy except in foreign affairs and defense. It will continue in that status for fifty years, at which time it will come under the direct administration of China. The Joint Declaration precipitated a capital drain and brain drain in Hong Kong, with many fearing that China will dismantle the colony's capitalist institutions. Well-to-do Hong Kongese relocated themselves and their businesses to North America and other parts of the world. Many talented businesspeople left to seek their fortunes elsewhere.

In the last few years, however, confidence in Hong Kong's commercial future has grown enormously. One reason is that China's own economy has grown in leaps and bounds since the Joint Declaration, tilting strongly in the free-market and private-sector directions. (See "China.") A second reason is that China has signaled in various ways its intention to permit Hong Kong to continue its commercial activities; for instance, China approved the construction of a new $6 billion airport and agreed to other infrastructure improvements. A third and more telling reason is the importance of Hong Kong to China as an international trading and finance center. Fully 40 percent of China's trade now goes through Hong Kong, and Hong Kong is functioning as a point of entry for much of China's new foreign investment. There is little chance that China will permit this substantial link in its expanding economy to deteriorate.

So Hong Kong, considered by many the world's foremost international business center, is booming once again. There remains concern over 1997, and the British continue to press for democratic political reforms that will survive the transition to Chinese sovereignty. But all this takes a backseat to business. Business is in the air: throughout Hong Kong people are buying, selling, trading, planning, and plotting.

A kinetic pace is characteristic of Hong Kong business. An old Hong Kong proverb goes: "Register a business in the morning. Open in the afternoon. Have a profit by nightfall"—and traditionally Hong Kong is a city of small businesses. It does have its huge houses, such as Jardine Matheson and Hutchison Whampoa, as well as the regional offices of some of the world's largest multinational corporations. However, the vast majority of economic activities in Hong Kong are carried out by businesses with fewer than twenty-five employees. In keeping with collectivist culture, these businesses are invariably family-owned and

family-run. But Hong Kong is also highly entrepreneurial. Sons and daughters and siblings and cousins in family-owned businesses—and many others—are continually striking out to start a new business and "have a profit by nightfall." Opportunities are seldom overlooked, and competition is keen.

The commercial history of Hong Kong is surprisingly modern, and it started with a bang—the Anglo-Chinese War of 1839–1842, referred to sometimes as the Opium War. The Chinese, concerned with the expanding opium trade in the region, drove British and other foreign traders out of Guangzhou in 1839. The British took refuge at the port of Hong Kong. A period of posturing and limited military engagements followed, ending with the British establishing Hong Kong as a Crown Colony in 1843 and the Chinese ceding the Kowloon Peninsula to the British in 1859.

International commerce became active in Hong Kong at that time. Commercial interests thrived, and in 1898 the British, to protect these interests, negotiated a ninety-nine-year lease from China of the New Territories, a large area immediately to the north of Hong Kong Island and the Kowloon Peninsula. It is the expiration of the lease on the New Territories that led the governments of the People's Republic of China and Great Britain to negotiate and sign the Joint Declaration. When Hong Kong is returned to China in 1997, it will have been under continuous British rule for over 150 years, except for 4 years of occupation by the Japanese during World War II.

Hong Kong's population of about 6 million people is largely Chinese— mostly from China's adjacent Guangdong Province—but it includes a large expatriate business community. This energetic multitude is crammed onto about 412 square miles of land area consisting of Hong Kong Island, Kowloon Peninsula, the New Territories, and a cluster of small islands on the southeast coast of China.

> ### ICD Prevention Tip— Good Luck
>
> *With the superstitious Hong Kong Chinese, heed their suggestions that a product be introduced, a meeting held, or a contract signed on a certain day or in a certain manner.*

An important characteristic of Hong Kong Chinese is that they tend to be superstitious, acutely aware of lucky and unlucky days, places, colors, and events. The principles of *feng shui* are keenly observed: even prominent Western architects will consult a practicioner before embarking on building projects. For more on *feng shui*, as well as auspicious colors and numbers, see Chapter 3.

▲ ▲

Country Data: Hong Kong

Formality Factor • Moderate

Population • 5.8 million

Gross Domestic Product • $107.4 billion

Income per Capita • $18,520

Average Growth Rate, 1985–1992 • 5.6 percent

Government • Chinese terrritory under British administration

Ethnic Groups • Chinese 95%

Religion • Hong Kong's principal religions are Buddhism and Taoism (85%), Christianity (8%); sizable Muslim, Hindu, and Sikh communities also exist.

Business Hours • Normal business hours are Monday through Friday, 9:00 A.M. to 5:30 P.M., with an hour for lunch taken from 1:00 P.M. to 2:00 P.M. Some offices are open on Saturday morning.

Literacy • 77%

Languages • English and Chinese—written and spoken—are the two official languages of Hong Kong. English is widely used in commercial and financial circles. Cantonese is the principal Chinese dialect spoken, but Mandarin is now coming into wider use. The written Chinese language is ideographic and is uniform regardless of dialect.

Telecommunications • Telecommunications are excellent in Hong Kong. Fax machines are in wide use. International direct dialing is available throughout the city. The postal service is excellent as well. International courier services are widely available.

Sports • Horse racing, cricket, and soccer are the popular sports.

Money • Currency is the Hong Kong dollar, signified by the prefix "HK$." Cash is easily obtained at banks and hotels. Major credit cards and international traveler's checks are accepted throughout Hong Kong.

One U.S. dollar is equal to about HK$7.3.

MAJOR HOLIDAYS

New Year's Day	January 1
Lunar New Year	Late January or early February

Good Friday, Easter	March or April, four days including the following Monday	
Ching Ming Festival	April 5	
Queen's Birthday	A Monday in early June	
Tuen Ng Festival	June	
Liberation Day	Late August	
Day following Mid-Autumn Festival	September	
Chung Yeung Festival	October	
Christmas Day	December 25	
Boxing Day	December 26	

USEFUL PHRASES

English	Cantonese*	Phonetic Pronunciation
Hello	Neih hau	Nay hoe
Good morning	Jou sahn	Joe sun
Good afternoon	M'an	Mm-on
Good night	Jou tau	Joe tow
Good-bye	Joi gin	Joy gin
Yes	Haih	High
No	Mhaih	Mm-high
Please	Ching neih	Ching-nay
How much?	Geih do tsing?	Gay doh tsin?
Thank you	Do jeh	Doh-jay
You're welcome	Mmsaih do jeh	Mm-sigh doh-jay
Cheers	Yum tsing	Yum-sin
I don't understand	Mming baak	Mm-ing bahk

▼ ▼

INDONESIA

Subtle Giant

Not long ago an American waited months for word from Indonesia that an important transaction had received necessary governmental

---

* See "China" for Mandarin.

clearance. His colleagues in Jakarta were vague on the telephone and in correspondence about why the clearance was taking so long. He finally learned that one of the Indonesian links in the transaction chain had delayed paying an excise tax that was due. His colleagues had been reluctant to identify the problem in their communications for fear that any criticism of the Indonesian would be overheard or reported and might further complicate the problem—or that the reluctant link would demand more money to complete the transaction on realizing its value to the parties concerned.

In Indonesia much goes on—or fails to go on—that a foreign businessperson, even one with good communicating abilities, will never hear about. This is certainly true when long-distance communications are involved. It is also true for foreigners who live and work in Indonesia. For Indonesians there is more to be gained by subtlety and indirection than by clear communications. A corollary is that there is often no "sticker price" on products and services in Indonesia. The price of most things is arrived at by negotiation. Even if prices are stated, they can often be negotiated down. As Indonesians will say, "Anything is possible"—for a price or other consideration, that is.

On a small scale, the value of action or inaction is found in favors and little payments made to officials at lower levels of government to carry out, or to refrain from carrying out, their responsibilities. For example, imported goods

> ### ICD Prevention Tip—Interpretations
>
> *Don't take things at face value in your communications with Indonesians. Tactfully press for clarification. Develop relationships with people in Indonesia upon whom you can rely to assist you in interpreting and delivering communications.*

are often not cleared by customs until a customs official receives something of value from an importer, and a licensing infraction sometimes becomes a legal prosecution unless a court official is paid to overlook it. On a larger scale, various permits and contracts seem never to materialize unless payments are made to a person of influence. While payments like these occur throughout the world, in Indonesia the practice is cultural, part of a tradition of honoring important personal relationships, spreading the wealth, and paying deference to one's hierarchical superiors (even lowly bureaucrats are considered superiors since they represent the government). Low salaries also play a part in the case of payments to bureaucrats. It is an accepted premise that civil servants derive a portion of their compensation from such payments, not unlike the premise that waitresses and taxi drivers derive a portion of their compensation from tips.

> **ICD Prevention Tip—Local Assistance**
>
> *If your own culture prevents you from dealing effectively with the Indonesian value system, establish a relationship with people in Indonesia who are accustomed to the system and can help you accomplish your objectives within the parameters of the country's culture and laws.*

Although most business is done in the capital city of Jakarta, communications are complicated by the sheer size and diversity of the country. Indonesia is the largest of the Southeast Asian countries, consisting of over 13,500 large and small islands stretching over 3,200 miles east to west and over 1,100 miles north and south. Its geographic expanse is therefore similar to that of Australia or the continental United States. Each one of its principal islands—Java, Sumatra, Sulawesi, Borneo (Kalimantan is the portion belonging to Indonesia), and New Guinea (Irian Jaya is the Indonesian portion)—is in itself the size of a small country. Of its smaller islands perhaps the best known is Bali.

Indonesia's population of 182 million makes it the fourth largest country in the world, after China, India, and the United States. Its people are predominantly Malay but otherwise ethnically diverse. (There are more than 300 ethnic groups in Indonesia.) Chinese constitute a small but economically important minority. Approximately two-thirds of the population live on the island of Java, where Jakarta is located. About three out of four Indonesians live in rural areas, and about one out of two work in the agricultural sector.

The vast majority of the population, about 85 percent, follow the Islamic religion, and government policies often reflect religious conservatism. Postal regulations prohibit materials that offend Islamic beliefs. Sexually oriented materials are often confiscated by postal authorities on this basis. In one instance, a videocassette tape of the recent marriage of an American woman (in a Methodist ceremony) was mailed to her in Jakarta from the United States. Postal authorities refused to release it. The woman guessed that the authorities objected to a scene of the married couple kissing at the conclusion of the ceremony. Kissing in public is offensive to Muslims in Indonesia.

During the early history of Indonesia, Malay people migrated from the Asiatic mainland, and Indian and Asian kingdoms colonized the region. Dutch, Portuguese, Indian, and Persian traders plied its waters. Gradually, the Dutch brought the area under their control as the Netherlands East Indies. Dutch rule continued for some 300 years, until the Japanese occupied the country during World War II. The Dutch returned after the war but were soon ousted by Indonesian nationalists led by Sukarno. Sukarno's government was marked by political instability and a stumbling economy. An unsuccessful coup attempt in 1965 led to transfer of leadership in 1967 to General Suharto. Suharto continues to lead the country, and his administration has compiled a remarkable record of economic progress and national unification.

> **ICD Caution— Government Sensitivities**
>
> *Although Indonesia embraces many democratic principles, the Suharto administration is highly sensitive to criticism, especially of the business interests and influence of Suharto's children and of the Chinese community in Indonesia, who are each said to profit substantially from close relations with the administration. In your communications with Indonesians, be careful not to criticize the government on these counts—or others, for that matter. Even though your correspondents might agree, they will not want to be visibly associated with the criticism.*

An important factor in the unification of this vast and diverse country has been the government's promotion of five fundamental social principles known as the *Pancasila:* belief in one god, nationalism, humanitarianism, representative government, and social justice. The *Pancasila* have been used by the government at times to suppress divisive factions, but there is no doubt that they give the diverse Indonesians a common philosophical touchstone.

▲ ▲

COUNTRY DATA: INDONESIA

FORMALITY FACTOR • High

POPULATION • 181.3 million

GROSS DOMESTIC PRODUCT • $494.9 billion

INCOME PER CAPITA • $2,730

AVERAGE GROWTH RATE, 1985–1992 • 4.7 percent

GOVERNMENT • Republic

ETHNIC GROUPS • Javanese 45%, Sundanese 14%, Madurese 8%, coastal Malay 8%, others

RELIGION • Islam is the principal religion of Indonesia; Muslims constitute about 85% of the population. Other prominent religions are Christianity (about 6%), Buddhism (about 2%), and Hinduism (about 1%).

BUSINESS HOURS • Most business offices are open Monday through Friday, 8:00 A.M. to 5:00 P.M. Government offices and some business offices are open on Saturday from 8:00 A.M. to 1:00 P.M. A lunch hour is normally taken on weekdays at noon or 12:30 P.M.

LITERACY • 77%

LANGUAGES • There are about 365 languages and dialects spoken in Indonesia, but Malay-based Bahasa Indonesia is the official language and is understood by most Indonesians. English is spoken at senior levels of business and government and by many Indonesians who are in frequent contact with international visitors.

TELECOMMUNICATIONS • Telecommunications are excellent in hotels and business offices in Jakarta. Fax machines are in wide use there, and international courier services are available. Elsewhere in Indonesia facilities are not so satisfactory.

SPORTS • Soccer is the primary spectator and competitive sport of Indonesia. Golf, tennis, and water sports are enjoyed by many.

MONEY • The unit of currency is the rupiah (Rp.). Cash is easily obtained at banks and hotels. Major credit cards are widely accepted throughout Indonesia. International traveler's checks are accepted in hotels but often not in shops. One U.S. dollar is equal to about 2,170 rupiahs.

MAJOR HOLIDAYS

New Year's Day	January 1
Lailat Al-Mi'raj	January/February*
Good Friday	Friday before Easter*
Easter	March/April*
Lebaran	April (two days)*
Waisak	May*
Ascension Day	May*
Idul Adha	July*
First Muharan	July*
Independence Day	August 17
Birthday of Prophet Muhammad	October*
Christmas Day	December 25

USEFUL PHRASES

English	Bahasa Indonesia	Phonetic Pronunciation
Welcome	Selamat datang	Suh-lah-maht da-tahng
Good morning	Selamat pagi	Suh-lah-maht pah-gee
Good afternoon	Selamat sore	Suh-lah-maht so-ray
Good evening	Selamat malam	Suh-lah-maht mah-lahm
Good night	Selamat tidur	Suh-lah-maht tee-duhr
Good-bye (to guest)	Selamat jalan	Suh-lah-maht jah-lahn
Good-bye (to host)	Selamat tinggal	Suh-lah-maht teen-gahl
Yes	Ya	Yah
No	Tidak	Tee-dahk
Please	Silakan	See-lah-kahn
How much?	Barapa harganya?	Bar-ah-pah har-gahn-yah?
Thank you	Terima kasih	Teh-ree-mah cah-see
You're welcome	Kembali	Kem-bah-lee
Cheers	Selamat	Suh-lah-maht
I don't understand	Saya tidak mengerti	Sah-ya tee-dahk men-gehr-tee

---

* Date varies

In pronouncing Bahasa Indonesia, place the accent on the next-to-last syllable of each word. For example, *silakan masuk* (come in) is pronounced "see-LAH-kahn MAH-sook." [Note: Bahasa Indonesia is similar but not identical to Bahasa Malaysia, another Malay-based language.]

▼ ▼

JAPAN

Trying Hard

One of the international executives interviewed for this book, who runs a consumer products marketing company that has been doing business in Japan for many years, says that in dealing with the Japanese it helps to "out-Japanese them." According to this executive, diligence is the key characteristic of the Japanese. If you want to do business with them successfully, you must equal or exceed their efforts. This means putting in long hours, going over things time and time again, responding promptly, following up faithfully, and continually improving your products and services.

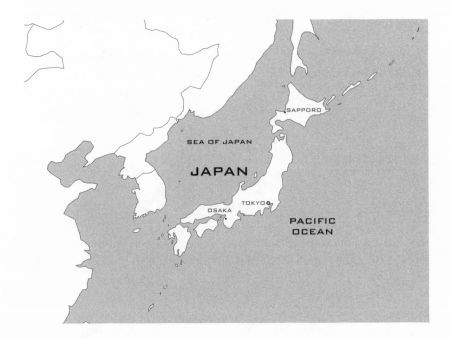

In recent years, when U.S. trade representatives complained to Japanese officials about Japanese trade barriers, the Japanese often responded, "Americans must try harder." Although their rhetoric on this subject became more subdued following the economic reversals and political scandals that have surfaced during the past few years, they continue to set high standards for themselves and others.

Following World War II, Japan founded its economic revival on an increasingly advanced and innovative manufacturing base. Its growth strategies, at first export-driven, now concentrate on domestic economic growth and investment outside Japan.

> ## ICD Prevention Tip— Diligent Efforts
>
> *Maintain an active correspondence with your Japanese contacts. Acknowledge receipt of their communications. Send interim status reports and other information that might interest them. Let them know about your activities. If a personal relationship develops, send holiday greetings.*

Japan's economy is currently the second largest in the world, after that of the United States. For an island nation having few natural resources and limited land area—a nation severely depressed fifty years ago, at the end of World War II—Japan's economic strength is remarkable. Although the Japanese economy has been in recession in recent years, it remains formidable. In particular Japan continues to export more than it imports, maintaining major trade surpluses with most of its large trading partners, notably the United States. This has led to international pressures on Japan to make its markets more accessible to foreign competition. It has also led to a gradual strengthening of the yen against other currencies, making Japanese products more costly overseas and foreign products less expensive in Japan.

International business firms that succeed in Japan normally credit their own diligence, perseverance, and adaptability: their efforts to modify their products and services to fit the Japanese market, their willingness to "conform to the system" rather than try to change it, and their ability to sustain early setbacks. Firms that succeed in Japan claim that market knowledge and cultural understanding are especially important there because Japanese society is so unique. This uniqueness stems in part from Japan's long isolation from the Asian continent. Early Asiatic migrants to Japan, mostly from China and Korea, coalesced into a largely homogeneous race. A military class began to

ICD Prevention Tip— Method

In communications, follow the lead of your Japanese contacts. Conformity is a form of sincere flattery for the Japanese, and it can help to alleviate any concerns they may have about the proper method of communication. If they prefer to correspond by letter, do the same. If they prefer using faxes, do that instead.

develop in the tenth century and was dominated by the seventeenth century by the Tokugawa Shogunate. The nation was then ruled by a succession of warlords, remaining essentially a rural economy largely closed to foreign trade and influences until in the mid-1800s commercial treaties were concluded with the United States, Britain, Russia, France, and the Netherlands. In 1868 the Tokugawa Shogunate restored the reins of government to Emperor Meiji, marking an opening of the country to Western civilization and the beginning of its transformation from a feudal, militaristic society to a modern industrialized state.

From the beginning of their civilization, the Japanese have had to conserve in many ways. They learned to live in close quarters, to be precise in their activities, to use materials economically, to be self-sufficient, and to save for an uncertain future. They also developed strong collectivist attitudes and traditions, which prevail today. The group orientation of Japanese, for example, accounts in part for the difficulties that non-Japanese often face in breaking into Japanese markets, and in establishing joint ventures and other business relationships in Japan. Japanese firms tend to set up exclusive networks with other Japanese firms, even overseas. Most of these networks are informal, but there are a number of large groupings of companies, called *keiretsu*, such as Mitsui and Fuji, which have cross-holdings of large blocks of each other's stock. (*Keiretsu* means "linkage" in Japanese.)

In keeping with their collectivist culture, the Japanese have a strong urge to conform in group behavior—a "herding instinct." This is often apparent in their choice of products and services. Combining traditions that value high quality and group acceptance, they tend to

ICD Prevention Tip— Success

Where possible, without being boastful, do not hesitate to identify yourself or your organization with prominent people, companies, and products. The Japanese like to be associated with success.

prefer products and services with established reputations and brand names.

A consequence of their conformity and commitment is that the Japanese are great customers and colleagues. Once they are sold or committed, they are loyal and steadfast. If a relationship becomes well established, it can flower. If a product "catches on" in Japan, sales can skyrocket. However, because of their dedication to high standards of quality and the long isolation of their society, Japanese tend to be resistant to products and services that fail to measure up to exacting standards of quality, to things that are new or different, and to things that do not appeal to their sense of scale and precision.

> ### ICD Prevention Tip—Women
>
> *If you are a woman dealing with Japanese, be clear about your title and responsibilities at the outset. Do not hide your gender (for example, by using only your first initials); confusion could do harm later.*

Japanese society is also highly male-oriented. Do not expect to see many women in senior positions at Japanese firms. A foreign businesswoman might be annoyed to find that a Japanese businessman will often pay greater deference to her male assistant. However, once a Japanese man is made aware of her authority, he has no difficulty in dealing with a woman as an equal.

▲ ▲

COUNTRY DATA: JAPAN

FORMALITY FACTOR • Very high
POPULATION • 123.9 million
GROSS DOMESTIC PRODUCT • $2.4 trillion
INCOME PER CAPITA • $19,390
AVERAGE GROWTH RATE, 1985–1992 • 4.0 percent
GOVERNMENT • Constitutional monarchy
ETHNIC GROUPS • Japanese 99%, Korean
RELIGION • Buddhism and Shintoism are the principal religions of Japan. Less than 1% of the population is Christian.
BUSINESS HOURS • Offices are open Monday through Friday, 9:00 A.M. to 5:00 P.M., with an hour for lunch normally taken at noon. Workers are also often at their desks well into the evenings and on

Saturday mornings, but they do not welcome telephone calls or office visits at these times. Further, the practice of long hours is gradually beginning to abate.

LITERACY • 99%

LANGUAGES • A standard dialect of Japanese is understood throughout Japan, and the written language, in addition to ideographic (kanji) characters, is in a standardized script.

English is the most frequently taught foreign language in Japanese schools, and many Japanese, especially members of younger generations, understand English. However, the Japanese tend to read and write English better than they understand spoken English or speak English.

TELECOMMUNICATIONS • Communications—telephones with international direct dialing, fax machines, the postal service, courier and messenger services—are all excellent and readily available in Japanese cities. Automatic fax machines are even available in the twenty-four-hour convenience stores that are found throughout urban areas.

SPORTS • Baseball and sumo wrestling are the primary spectator sports in Japan. Golf is a fanatically popular recreational sport.

MONEY • The unit of currency in Japan is the yen (¥). Cash is easily obtained at banks and hotels. Major credit cards and international traveler's checks are widely accepted throughout Japan except in small establishments. One U.S. dollar is equal to about ¥97.

MAJOR HOLIDAYS

New Year's Day	January 1
Adults' Day	January 15
National Foundation Day	February 11
Spring Equinox	Around March 21*
Greenery Day	April 29
Constitution Day	May 3
National Holiday	May 4
Children's Day	May 5
Respect for the Aged Day	September 15
Autumnal Equinox	Around September 23*
Physical Fitness Day	October 10

---

* Date varies

Cultural Day	November 3
Labor Thanksgiving Day	November 23
Emperor's Birthday	December 23

(Holidays falling on a Sunday are observed on the following Monday.)

Little business is done in Japan during the last ten days of December and first ten days of January, and many Japanese are on vacation during the month of August.

USEFUL PHRASES

English	Japanese	Phonetic Pronunciation
Hello	Hajimemashite	Hah-jee-meh-mahsh-tay
Good morning	Ohayo gozaimasu	O-hah-yo go-zye-mahs
Good afternoon	Konnichi wa	Kon-nee-chee wah
Good evening	Konban wa	Kon-bahn wah
Good-bye	Sayonara	Sigh-oh-na-ra
Yes	Hai	Hi
No	Iie	Ee-yeh
Please	Dozo	Doh-zo
How much?	Ikura desu ka?	Ee-koo-rah des kah?
Thank you	Arigato gozaimasu	Ah-ree-gah-toh go-zye-mahs
You're welcome	Do itashimashite	Doh ee-tahsh-ee-mahsh-tay
Cheers	Kampai	Kam-pie
I don't understand	Wakarimasen	Wah-kah-ree-mahs-sen

▼ ▼

MALAYSIA

Marching Well Together

Malaysia is a nation of great diversity. It is endowed with a variety of natural resources and has long been a major producer of oil and gas, tin, palm oil, natural rubber, cocoa, and hardwood. Its population is

mixed, with two prominent ethnic groups, Malay and Chinese. And its government is a parliamentary monarchy with a rotating hereditary monarch.

Ethnically, Malaysia is a heady mixture of people. Its population of 18 million is about 56 percent Malay, 34 percent Chinese, 8 percent Indian, and 2 percent "other." With political power in the hands of the Malays and economic power in the hands of the Chinese, Malaysia has had its share of racial friction. Businesspeople are predominantly Chinese Malaysians. However, people of different ethnic backgrounds often work in the same organization. Women are not normally active in business in Malaysia, but there are many women in high positions in government and the professions.

Following racial disturbances in 1969, the government introduced numerous policies to enhance the status of native Malays (called Bumiputras) and promote a more equitable distribution of wealth. Steps were taken to transfer some of the economic power held by Chinese Malaysians and others to Bumiputras. Some progress has been made (corporate equity in Bumiputra hands has increased from negligible amounts to about 24 percent). While these steps generated ill feelings on the part of Chinese Malaysians, economic development policies produced enough growth to satisfy the commercial appetites of all.

In Malaysia's rotating monarchy the royalty of the nine sultanates shares power with a strong federal government and a representative parliament. Every five years the hereditary rulers of these nine states elect one of their members to serve as king. The king rules on the advice of a cabinet led by a prime minister. In practice, substantial power is exercised by the prime minister and his cabinet ministers.

Malaysia's political system is the result of an unusual national history. Peninsular Malaysia was first settled by Asiatic people from the north. (Geographically, the country is divided into two parts: Peninsular Malaysia to the west, where about 85 percent of the population lives, and East Malaysia on the island of Borneo.) In the fifteenth century the rich silk and spice trade between Europe and the Far East established the port of Malacca (on the west coast of Peninsular Malaysia on the Straits of Malacca) as an important trading center. At first Portuguese traders controlled Malacca, then Dutch traders, and finally the British. Gradually all of Malaysia came under British influence and control. Tin mines and rubber plantations were developed with imported Chinese and Indian labor, and trade and industry steadily grew.

Except for three years of Japanese occupation during World War II, the British continued to control Malaysia (which they called Malaya) until 1957. In that year, as a result of a nationalist movement born out of the disruption of World War II, Malaysia declared its independence. A federation of thirteen states was formed. (Singapore was originally one of fourteen states of Malaysia, but it withdrew in 1965 to become an independent republic.) Nine of Malaysia's states are governed by the heirs of the sultans who once ruled them as kingdoms. The remaining four states are governed by appointed heads of state.

> **ICD Prevention Tip— Communications Style**
>
> *Use a fairly formal style in communicating with Malaysians. Owing in part to the long British presence in Malaysia and in part to the country's collectivist traditions, Malaysians' communications style tends to be formalistic.*

Malaysia has achieved some of the highest growth rates in Asia in recent years. Exports of its abundant natural resources have long supported Malaysia's economy. More recently, however, successful promotion of foreign investment in manufacturing and various value-added activities have resulted in a manufacturing sector that now accounts for 55 percent of all exports. Malaysia's economic development promises to continue at a rapid pace. Under a planning program dubbed Vision 2020, Malaysia expects to be "fully industrialized" by the year 2020. The current five-year plan anticipates growth rates averaging 7.5 percent and emphasizes continued development of the manufacturing sector and a substantial infrastructure buildup.

In addition, Malaysia is increasingly committed to free trade. Trade barriers have been steadily lowered in recent years. Moreover, the government has participated in a number of free trade initiatives as a member of the Association of Southeast Asian Nations (ASEAN) and the Asia Pacific Economic Cooperation forum (APEC). However, Malaysia is actively promoting an Asia-only trade group, called the East Asian Economic Caucus, that would exclude the United States, Canada, Australia, and New Zealand. Malaysia's reason for wanting such a group, it claims, is that Western trading styles promote governance styles that stress individual liberties over economic development.

> **ICD Prevention Tip—
> Government Sensitivities**
>
> *Be sensitive to the political and ethnic winds of Malaysia. If you are dealing with government officials, expect them to be highly development-oriented and critical of Western trade policies. If you are dealing with Malaysian businesspeople, anticipate that transactions involving relations with their own government can sometimes be delicate.*

The Malaysian government tends to be highly sensitive in international relations. Its prime minister, Dr. Mahathir bin Mohamad, was the only leader of an APEC nation who declined to attend the 1993 meeting of the sixteen-member organization, apparently in opposition to trade groups that include Western nations. When the prime minister of Australia, Paul Keating, referred to Mahathir as "recalcitrant," the Malaysian government banned Australian-made TV shows from broadcast in Malaysia and canceled an exchange program for Malaysians studying in Australia.

The attitudes of the Malaysian government are conservative. Criticism of the government by the media and others is not tolerated; pornographic materials (even soft porn such as *Playboy* magazine) are confiscated by customs officials; convicted drug traffickers are put to death.

▲ ▲

COUNTRY DATA: MALAYSIA

FORMALITY FACTOR • High

POPULATION • 18.2 million

GROSS DOMESTIC PRODUCT • $134.7 billion

INCOME PER CAPITA • $7,400

AVERAGE GROWTH RATE, 1985–1992 • 5.7 percent

GOVERNMENT • Constitutional monarchy

ETHNIC GROUPS • Malay and other indigenous 56%, Chinese 34%, Indian 8%, others 2%

RELIGION • Islam is the national religion, and Muslims constitute about 53% of the population. Other prominent religions are Buddhism (about 17%), Taoism and Confucianism (about 12%), Hinduism (7%), and Christianity (about 3%).

BUSINESS HOURS • Offices are normally open Monday through Saturday, with weekday hours from 8:00 A.M. to 4:30 P.M. and Saturday hours from 8:00 A.M. to 12:30 P.M. A lunch hour is usually taken around 1:00 P.M.

LITERACY • 78%

LANGUAGES • Bahasa Malaysia is the national language. Because Malaysia is a former British colony, many Malaysians speak and write English, which is often spoken with a British accent. English is widely used in business circles.

TELECOMMUNICATIONS • Telecommunications are excellent in the better hotels in Kuala Lumpur and in most business offices. Fax machines are in wide use there, and international courier services are available. Communications are good to excellent elsewhere in Malaysia.

SPORTS • Soccer, men's field hockey, badminton, and golf are the primary sports.

MONEY • The ringgit (dollar) is Malaysia's unit of currency, indicated by "M$." Cash is easily obtained at airport currency exchanges on arrival (during the day) and at banks and hotels. Major credit cards are accepted at hotels and larger establishments but not in most shops. International traveler's checks are accepted in hotels but not in most shops. One U.S. dollar is equal to about M$2.50.

MAJOR HOLIDAYS

New Year's Day	January 1
Chinese New Year	Late January or early February*
Federal Territory Day	February 1
Hari Raya Puasa	March/April*
Labor Day	May 1
Wesak Day	May*
King's Birthday	June 6
Hari Raya Raji	July*
Awal Muharram	July*
National Day	August 31
Birthday of Prophet Muhammad	October*
Deepavali	October/November*
Christmas Day	December 25

Muslims fast from dawn to dusk during Ramadan, the lunar month immediately preceding Hari Raya Puasa. They tend not to be available for daylight functions during that period, although functions after 8:00 P.M. are often feasible.

USEFUL PHRASES

English	Bahasa Malaysia	Phonetic Pronunciation
Welcome	Selamat datang	Slah-maht da-tahng
Good morning	Selamat pagi	Slah-maht pah-gee
Good evening	Selamat petang	Slah-maht puh-tahng
Good night	Selamat malam	Slah-maht mah-lahm
Good-bye	Selamat tinggal	Slah-maht ting-gahl
Yes	Ya	Yah
No	Tidak	Tee-dahk
Please	Sila or Tolong	See-lah or Toh-long
How much?	Berapa?	Buh-rah-pah?
Thank you	Terima kasih	Tuh-ree-mah cah-see
You're welcome	Sama-sama	Sah-mah sah-mah

---

* Date varies

English	Bahasa Malaysia	Phonetic Pronunciation
Cheers	Selamat minum	Slah-maht mee-num
I don't understand	Saya tidak faham	Sah-yah tee-dahk fah-hahm

[Note: Bahasa Malaysia is similar, but not identical, to Bahasa Indonesia, another Malay-based language.]

▼ ▼

NEW ZEALAND

Frugal Beauty

New Zealand is known for its lush beauty and its abundant agricultural and dairy production—wool, meat, butter, kiwifruit, apples, and all manner of wonderful produce. The land is New Zealand's principal resource, and the nation's character is strongly influenced by the close association of its people with the land: New Zealand is a nation of independent, self-sufficient, resourceful people.

The Maoris, who inhabited New Zealand before the Europeans started settling there, add to this strength. Captain James Cook, who explored New Zealand for six months in 1769–70, described the Maoris as "a brave, open, warlike people." In later years Maoris and

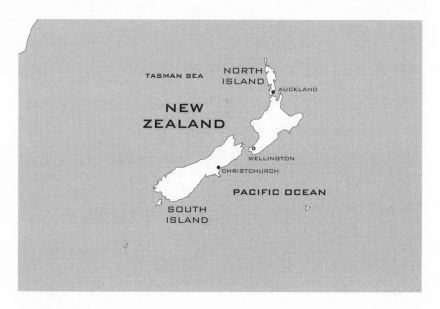

white settlers had many bloody confrontations, but today they share a mutual respect. Maoris constitute approximately 9 percent of New Zealand's population.

There is a friendly rivalry between New Zealand and its larger neighbor, Australia. Gough Whitlam, a former Australian prime minister, once referred to New Zealand as an "offshore farm," lacking Australia's mineral wealth but rich in fertile soil. For better or for worse, Australians tend to make light of New Zealanders and their largely pastoral lives. A favorite Aussie quip is "I went to New Zealand last week, but it was closed."

One important distinction between New Zealanders and Australians lies in their respective attitudes toward Great Britain. New Zealanders have a strong affinity for the British. Australians, on the other hand, often have an antipathy toward Britain. The difference can be traced to Australia's origin as a British penal colony; in contrast, New Zealand was colonized by free settlers who came voluntarily for a better life. Many of the settlers were said to be "second sons," who left Great Britain because their parents bestowed responsibility or fortune on another member of the family.

New Zealand's natural affinity for Great Britain was reinforced over the years by strong trade ties. Until recently, more than half of New Zealand's exports went to Great Britain. Now that Britain's trade is open to the European Economic Community, however, New Zealand is actively and successfully promoting its ties to Asia.

In keeping with an affinity for the British, New Zealanders tend to be reserved and formal in their communications. But, they are very practical people (probably as a result of living close to the land) and claim "not to stand on formality." Farmers at heart, they are especially resourceful in making something out of little—as one has asserted, "A New Zealander can fix a whole machine with a piece of wire."

Frugality and conservatism are other New Zealand characteristics, results in part of decades as a sub-

> **ICD Prevention Tip—
> National Sensitivities**
>
> *When communicating with New Zealanders, bear in mind their rivalry with their Australian neighbors and their affinity for Great Britain. Avoid comparisons to Australians. Avoid references that might be disparaging of an agricultural economy or of British ways.*

sistence economy. In terms of communications, this can translate into a reluctance to spend money on overseas faxes and telephone calls or to send interim progress reports to colleagues overseas. It can also mean a slower, more deliberate response time and deficient efforts in following through. Some claim that New Zealanders are lacking in responsiveness and follow-through as a consequence of having lived for many years under a socialist, welfare government, where many personal decisions were left for government to make, and high taxes left little discretionary income for enterprise.

More than any other national group in the Asia-Pacific region, New Zealanders take pride in their proficiency with the English language. This is again tied to their affinity to Great Britain. Many British expressions and usages appear in their speech and writings. For example, New Zealanders follow the British practice in using words such as *corporation, company,* and *government* as collective terms, as in "The company have issued a statement."

Notwithstanding adherence to high standards in speaking English, New Zealanders often have an accent that can be difficult for a non–New Zealander to understand. For example, "red dress" sounds like "rid driss," and a "dairy" is a "dearie." New Zealanders also enjoy their slang expressions. One favorite is "muck in," meaning to go about something informally, as in "Let's all muck in and get this job done." On the following table are a few more that international businesspeople will sometimes hear; some of these are also prevalent in Australia, or have British roots.

WORD OR PHRASE	MEANING
Cobber	Friend
Crikey	An all-purpose exclamation
Godzone	New Zealand (from "God's own country")
Kiwi	A New Zealander or anything associated with New Zealand
The lot	The whole thing. All of it.
Too right!	Definitely!

▲ ▲

COUNTRY DATA: NEW ZEALAND

FORMALITY FACTOR • Moderately low

POPULATION • 3.4 million

GROSS DOMESTIC PRODUCT • $47.5 billion

INCOME PER CAPITA • $13,970

AVERAGE GROWTH RATE, 1985–1992 • –0.4 percent

GOVERNMENT • Parliamentary state

ETHNIC GROUPS • European origin 86%, Maori 9%, Samoan and other Pacific islanders 3%

RELIGION • Most New Zealanders are Christian: Anglican 24%, Presbyterian 18%, Roman Catholic 15%, Methodist 5%.

BUSINESS HOURS • Normal business hours are Monday through Friday, 9:00 A.M. to 5:00 P.M., with an hour for lunch taken at noon.

LITERACY • 99%

LANGUAGES • English is spoken throughout New Zealand.

TELECOMMUNICATIONS • International direct dialing is available throughout New Zealand. Locally purchased phone cards are in common use. On rotary dial telephones, numbers go in the opposite direction from those on rotary dial telephones elsewhere. Instead of progressing from 1 to 0 in a counterclockwise direction, they descend from 9 to 0. However, push button telephones are now in wide use in New Zealand.

SPORTS • New Zealanders favor team sports and activities that take advantage of their striking outdoors. Rugby, cricket, tennis, sailing, fishing, skiing, and hiking are favorites. The Milford

Track, a four-day walk through breathtaking scenery on the South Island to the edge of Milford Sound, is one of the world's most beautiful hikes.

MONEY • New Zealand currency is denominated as the dollar, expressed internationally as "NZ$." The exchange rate of the New Zealand dollar is presently about US$0.62. International banking transactions are sophisticated. Major international credit cards are accepted throughout the country.

MAJOR HOLIDAYS

New Year's Day	January 1
Waitangi Day	February 5
Good Friday, Easter	March or April, four days including the following Monday
Anzac Day	April 25
Queen's Birthday	A Monday in early June
Labour Day	Fourth Monday in October
Christmas Day	December 25
Boxing Day	December 26

▼ ▼

THE PHILIPPINES

East or West?

The Philippines is a nation of contrasts struggling to form a single identity. It is a collectivist society, yet its institutions are primarily Western. It is rich in human and natural resources, yet in recent years it has had a stagnating economy. Its population is well educated and possesses a high degree of literacy, yet there are large pockets of poverty. It is a working democracy, yet political and economic power is vested in a few. Unlike in its Asian neighbors, Christianity is its principal religion, and English is the language of choice in business, government, and schools. (In terms of population, the Philippines is the third largest English-speaking nation in the world, after the United States and Great Britain.)

As collectivists Filipinos value group goals and long-term relation-

ships more highly than personal goals and short-term results. They also emphasize harmony, politeness, and modesty more highly than their Western counterparts. Hierarchical positions are closely observed, and older people are accorded special deference.

The Philippines' early identity was as a Spanish colony. The islands' first contact with the Western world came in 1521 with the arrival of Ferdinand Magellan, the Portuguese navigator. (Magellan was killed in the Philippines by the warrior king Lapu-Lapu.) The Spanish later colonized the islands, exerting largely political and religious influences. Philippine trade developed primarily with China and Mexico. Trade was ultimately dominated by Chinese merchants in the nineteenth century.

For much of the Philippines' modern history, its national identity has been as an American protectorate. Except for four years of Japanese occupation during World War II, the United States ruled the

> **ICD Prevention Tip—Business Style**
>
> *Do not assume that Western business styles work well in the Philippines. Make an effort to build warm personal relationships with your Filipino counterparts. Also, do not interpret a Filipino's politeness as acceptance of a business proposal. Tactfully press for a clear understanding of a positive response before you celebrate.*

Philippines from 1898—when the Spanish ceded the islands following the Spanish-American War—until 1946, when the Philippines became independent following liberation from Japanese rule by American forces. The two countries maintained close ties, in part as a result of American regional military strategies. In pursuit of these strategies, the United States collaborated with the regime of Ferdinand Marcos, who became president in 1965 and gradually accumulated dictatorial powers. Marcos declared martial law in 1972, to deal with increasing guerrilla activities. Fol-

lowing a long period of political turmoil, he was removed from office in 1986 with the election of president Corazon Aquino.

Close ties between the United States and the Philippines continued throughout this period. In 1991, however, the Philippines denied further tenure of the U.S. military bases at Subic Bay and Clark Air Base and placed a substantial chill on relations between the two countries. Since that time the Philippines has sought to remake its relationship with the United States on the basis of equal partnership as sovereign nations and economic cooperation. The United States continues to be the Philippines' largest trading partner and its major source of foreign investment.

Filipinos are not unlike Canadians in feeling smothered by the United States. However, in contrast to the Canadians, who tend to view the United States as a noisy, overbearing neighbor, Filipinos see it as more of a domineering parent or sibling. While the relationship is warm, it is often resentful, and always intense. On the other hand, Filipino relations with Japan, Taiwan, South Korea, and other Asian nations are ever-improving. Japan is the Philippines' second largest trading partner and its largest provider of development assistance. Japanese, Taiwanese, and South Korean companies are substantial investors in new ventures there.

The Philippines has much social and economic potential. It is a large island nation well positioned in the Asia-Pacific region, just north of the equator between the South China Sea and the Pacific

Ocean. It has over 7,000 islands, with the eleven largest possessing 94 percent of the country's land area. Luzon, to the north, where Manila is located, is the largest island; Mindanao, to the south, is the next largest. The country's 63 million people are mostly of Malay stock, and there are many ethnic and cultural subgroups. Seventy percent of the population lives in rural areas.

On the debit side, political unrest, official corruption, and the vested interests of powerful landed gentries dampen moves at economic reform, impede trade liberalization, and discourage foreign investment. The Philippines is also energy-dependent, with only about 40 percent of its recent energy requirements being domestically produced. In addition, its infrastructure, such as electrical power capacity and the system of roads, is either inadequate to meet a rapid expansion of the economy or badly in need of repair.

▲ ▲

COUNTRY DATA: THE PHILIPPINES

FORMALITY FACTOR • Moderate

POPULATION • 62.9 million

GROSS DOMESTIC PRODUCT • $153.5 billion

INCOME PER CAPITA • $2,440

AVERAGE GROWTH RATE, 1985–1992 • 1.9 percent

GOVERNMENT • Republic

ETHNIC GROUPS • Christian Malay 92%, Muslim Malay 4%, Chinese 2%

RELIGION • Roman Catholic 83%, Protestant 9%, Muslim 5%, Buddhist and others 3%. Muslims are located primarily in the southern regions (on Mindanao and in the Sulu archipelago).

BUSINESS HOURS • Offices are normally open Monday through Friday, from 8:00 A.M. to 5:00 P.M., with a lunch hour from noon to 1:00 P.M. Some offices are open Saturday from 8:00 A.M. to noon.

LITERACY • 90%

LANGUAGES • The official language of the Philippines is Pilipino (a form of the Tagalog dialect), which is used mainly in Metro Manila and by the mass media. English is widely spoken as a first or second language and is the basic language in business, government, and schools. Altogether there are some eighty-six spoken languages, the principal ones being Tagalog, Ilocano, and Cebuano.

TELECOMMUNICATIONS • In recent years, telecommunications have been badly handicapped by electrical brownouts and an inadequate number of telephone lines, especially in Manila. Telecommunications are good, however, in the better hotels in Manila and in most business offices. Fax machines are in wide use there, and international courier services are also available. Communications are only fair elsewhere in the Philippines. To avoid delays and hotel surcharges, it is a good idea to arrange for your office or home to place calls to you at appointed times.

SPORTS • Soccer, basketball, baseball, and cockfighting are popular.

MONEY • The Philippines's unit of currency is the peso, indicated by a "P." Cash is easily obtained at airport currency exchanges on arrival (during the day) and at banks and hotels. Major credit cards are accepted at hotels and larger establishments but not in most shops. International traveler's checks are accepted at hotels and banks but rarely elsewhere. One U.S. dollar is equal to about P25.

MAJOR HOLIDAYS

New Year's Day	January 1
Maundy Thursday	Thursday before Easter*
Good Friday	Friday before Easter*
Easter	March/April*
Bataan and Corregidor Day	April 9
Labor Day	May 1
Independence Day	June 12
National Heroes Day	Last Sunday of August
All Saints' Day	November 1
Bonifacio Day	November 30
Christmas Day	December 25
Rizal Day	December 30
Last day of the year	December 31

---

* Date varies

English	Tagalog	Phonetic Pronunciation
Hello	Kumasta	Koom-ah-stah
Good morning	Magandang umaga po	Ma-gahn-dahng oo-mah-gah po
Good afternoon	Magandang hapon po	Ma-gahn-dahng ha-poan po
Good evening	Magandang gabi po	Ma-gahn-dahng ga-bee po
Good-bye	Paalam	Pa-ah-lahm
Yes	Opo	O-po
No	Hindi po	Heen-dee po
Please	Paki	Pah-key
How much?	Maghano ba ito?	Mahg-hah-no bah eetoh?
Thank you	Salamat po	Sah-lah-maht po
You're welcome	Walang anu man	Wah-lahng ah-noo mahn
Cheers	Mabuhay	Mah-boo-hay
I don't understand (Please repeat)	Paki ulit po	Pah-key oo-lit po

▼ ▼ ▼ ▼ ▼ ▼ ▼ ▼ ▼ ▼ ▼ ▼ ▼ ▼ ▼ ▼ ▼ ▼ ▼ ▼

SINGAPORE

Managed Trader

The key to understanding Singapore lies in understanding its parallels to Hong Kong. Like Hong Kong, Singapore was founded by the British as a trading center, strategically positioned near Asia's busiest shipping routes. Its population is also primarily ethnic Chinese. And, like Hong Kong, Singapore is a small territory (Singapore Island and some fifty-seven smaller islands) with virtually no natural resources other than a deep-water port.

Unlike Hong Kong, however, Singapore is a tightly controlled society. Instead of frenzied business activity, there is deliberately implemented central planning. Public and private affairs alike are overseen by a visionary, hands-on government that leaves nothing to

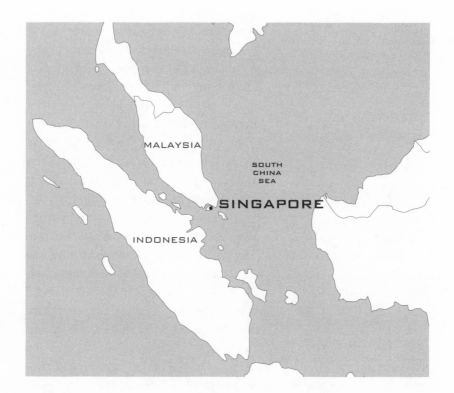

chance and involves itself deeply in the affairs of its people and their welfare; this is no helter-skelter growth economy. Citizens are told what to do and when and where to do it. For example, voting is compulsory, saving a part of one's salary is mandatory, long hair on men is officially discouraged, and even spitting on the sidewalk is prohibited.

Singapore was established as a trading post for the British East India Company in 1819 by Sir Stamford Raffles. From that time, except for three years of Japanese occupation during World War II, Britain controlled Singapore until it became self-governing in 1959. British influence is still felt: English, spoken with a British accent, is the principal language of business, government, and education; the legal and governmental systems are also based on those of the British. In these respects Singapore is similar to Malaysia, its immediate neighbor to the north, except that the ethnic composition of the population is about reversed. Whereas Malaysia is 56 percent Malay and 34 percent Chinese, Singapore is 76 percent Chinese and 15 percent Malay.

Singapore is now the modern essence of its origin: a technology-oriented manufacturing, financial, and services center of the first order. But, instead of Hong Kong's chaotic pace, there is an atmosphere of brisk efficiency. Its airport is one of the best in the world, but travelers are in and out of it so fast that they barely notice. Visitors are whisked into the city by taxis along attractive, tree-lined highways, arriving at one of many modern hotels within a half hour. They come away highly impressed with Singapore's modern office buildings, new subway system, cleanliness, and fine dining.

Critics of Singapore's carefully managed society assert that it is overregulated, that its pervasive governmental regulations dampen spontaneity and innovation, and that, while clean and efficient, it is very dull. But such criticism overlooks Singapore's achievement as the Economic Miracle of Southeast Asia. In less than thirty years, since leaving the Malaysian Federation in 1965 to become an independent republic, Singapore has forged one of the strongest economies in Asia, boasting the highest per capita income in Asia after Japan. The discretionary income of Singaporeans is also high because government policies discourage spending money on various big-ticket items such as single-family homes and expensive cars—and these policies effectively control land usage and traffic congestion. Singapore's tight government controls also provide a number of tangential benefits to foreign businesspeople. Intellectual property protection (copyright) is good, there is virtually no corruption, and the bureaucracy is reasonably efficient.

During the 1970s and 1980s, Singapore's economic growth was export-driven. A large manufacturing sector was established on the basis of an ample, educated workforce and liberal foreign investment policies. In recent years Singapore's economic success has produced a tight labor supply and higher wages. As a result, the government has shifted its economic policies to discourage investment in labor-intensive activities and promote technology-based, value-added manufacturing. Singapore today claims a global niche as Southeast Asia's primary commercial and financial center in the Age of Information and Technology. Fittingly, its financial services sector has been its growth leader in recent years, and high-tech manufacturing continues to advance. In addition, Singapore's growing wealth has enabled it to expand its economic base with direct foreign investment elsewhere, primarily in Southeast Asia.

▲ ▲

COUNTRY DATA: SINGAPORE

FORMALITY FACTOR • Moderate

POPULATION • 2.8 million

GROSS DOMESTIC PRODUCT • $44.1 billion

INCOME PER CAPITA • $15,760

AVERAGE GROWTH RATE, 1985–1992 • 5.9 percent

GOVERNMENT • Republic

ETHNIC GROUPS • Chinese 76%, Malay 15%, Indian 6%

RELIGION • There is tolerance toward all religions in Singapore, and many are practiced. The approximate breakdown is Taoist 29%, Buddhist 27%, Muslim 16%, Christian 10%, and Hindu 4%.

BUSINESS HOURS • Offices are normally open Monday through Friday from 9:00 A.M. to 5:00 P.M., and Saturday from 9:00 A.M. to 1:00 P.M. A lunch hour is taken on weekdays from 1:00 P.M. to 2:00 P.M.

LITERACY • 88%

LANGUAGES • Singapore's official languages are English, Chinese (Mandarin), Malay, and Tamil. However, English is the principal language of business and government and is widely used throughout Singapore. Several Chinese dialects (Hokkien, Teochew, Cantonese, Hainanese, Hakka, and Foochow) are spoken, but the government encourages the use of Mandarin in their place.

TELECOMMUNICATIONS • Telecommunications are excellent. Fax machines are in wide use. International direct dialing is available throughout the city. The postal service is excellent. International courier services are widely available.

SPORTS • Badminton, basketball, swimming, and boxing are popular.

MONEY • The unit of currency is the Singapore dollar, signified by the symbol "S$." Cash is easily obtained at banks and hotels and at currency exchanges at the airport upon arrival. Major credit cards are accepted throughout Singapore except at smaller shops. International traveler's checks are accepted at banks and hotels and some of the larger establishments that cater to visitors. One U.S. dollar is equal to about S$1.47.

MAJOR HOLIDAYS

New Year's Day	January 1
Chinese New Year	Late January or early February*
Good Friday	Friday before Easter*
Hari Raya Puasa	March/April*
Labor Day	May 1
Vesak Day	May 2
Hari Raya Haji	July*
National Day	August 9
Deepavali	October/November*
Christmas Day	December 25

USEFUL PHRASES

English	Mandarin[†]	Phonetic Pronunciation
Hello	Ni hao	Knee how
Good morning	Zao shang hao	Tzaow shang how
Good evening	Wan shang hao	Wahn shang how
Good night	Wan an	Wahn ahn
Good-bye	Zai jian	Dzye jee-en
Yes	Dui	Doo-ee
No	Bu dui	Boo doo-ee
Please	Qing	Ching
How much?	Duo shao?	Doo-oh shah-oh?
Thank you	Xie xie	Shee-yeh shee-yeh
You're welcome	Bu xie	Boo shee-yeh
Cheers	Gan bei	Kahm pie
I don't understand	Wo bu dong	Wah boo dong

▼ ▼

---

* Date varies
† See "Hong Kong" for Cantonese and "Malaysia" for Bahasa Malaysia.

SOUTH KOREA

Asian Individualists

In some ways Koreans are similar to people from individualist cultures. They are at times referred to as the "Irish of the East" because their style tends to be more boisterous, emotional, and confrontational than that of other Asian ethnic groups—characteristics other Westerners often attribute to the Irish. Occasional student riots and labor unrest in South Korea are vivid reminders of such characteristics. In a business context Koreans are often tough, emotional negotiators. They tend to be more direct in their communications than other Asians. For example, while other Asians might say yes rather than no because they wish to avoid giving offense, Koreans will say, "Yes, but. . . ."

Koreans also tend to be more individualistic than other Asians. They take more risks. They are often more entrepreneurial. They are more sensitive to deadlines and schedules. They also value more highly various personal factors such as titles and executive perks.

Koreans, believed to have migrated from central Asia to the Korean Peninsula, have much to be emotional about. For centuries Korea was "the meat in the sandwich." With China to the west, Japan to the east, and the Russian Empire to the north, it was occupied or invaded by one or another of its neighbors for much of its history. Japan annexed Korea outright in 1910. Following World War II, the

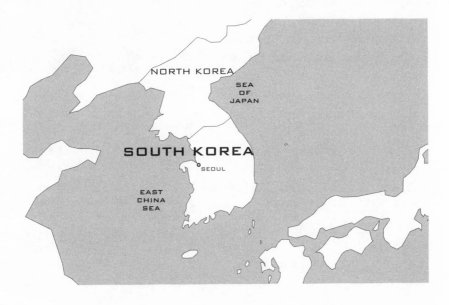

ICD Prevention Tip—
Recognition

*Be sure to address Koreans by
their proper titles and favor them
with individual recognition when
it seems appropriate—for example, when a Korean is personally
responsible for a sale or other
business success.*

Soviet Union and the United States occupied the peninsula, dividing it at the thirty-eighth parallel of latitude into North Korea (the People's Republic of Korea) and South Korea (the Republic of Korea). In 1950, perceived Soviet ambitions in the region led to the invasion of South Korea by North Korea, and to the three-year Korean War.

Perhaps it is this history of siege that has forged a distinctive national character. Koreans remain ethnically homogeneous, preserving a comparatively unique society. They tend to be suspicious of foreigners and highly nationalistic. For example, in their patriotic and single-minded quest for economic prowess, South Koreans often shun imported products and save or invest the bulk of their discretionary income.

Koreans are distinctive from other Asians in many ways. Their language is very different. In the fifteenth century King Sejong of Korea invented a national written script, called *hangul*. The beauty of *hangul* is that it does not require a person to memorize countless Chinese ideograms, as was the case before its adoption. Korea is the only country that has a holiday celebrating its script: Korean Alphabet Day, or *Hangul* Day.

In addition, many Asian cultural distinctions are even more prominent in the Korean mind than for other Asians. Hierarchy, status, age, and respect for elders are especially important. Shame, or loss of face, can be a heavy emotional burden. Hard work, education, and group commitment are viewed as vital to society's interests. South Koreans work long and hard, industrial workers averaging fifty-six hours on the job during a six-day workweek, the highest average in the world. Children go to school six days a week, 240 days a

ICD Prevention Tip—
National Sensitivities

*Today Japanese and Ameri-
cans need to be especially
sensitive to Koreans' feelings
toward them: the Japanese
because of atrocities committed during World War II,
the Americans because of the
long U.S. military and diplomatic presence in South
Korea.*

year, compared with children in the United States who go five days a week, 180 days a year. Vacations for South Koreans of all ages are few and short.

South Korea is highly male oriented. Women are accorded great respect in their roles as mothers and wives and exert considerable influence over families' buying decisions, but they are seldom found in the upper echelons of business or government.

South Korea came into its own after the Korean War. Whereas the 1950s in Korea were marked by political upheaval, the 1960s and 1970s saw growing stability and economic improvement. Then, in the 1980s, South Korea's economy boomed. Growth rates in 1986, 1987, and 1988 exceeded 12 percent, and growth continues. This success can be credited to two principal factors: the hard work and dedication of its people, and the close collaboration of business and government. During the 1960s President Park Chung Hee laid the foundation of a business/government partnership by setting up large government-owned corporations to develop key segments of the economy. These corporations, called *chaebols,* received the full financial and planning support of the government, and they thrived. They were gradually turned over to private, family-led ownership, but their close relationships with the government continue. The government coordinates their activities and dictates in large part the industries in which each may participate. Today large *chaebols* such as Samsung, Hyundai, Daewoo, and Lucky-Goldstar dominate business in South Korea.

> **ICD Prevention Tip—Marketing**
>
> *If your communications to Koreans relate to markets for goods and services to be used in the home, be sure to mention the appeal to Korean women.*

The international communications systems and abilities of the *chaebols* are excellent. Those of smaller Korean enterprises are also quite good. Such smaller enterprises are often found in or near "OfficeTels," commercial complexes where trading companies, lawyers, translation and secretarial firms, and other businesses are located.

South Korea's economy is largely export-driven, with manufactured goods constituting over 90 percent of exports. The electronics industry has had the highest rates of growth in recent years. However, the country has limited natural resources and must import many commodities for manufacturing. It is also energy-dependent, with only 22 percent of its energy needs domestically produced.

Like many developing countries, South Korea has a history of trade protection. This is slowly being liberalized, responding to pressure from other nations to lower barriers. On the political side, with an eye to economic implications, the government has taken a number of steps to improve relations with China, Japan, and North Korea. The reunification of the Korean Peninsula is a primary political objective.

▲ ▲

COUNTRY DATA: SOUTH KOREA

FORMALITY FACTOR • High to very high

POPULATION • 44.2 million

GROSS DOMESTIC PRODUCT • $360.3 billion

INCOME PER CAPITA • $8,320

AVERAGE GROWTH RATE, 1985–1992 • 8.5 percent

GOVERNMENT • Republic

ETHNIC GROUP • Korean 99%

RELIGION • Buddhist 20%, Roman Catholic 16%, Protestant 5%, Confucian 1%. Other religions, including Islam and Taoism, are also followed. In addition, there is an undercurrent of native shamanism in the religious beliefs of many Koreans.

BUSINESS HOURS • Office hours are normally Monday through Friday from 9:00 A.M. to 6:00 P.M. and Saturday from 9:00 A.M. to 1:00 P.M. A lunch hour is taken on weekdays from about 12:30 P.M. to 1:30 P.M.

LITERACY • 96%

LANGUAGES • Korean is the official language of South Korea. Although Korean has many Chinese words and its grammar is similar to that of Japanese, it is a distinct language. Written Korean, in contrast to the Chinese ideographic system, employs a phonetic alphabet with relatively few characters. This unique phonetic system helps account for South Korea's high literacy rate. English is understood and spoken to only a limited extent, although there are many in the senior ranks of business and government who speak and write English.

TELECOMMUNICATIONS • Telecommunications are excellent in South Korea. Fax machines are in wide use. International direct dialing is available throughout the country. International courier services are also widely available.

SPORTS • Soccer, baseball, tae kwon do (a martial art), and golf are the most popular sports.

MONEY • South Korea's unit of currency is the won, indicated by the symbol "KW." Cash is easily obtained at banks and hotels and, except at night, at currency exchanges at the airport upon arrival. Major credit cards are accepted in hotels and larger shops and restaurants. International traveler's checks are normally accepted only at banks and hotels. One U.S. dollar is equal to about KW800.

MAJOR HOLIDAYS

New Year's Day	January 1
New Year's holiday	January 2
Independence Movement Day	March 1
Arbor Day	April 5
Buddha's Birthday	May*
Children's Day	May 5
Memorial Day	June 6
Constitution Day	July 17
Liberation Day	August 15
Thanksgiving (two days)	September/October*
National Foundation Day	October 3
Christmas Day	December 25

USEFUL PHRASES

English	Korean	Phonetic Pronunciation
Hello	Yôboseyo	Yah-bo-say-oh

---

* Date varies

English	Korean	Phonetic Pronunciation
Good morning	Annyong hashimnika	Ahn-yohng hah-shim-nee-kah
Good evening	(same)	(same)
Good night	(same)	(same)
Good-bye	Annyonghee kaseyo	Ahn-yohng-hee kah-say-o
Yes	Ne	Neh
No	Aniyo	Ah-nee-yo
Please	Chom	Chohm
How much?	Ôllma imnika?	Ole-mah im-nee-kah?
Thank you	Kamsa hamnida	Kahm-sah hahm-nee-dah
You're welcome	Ch'onmaneyo	Chon-mahn-ay-yo
Cheers	Kônbae	Kohn-bai
I don't understand	Chal morûgetsumnida	Chahl mor-oo-get-soom-nee-dah

▼ ▼

TAIWAN

An Offshore Dynamo

International communications have a decidedly political slant in Taiwan, the Republic of China (ROC). From its founding—that is, from the time Chiang Kai-shek's Nationalist Party lost China's civil war to Mao Ze-dong's Communist Party in 1949 and retreated to Taiwan—the present government has claimed to be the true government of all of China. In earlier years Taiwan frequently and steadfastly invoked its policy of the "Three Nos" toward mainland China, the People's Republic of China (PRC): no negotiation, no compromise, no contact. Today, however, ROC leaders call for open economic and cultural exchanges with the PRC and give tacit approval to Taiwanese citizens increasing their contacts with the mainland through indirect investments (primarily via Hong Kong) and family visits. And the reunification of China remains high on the national agenda.

The catalyst for this move toward expanded communications overseas was Taiwan's economic success, fueled by the power of the

global marketplace. Now the world's thirteenth largest trading economy, Taiwan began its long march to economic prominence when the United States poured military aid into the country during the Korean War (1950–1953). Taiwan's leaders took the opportunity to move the country swiftly toward an export-driven, free-enterprise economy. Large government-owned corporations were set up to develop strategic industries, such as steel, petrochemicals, shipbuilding, and energy. New airports, highways, railways, seaports, and communications systems were built. Foreign investment was encouraged, and the economy thrived.

For its part, the PRC refused to acknowledge Taiwan's growth, and its claim to status as an independent nation. However, the PRC is now softening its own rigidity on the subject. At the 1993 summit of the Asia Pacific Economic Cooperation organization in Seattle, the PRC posed no objection to Taiwan's inclusion in the meetings, and with the PRC's own economic reforms rapidly moving toward a market economy, there is growing respect for Taiwan on the mainland.

Westerners once knew Taiwan as Formosa, the name it was given in the 1600s by the Portuguese, for whom *Ilha Formosa* meant "Beautiful Island." Its present name means "Terraced Bay" in Chinese. Owing to its proximity to trade routes (it lies off the east coast of China, between Japan and the Philippines), Taiwan was occupied from time to time by the Dutch, the Spanish, and the French. In 1894 it was invaded by the Japanese and remained under Japanese control until the end of World War II, when it was returned to Chinese rule. Culturally, politically, and economically, Taiwan has remained predominantly Chinese throughout its history. Some 85 percent of its inhabitants are descendants of emigrants from mainland China's neighboring Fukien and Guangdong provinces; the bulk of the remainder of the population are "mainlanders" who have arrived from various Chinese provinces since 1949.

Although Taiwan is Westernized in many ways, it does remain fundamentally traditionally Chinese. Age is venerated; social and organizational hierarchy is carefully observed; men dominate the senior levels of business and government (although there are many professional women, and family businesses are sometimes headed by a daughter and only child of the patriarch). Nonetheless, Taipei, Taiwan's capital city and commercial heart, is bursting with vitality. Its traffic jams and sprawling growth are characteristic of Taiwan's urgent quest for achievement.

Ethnic and cultural homogeneity aside, Taiwan is a country of great diversity. There are both high mountains and open seas; half of the island is covered with forests, so there are both forestry and fishery industries. One-third of the land is arable, producing rice, wheat, corn, and other crops as well as supporting livestock. However, agriculture now accounts for only about 5 percent of Taiwan's gross national product. Manufacturing accounts for about 37 percent and services for about 54 percent. Manufacturing now produces virtually everything from low-tech garments to high-tech computers, from household television sets to industrial shipbuilding.

Personal computer manufacturing is a major industry in Taiwan. General Kuo Yun, vice chairman and president of the Institute for the Information Industry in Taipei, claims that 80 percent of the world's personal computers are made in Taiwan. "ROC stands for Republic of Computers, not Republic of China," he often jokes.

Despite the significant influence of Taiwan's large, government-owned corporations, the strength of its economy lies principally in small, entrepreneurial

> ### ICD Prevention Tip— National Sensitivities
>
> *Although relations between Taiwan and the PRC are warming, outsiders should faithfully observe the autonomy of Taiwan in their communications with Taiwanese. For example, references to the PRC and "Greater China" (a phrase used by some to refer inclusively to mainland China, Taiwan, and Hong Kong) should be avoided, and one should never refer to Taiwan as the People's Republic of China. Taiwan's official name is the Republic of China (ROC).*

firms. In the manufacturing sector, fully 85 percent of Taiwan's factories employ fewer than fifty workers. The Taiwanese are especially proficient in product development, designing new products and bringing them to market faster than anywhere else in the world. Where they are weak, in the view of some observers, is in marketing and advertising. Also, according to one of the Taiwanese executives interviewed for this book, Taiwanese manufacturers need to sharpen their international product services, in particular by providing better manuals and instructions with their products.

A major impediment to communications with Taiwanese business enterprises is that so many of them are small. Another is that there are so many players in a given industry. Consequently, international firms have difficulty approaching potential Taiwanese suppliers and customers in an efficient manner.

This complex economy is not becoming any more manageable. Recently the government has taken steps to encourage businesses to move more rapidly into high-tech, value-added activities and to invest in production facilities in countries (largely in Southeast Asia) where labor costs are lower. Steps have also been taken to privatize some of Taiwan's government-owned industries. Government-held stock has already been sold in the China Steel Corporation and several public commercial banks. Other industries, including paper, chemicals, and construction, are targeted for privatization.

Substantial infrastructure improvements are also in the works. In 1991 Taiwan approved an ambitious Six-Year Economic Development Plan calling for $302 billion to be spent by the government and private industry on public works and industrial projects from 1991 to 1996. The plan contemplates antipollution projects, technology gains, energy diversification, and capital-intensive industrial developments. It also provides for various trade and financial liberalization measures designed to help the country achieve its economic targets.

▲ ▲

COUNTRY DATA: TAIWAN

FORMALITY FACTOR • Moderate

POPULATION • 20.7 million

GROSS DOMESTIC PRODUCT • $280 billion

INCOME PER CAPITA • $13,527

AVERAGE GROWTH RATE, 1985–1992 • 5.7 percent

GOVERNMENT • Republic

ETHNIC GROUPS • Taiwanese 84%, Chinese 14%, aboriginal 2%

RELIGION • Buddhism, Confucianism, and Taoism (together about 93%) are the predominant religions. About 5% of the population are Christian, and a small minority are Muslim. There are temples and churches of various faiths throughout the country.

BUSINESS HOURS • Offices are normally open Monday through Friday from 8:30 A.M. to 5:30 P.M. and Saturday from 8:30 A.M. to noon. Lunch on weekdays is normally taken from noon to 1:00 P.M.

LITERACY • 91%

LANGUAGES • Mandarin is the official language of Taiwan and the language of instruction in schools. English is spoken as a second language by about 50 percent of the population, especially in business circles and among young people; it is taught to all students as their first foreign language, beginning in the seventh grade. Taiwanese, a southern Fukien dialect, is also widely spoken and is increasingly popular. Taiwanese is frequently heard on television and in public activities, and speaking Taiwanese is becoming fashionable among the younger generation.

TELECOMMUNICATIONS • Telecommunications are excellent in Taiwan. International direct dialing is available throughout the country. Fax machines are in wide use. International courier services are also widely available.

SPORTS • Baseball, soccer, and basketball are the most popular sports.

MONEY • Taiwan's unit of currency is the New Taiwan dollar, indicated by the symbol "NT$." Cash is easily obtained at banks and hotels and at currency exchanges at the airport upon arrival. Major credit cards are accepted in hotels and larger shops and restaurants. International traveler's checks are accepted at banks, hotels, and some of the larger shops and restaurants. One U.S. dollar is equal to about NT$26.

MAJOR HOLIDAYS

New Year's Day, Founding Day	January 1
Chinese New Year	Late January or early February*
Youth Day	March 29
Children's and Women's Day	April 4
Tomb-Sweeping Day	April 5
Labor Day	May 1
Dragon-Boat Festival	May*
Midautumn Festival	August*
Confucius's Birthday	September 28
National Day	October 10
Taiwan Restoration Day	October 25
Chiang Kai-shek's Birthday	October 31
Sun Yat-sen's Birthday	November 12
Constitution Day	December 25

(Holidays falling on a Sunday are observed on the following day.)

USEFUL PHRASES

English	Mandarin[†]	Phonetic Pronunciation
Hello	Ni hao	Knee how
Good morning	Zao shang hao	Tzaow shang how
Good evening	Wan shang hao	Wahn shang how
Good night	Wan an	Wahn ahn
Good-bye	Zai jian	Dzye jee-en
Yes	Dui	Doo-ee

---

[*]   Date varies

[†]   Pinyin romanization

English	Mandarin[†]	Phonetic Pronunciation
No	Bu dui	Boo doo-ee
Please	Qing	Ching
How much?	Duo shao?	Doo-oh shah-oh?
Thank you	Xie xie	Shee-yeh shee-yeh
You're welcome	Bu xie	Boo shee-yeh
Cheers	Gan bei	Kahm pie
I don't understand	Wo bu dong	Wah boo dong

▼ ▼

THAILAND

Sweet Success

A favorite expression of Thais is *mai pen rai,* meaning "never mind; it doesn't matter; everything will be all right," an expression that says much about the agreeable Thai temperament. And one of the most popular stories about Thailand is *Anna and the King of Siam* by Margaret Landon, on which the musical comedy and movie *The King and I* were based. But let a foreigner speak admiringly of *Anna and the King of Siam* or *The King and I* and there will be no utterance of *mai pen rai.* In Thailand's constitutional monarchy, the king is held in high esteem. The subject of these works was Rama IV, king of Siam from 1851 to 1868 and a remarkable, farsighted leader who opened the doors of his kingdom to new ideas in science, education, and historical research. Thais deeply resent the portrayal of their beloved Rama IV in *The King and I* as something of a buffoon, and they hotly dispute the historical accuracy of *Anna and the King of Siam.*

The name Siam was changed to Thailand, meaning "Land of the Free," in 1939. Since 1932, despite frequent changes in leadership, Thailand has been governed by a unique collaboration of the military, a strong central bureaucracy, and a revered monarch. The military has generally been content to let the bureaucracy and key politicians run the government. The king's governmental role and indirect powers are often compared with those of the British throne but are in fact stronger owing to the respect he commands: the bloody 1992 pro-

---

† Pinyin romanization

CHIANG MAI

THAILAND

BANGKOK

ANDAMAN
SEA

SONGKHLA

SOUTH
CHINA
SEA

democracy riots in Bangkok were quelled following the king's scolding of Prime Minister Suchinda Kraprayoon and his opponent Chamlong Srimuang as the two kneeled before him.

Thailand is part of continental Southeast Asia, lying just north of the Malay Peninsula. About 84 percent of its population of 58 million is ethnic Thai, descended in part from tribes that migrated long ago from southern China. Other ethnic groups include Chinese, Laotians, Vietnamese, Malays, Cambodians, Burmese, and hill tribe peoples. Many of these, or their ancestors, entered Thailand as refugees from neighboring countries in times of war.

The culture of Thailand is clearly collectivist, but three factors stand out. First, the predominant religion of the country, Buddhism, is in greater evidence than predominant religions in other countries. Legions of Buddhist priests in orange robes are commonly seen in the streets. Second, a generous nature and a pleasant manner are very important to Thais. Conduct to the contrary can be embar-

rassing and demeaning. Third, individualistic behavior is more acceptable here
than in other collectivist countries.
Thais comfortably receive personal
credit for business success and other
achievements. They are also more
direct in expressing their thoughts,
although they do so politely.

Like many Asian countries, Thailand is male-oriented. Although the constitution gives women fully equal rights,
Thai women are traditionally submis-
sive toward men, and there are few
women in the senior ranks of business
and government. However, there are
many women in the professions, and
Queen Sirikit is prominent in active efforts to improve women's
rights.

In terms of economic performance, Thailand is one of the
strongest and fastest-growing countries in Asia. It achieved annual
growth rates averaging 12 percent in the period 1988–1990 while
maintaining low inflation rates and a stable currency. Exports boomed
in the late 1980s. Direct foreign investment, much of it from Japan,
jumped 54 percent in 1989. Growth has presently slowed somewhat,
but there are overall indications that Thailand's strong economic
expansion will continue.

The key to Thailand's economic success has been a series of pro-
business administrations in government that have implemented liberal, free-market development policies. Visitors to Bangkok, bogged
down in traffic and confounded by an
apparent lack of planning and coordina-
tion at every turn, may wonder at Thailand's achievements; however, the chaos
they encounter is largely the by-product
of Thailand's economic vitality.

Thailand has plenty on which to
base economic growth. A large pool of
inexpensive labor enables the country to
attract foreign investment for the expan-

sion of export-driven manufacturing industries. Thailand is also relatively rich in natural resources, with high-yielding agricultural lands and extensive reserves of tin, lead, zinc, potash, and oil and gas. Thailand is the world's leading exporter of rice and tapioca, and a major exporter of rubber, corn, and sugar.

While agriculture employs 65 percent of the working population, manufacturing is now the largest sector of the economy, producing about 25 percent of the gross domestic product compared with agriculture's 17 percent. Most manufacturing is located in the Bangkok area, where it expanded during the 1970s and 1980s from import-substitution activities (producing goods such as beverages and vehicles that were otherwise imported) to export-oriented activities such as the manufacture of clothing, electronics, and chemicals. Long-range government plans are to develop manufacturing centers in other parts of Thailand. Two new ports, a petrochemical complex, a fertilizer plant, and export-processing zones are planned for the eastern seaboard, southeast of Bangkok. On the services side, the government is pushing the development of tourism (the principal destinations are Chiang Mai, Pattaya, and Phuket) and Thailand's growing importance as a convention center.

The most pressing economic challenge for Thailand in the foreseeable future is to build infrastructure fast enough to keep pace with the rapid expansion of the economy. Severe strains are appearing in the country's port facilities, transportation networks, and electrical generating systems. Existing roads need to be upgraded and new ones built; expressways are needed to divert congestion from the Bangkok area; and more seaports, airports, and railways are needed.

▲ ▲

COUNTRY DATA: THAILAND

FORMALITY FACTOR • Moderate

POPULATION • 57.2 million

GROSS DOMESTIC PRODUCT • $301.4 billion

INCOME PER CAPITA • $5,270

AVERAGE GROWTH RATE, 1985–1992 • 8.3 percent

GOVERNMENT • Constitutional monarchy

ETHNIC GROUPS • Thai 84%, Chinese 12%

RELIGION • Thailand is 98% Buddhist. About 1% of the population is Muslim (largely in the south), and there are some Christians, Hindus, and Sikhs.

BUSINESS HOURS • Offices are normally open Monday through Friday from 8:30 A.M. to 5:00 P.M. A lunch break is taken at noon.

Literacy • 93%

LANGUAGES • Thai, the national language, is spoken throughout the country with only minor differences, but various grammatical forms are used depending on the social status of the persons being addressed. Thai is a tonal language that foreigners find difficult to learn. The written language is a distinctive script. English, French, German, and several Chinese dialects are spoken. Some Malay is spoken in the south. Many people in business and government speak English.

TELECOMMUNICATIONS • Telecommunications are good in hotels and offices in Bangkok but lag elsewhere in Thailand. Fax machines and international courier services are available.

SPORTS • Soccer and baseball are the most popular sports.

MONEY • Thailand's unit of currency is the baht, indicated by the symbol "B." Major credit cards are accepted in hotels and larger shops and restaurants. International traveler's checks are accepted at banks and hotels. Cash may be obtained at currency exchanges at international airports and banks and hotels. However, exchange rates for money and traveler's checks at hotels tend to be unfavorable. One U.S. dollar is equal to about B25.

MAJOR HOLIDAYS

New Year's Day	January 1
Makha Bucha Day	February*
Chakri Memorial Day	April 6
Songkran Festival Day	April*
Labor Day	May 1
Coronation Day	May 5
Visakha Bucha Day	May/June*
Queen's Birthday	August 12
Chulalongkorn Day	October 23
King's Birthday	December 5
Constitution Day	December 10
New Year's Eve	December 31

(Holidays falling on a Saturday or Sunday are normally observed on the following Monday.)

USEFUL PHRASES

English	Thai	Phonetic Pronunciation
Hello	Sawat dee khrap (to a man)	Sah-waht dee kahp
	Sawat dee kha (to a woman)	Sah-waht dee kah
Good morning	(same)	(same)
Good evening	(same)	(same)
Good night	(same)	(same)
Good-bye	(same)	(same)
Yes	Khrap (to a man)	Kahp
	Kha (to a woman)	Kah
No	Mai khrap (to a man)	My kahp
	Mai kha (to a woman)	My kah
Please	Dai prod	Dye prod
How much?	Taorai?	Ta-oh-rye?

---

*   Date varies

English	Thai	Phonetic Pronunciation
Thank you	Khob khun khrap (to a man)	Cob koon kahp
	Khob khun kha (to a woman)	Cob koon kahp
You're welcome	Yindee	Yin-dee
Cheers	Chaiyo	Shay-yoh
I don't understand	Pom mai kaojai (to a man)	Pom my kah-o-jye
	Dichan mai kaojai (to a woman)	Dee-chahn my kah-o-jye
Never mind	Mai pen rai	My pen rye

▼ ▼

UNITED STATES OF AMERICA

An Open Door

In contrast to the great nations of Asia, the United States is predominantly a country of recently arrived settlers from all over the world. Starting with the religious outcasts who came to its shores in 1620 and followed by waves of English, Irish, Europeans, black Africans (who arrived as slaves), and—more recently—Latin Americans and Asians, the United States has represented an open door to opportunity and a better life. Since 1884 the Statue of Liberty has stood at the entrance of New York harbor, welcoming large numbers of new arrivals. On its base are the words from Emma Lazarus's poem "The New Colossus":

> *Give me your tired, your poor,*
> *Your huddled masses yearning to breathe free,*
> *The wretched refuse of your teeming shore.*
> *Send these, the homeless, tempest-tost to me,*
> *I lift my lamp beside the golden door!*

Today, with such a national kaleidoscope of ethnic and cultural origin, there are no typical Americans. But freedom and opportunity, concepts central to the American Revolution (1775–1783) and symbolized as well by the Statue of Liberty, constitute typical and funda-

mental values for Americans. These values fuel the civil rights movement and various causes that seek equality of status or representation, such as the currently strong women's movement. In business they fuel a strong entrepreneurial spirit and a belief in the free-enterprise system, which holds that an enterprise should be left to succeed or fail in an open market, unencumbered by government intervention. Americans tend to resist governmental authority over an individual's personal decisions but tolerate or support authority over activities that can abuse individual rights, such as stock market manipulation and employment discrimination. Many also resist religious authority, and a key constitutional concept is the separation of church and state, aimed at defeating a coalition that could wield pervasive powers over the population at large.

Except for Americans from collectivist cultural backgrounds, individualism is a prominent characteristic. The typical American tends to be self-centered, and many are cocky and demanding. In keeping with individualistic cultures, personal achievement for most Americans is more important than group achievement. One's career is more important than one's organization or group. Most Americans believe that individuals can control their own destinies and that outside influences—even fate—will bend to the determination and resourcefulness of the individual. As a consequence, Americans typically do not form many close personal relationships.

The self-sufficiency of the individualist places a greater emphasis on materialism than in collectivist cultures. Materialism and a need for personal recognition cause most Americans to be hardworking and ambitious. This accounts also for a quantitative, factual approach to life. Americans like to see things in writing, to have supporting data, to trust legal contracts more than personal relationships. These same characteristics tend to leave the individual less intuitive and less comprehending of subtlety. Accordingly, many Americans take things literally and require direct, explicit communications.

In addition to these basic American values and characteristics, international businesspeople who deal with Americans need to be aware of regional differences. Here are the country's seven principal regions and some of their more apparent features:

▲ New England: People from Boston and other cities and towns of this region tend to be among the most traditional, conservative, formal, and frugal of Americans. Speech is to the point, and telephone calls and meetings are brief.

▲ East: New York City, Philadelphia, Washington, D.C. and other cities along the eastern seaboard are known for their impatient, confrontational, and competitive style. Speech is often in the first-person singular, punctuated with plenty of superlatives. In Washington name-dropping and influence-peddling are art forms.

ICD Prevention Tip— Communications Style

Be specific in communications with Americans. Be clear about what you request, and supply all the information that they may need to make a decision.

▲ South: In cities such as Atlanta and New Orleans, as well as in smaller towns, the style is often slow and deliberate, and the traditions gracious and genteel. In the southwestern states, such as Texas and Arizona, the style is more informal and Mexican culture is much in evidence.

▲ Midwest: In both cities such as Chicago, Cleveland, and St. Louis, and in smaller towns, people are known for their open, friendly, down-to-earth manner. Because this region is in the middle of the country, attitudes can also be provincial, resistant to outside influences, and detached from the rest of the nation and world.

▲ Plains and Mountain States: In states such as Montana, Wyoming, Utah, and Idaho, people tend to be highly independent, utilitarian, and deliberate. As in the Midwest, attitudes are often provincial and preferences are for ample size and space.

▲ West Coast: Many here, in the cities of Seattle, Portland, San Francisco, and Los Angeles, and in cities and towns in between, consider themselves part of a "new" society, progressive and open. In southern California the style is more informal, even flashy. There are sizable Asian communities on the West Coast. Many Chinese live in San Francisco. Los Angeles has the largest Korean community outside Seoul and a large Vietnamese community. In addition, Latin Americans are heavily concentrated in southern California.

▲ Non-Contiguous Areas: Alaska and Hawaii are the two newest states, set apart by geography and attitude from people in the other states. Alaskans are hardy, independent frontier people who are happy to be as geographically isolated as they are. Many of the people in Hawaii are of Asian descent; Japanese Americans constitute the largest ethnic group, about 30 percent.

English is spoken throughout the United States except in various ethnic and immigrant enclaves and in some cities, such as Miami and Los Angeles, where there are large populations of recent immigrants whose first language is different. The English language is written with little clarity and proficiency by many Americans. Grammar, syntax, spelling, and vocabulary are often deficient.

For non-Americans regional accents and American slang present a challenge. Understanding the spoken words of a native of Vermont, or Mississippi, or Brooklyn, New York, can be an impossible task. To compound the problem, Americans often use slang and speak too rapidly. Here are a few examples of American business slang:

> **ICD Prevention Tip— Regional Differences**
>
> *In communicating with Americans, be alert to regional differences in style and attitude. Although individuals will vary, generally you can be more direct with easterners, more formal with New Englanders and southerners, and more informal with others.*

WORD OR PHRASE	MEANING
Ballpark figure	An estimate
Belly-up	Bankrupt
Cash cow	A business activity that provides good cash flow
Devil's advocate	One who takes an opposing view for purposes of argument
No-brainer	An obvious conclusion or decision
Proactive	Taking active steps, not simply reacting to others' actions
White knight	A rescuer, a friendly merger partner

▲ ▲

COUNTRY DATA: UNITED STATES

FORMALITY FACTOR • Low

POPULATION • 252.7 million

GROSS DOMESTIC PRODUCT • $5.59 trillion

INCOME PER CAPITA • $22,130

AVERAGE GROWTH RATE, 1985–1992 • 1.1 percent

GOVERNMENT • Republic

ETHNIC GROUPS • White 80%, black 11%, Hispanic 5%, Asian 3%

RELIGION • Protestant Christians 56%, Roman Catholics 28%, Jews 2%

BUSINESS HOURS • In most cities, 9:00 A.M. to 5:00 P.M. Monday through Friday, with an hour for lunch at about noon.

LITERACY • 97%

LANGUAGES • English is spoken except in various ethnic and immigrant enclaves and in parts of some cities with large immigrant populations.

TELECOMMUNICATIONS • Services are excellent throughout the country. International direct dialing is available everywhere. Credit card pay telephones are prevalent, but normally not phone card telephones such as those available in several Asian countries.

SPORTS • Baseball, American football, basketball, and hockey are the primary spectator sports. Tennis, golf, and soccer are also widely followed. Popular participative sports are tennis, golf, skiing, sailing, and various water sports.

MONEY • The national unit of currency is the U.S. dollar, expressed with the "$" sign. Credit cards and checks are widely used as means of payment. Automatic teller machines and banking offices are widely available.

New Year's Day	January 1
Martin Luther King, Jr., Day	Third Monday of January
Washington's Birthday	Third Monday of February
Memorial Day	Last Monday of May
Independence Day	July 4
Labor Day	First Monday of September
Columbus Day	Second Monday of October
Veterans' Day	November 11
Thanksgiving Day	Fourth Thursday of November (many offices remain closed the following day)
Christmas Day	December 25

▼ ▼

VIETNAM

The Ascending Dragon

One of the former names of Hanoi, the historical and political capital of Vietnam, was Thang Long, meaning "the Ascending Dragon," an apt description for present-day Vietnam. This war-ravaged country is at the threshold of emerging as a new star in the Asia-Pacific economic galaxy.

Like China, Vietnam is a communist country that is fast developing a market economy and is turning to the markets and investment of noncommunist countries to spur its growth. While until recently the United States and a few other countries maintained an embargo on trade and investment with Vietnam, other countries have rushed in to take advantage of Vietnam's low wage rates and natural resources. Taiwan, Hong Kong, and Australia are the largest investors to date. With the embargoes now lifted and diplomatic relations between Vietnam and Western countries returning to normal, many analysts predict that Vietnam's growth will soar in the coming decade.

Communicating with the Vietnamese presents a number of difficulties. First, because it is a developing country that has spent decades at war, Vietnam's transportation and communications infrastructure is

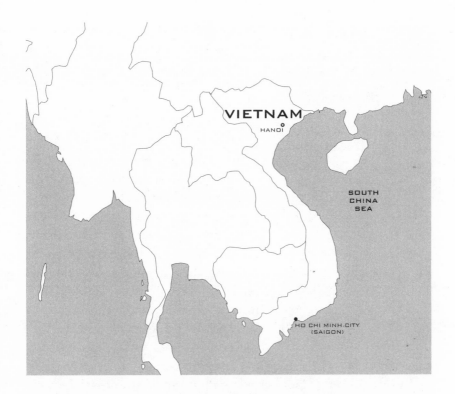

inferior or nonexistent. Roads, bridges, port facilities, electrical power, postal services, telecommunications, and their related management organizations, are all inadequate. Second, because of the country's long preoccupation with war, few Vietnamese possess the technical knowledge and management skills needed to interact with business counterparts from other countries. Third, few Vietnamese speak English, the lingua franca of international business. Their principal foreign languages are French and (especially in the north) Russian. Fourth, although the government now embraces capitalist concepts in developing a market economy, residual strains of communist ideology often present barriers to efficient business communications.

The Vietnamese are descendants of members of China's Han and Viet kingdoms who migrated from the north over centuries. Regional kingdoms were established as early as 2879 B.C. They maintained their independence at times, but at other times they were subjected to long periods of Chinese occupation. Following a long period of Chinese domination, a series of dynasties ruled Vietnam from 939 A.D. until the last century, with constant internal struggles and border conflicts with the Chinese.

The French entered the scene in 1801 when a French missionary, Pierre Pigneau de Behaine, began expanding the church's influence in the region. French colonial occupation of Vietnam commenced in 1858 and continued until invasion by the Japanese at the beginning of World War II. Anticolonialist sentiment grew throughout this period, spurred by news of the Russian Revolution and the earlier Kuomingtang revolution in China. Ho Chi Minh, perhaps Vietnam's best-known political figure, first became active in the anticolonialist movement in 1919 and gradually rose to power in the Vietnamese communist movement.

The disastrous modern history of Vietnam followed World War II. Commencing in 1946 the French sought to reassert control over Vietnam and wound up in a nine-year war with communist forces, who were supported in part by China. The conflict ended in 1954 with the division of the country into the Democratic Republic of Vietnam (North Vietnam) and the Republic of South Vietnam. The United States, pursuing a global policy of containment against communist influence, began supporting South Vietnam militarily and itself became embroiled in all-out war, not withdrawing until 1975. For fifteen years following the American withdrawal, Vietnam allied itself with Russia and continued in military conflict, occupying Cambodia and confronting China. Finally, in 1990, as a result of the crumbling of Soviet power and peace efforts of the United Nations in Cambodia, Vietnam entered its present course of social and economic reform, known as Doi Moi.

Notwithstanding Vietnam's presently weakened economic foundations, look for its large and industrious population to lift the nation's fortunes markedly in the next few years. Vietnam lies at the center of the world's most dynamic economic region, and many of that region's economies—for example, those of Japan, Taiwan, Singapore, and South Korea—with high wage rates at home now seek low-cost labor in other countries to maintain their industrial expansion. With such conditions prevailing in the region, Vietnam is clearly an Ascendant Dragon.

▲ ▲

COUNTRY DATA: VIETNAM

FORMALITY FACTOR • Moderately high

POPULATION • 67.7 million

GROSS DOMESTIC PRODUCT • $101.5 billion

INCOME PER CAPITA • $1,500

AVERAGE GROWTH RATE, 1985–1992 • Not available for these years

GOVERNMENT • Socialist republic

ETHNIC GROUPS • Kinh 87%, Hao 2%, Tay 2%

RELIGION • Buddhism, with some 36 million followers, is the principal religion. There are also about 4.5 million Roman Catholics. Other religions are Chondoist, Muslim, Confucian, and Animist.

BUSINESS HOURS • Offices are normally open Monday through Friday from 7:30 A.M. until 4:30 P.M., with an hour for lunch around noon. Offices are also generally open on Saturday mornings.

LITERACY • 88%

LANGUAGES • The national language is Vietnamese, which has its origins in Austro-Asiatic languages and is influenced by Sino-Tibetan Thai languages. In the eighteenth century French missionaries translated the language into its romanized form, Quoc Ngu, which now prevails. French is the principal second language. English is growing in use as a second language, especially in the south. Some Russian is spoken, especially in the north.

TELECOMMUNICATIONS • Most government offices and businesses have telephones. Few homes, other than those of wealthy individuals and high government officials, have telephones.

SPORTS • Basketball, soccer, and swimming are the popular sports.

MONEY • Vietnam's unit of currency is the dong, indicated by the symbol "d" following the amount, as in 500d. Certain credit cards are accepted in hotels and larger shops and restaurants. Cash, and sometimes checks on certain international banks, are the principal means of payment. Cash may be obtained at banks and some hotels. One U.S. dollar is equal to about 10,000d.

MAJOR HOLIDAYS

New Year's Day	January 1
Tet (Lunar New Year)	Late January or early February (three days)
Foundation of Vietnamese Communist Party	February 3
Liberation of Saigon	April 30
International Labor Day	May 1
Ho Chi Minh's Birthday	May 19
National Day	September 2

USEFUL PHRASES

English	Vietnamese	Phonetic Pronunciation
Hello	Chao ông (to a young man)	Chow awng
	Chao bác (to an older man)	Chow bahk
	Chao cô (to a young woman)	Chow ko
	Chao chi (to an older woman)	Chow chay
Yes (in the north)	Vâng	Vahng
Yes (in the south)	Dã	Yah
No	Không	Kohng
Please	Xin moi	Seen mah-ee
How much?	Bao nhiêu?	Bow nee-oo?
Thank you	Cám on	Kam un
You're welcome	Không có chi	Kohng gaw chee
Cheers	Moi	Mah-ee
I don't understand	Tôi không hiêu	Toy kohng hee-oo

▼ ▼

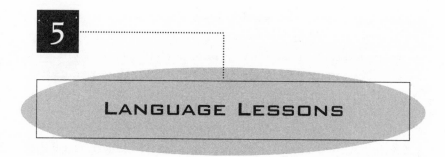

5

LANGUAGE LESSONS

The use and misuse of language are perhaps the greatest source of humor, social bonding, joy, abuse, and distraction in our lives. Language itself is more than a tool that communicates thought. It can be the glue that binds human relationships or the discordance that tears them asunder. In international business, if a common language is not understood by all parties, language is a major barrier to productive relationships, one that dominates any other cultural, ethnic, and national differences.

Businesspeople for whom English is the first language, or one in which they are skilled, are exceedingly fortunate, for English is the principal language of international business. However, even for those people, lack of understanding of another person's first language can induce International Communications Disorder. For anyone in international business, an understanding of general language concepts and practices can be very useful. It is the next best thing to an ability to speak the other person's language.

This chapter discusses characteristics and customs of the principal languages of the Asia-Pacific region. It reviews language factors that make a difference in the way international business is done in the region. It also suggests ways you can lessen the burdens of language barriers.

THE TROUBLE WITH ENGLISH

There is probably no reversing the growing use of English as the language of international communication, in business or otherwise. It is the language of countries that for many decades have substantially influenced international affairs and business, and it is the language of Britain and the United States, whose pop cultures fill so many of the airwaves and projection screens of the world. Moreover, its technical and definitional breadth suits the complex world in which we now live. It attained linguistic breadth in part because its speakers—individualistic Westerners, for the most part—required clarity and specificity in their communications because of the nature of their culture.

Even so, English is one of the most difficult languages to learn as a second language. It is filled with complex grammatical and semantic structures, numerous articles and pronouns, varieties of verb conjugations, and inconsistent spellings and pronunciations. Some words that have one spelling have different meanings and pronunciations depending on the verb form or other usage (e.g., "he *read* the book" versus "he will *read* the book"). Many words have different spellings but sound the same (e.g., *write* and *right*). Other words are similar in sound and must be distinguished by placement, punctuation, or emphasis (e.g., *ahead* and *a head,* as in "What's that in the road *ahead?*" and "What's that in the road, *a head?*").

> ### ICD Prevention Tip— Language Differences
>
> *English speakers can gain an appreciation of the difficulties of their language by taking a few minutes to analyze a passage of their own writing, noting different meanings that words can have and different meanings that can be conveyed by varying sentence structure and punctuation. The difficulties are compounded if the passage is spoken and the speaker uses different inflections and emphasis.*

Notwithstanding its difficulties, English is the language most widely taught as a second language. It is part of the required curriculum of countries such as China, Japan, Singapore, and Taiwan as early as age twelve, and it is the elective foreign language of choice in many countries. Where it is not part of the public school curriculum, private schools thrive by teaching it. In addition, other languages borrow words from it. Here are some Japanese words borrowed from English: for Western-style foods, *bifuteki, hamu, beikon, chïzu;* for tableware, *naifu, fōku;* for wearing apparel, *nekutai, hankechi;* for writing implements, *pen, inki.*

If English is your first language and you are traveling overseas, you will find that many people want to practice their English with you. People will approach you on the street to offer their assistance if you appear to be English-speaking and in need of directions. At social gatherings there will be no lack of guests wanting to speak with you. You will probably be frustrated if you who wish to practice their language with them.

DIFFERENCES RUN DEEP

While it may be enough for Asia-Pacific businesspeople to communicate in English alone, it pays them to have an understanding of how the region's languages differ. Let us review the basic differences.

For international business, the principal languages of the region are English, Chinese, Japanese, Korean, Thai, Vietnamese, and Malay (Bahasa Indonesia and Bahasa Malaysia). English is part of the Indo-European family, which includes the languages of Europe, the Mediterranean basin, and the Near East. The Chinese, Korean, Vietnamese, and Thai languages are part of the Sino-Tibetan language group. Japanese is a language group of its own, with a distant relationship to Korean. Malay is part of the Malayo-Polynesian group.

Spoken communication presents the most complex dimension of language. Dialects prevail in all languages, but especially in Chinese and Malay. Often people in an adjacent village who speak and write the same language cannot understand each other easily because their dialects are so different. In China there are many minor dialects and several major dialects. The principal dialect is Mandarin, designated the national tongue. It is the dialect of northern China (north of the Yangtze River) and of the former Imperial Court of Beijing. Other Chinese dialects are Cantonese of Guangdong, Wu of Shanghai, and Min of Fukien. North of the Yangtze, most people can understand another northern China dialect, but south of the Yangtze few people can understand another dialect. In Indonesia there are over 300 dialects and related languages, but most Indonesians can understand the national language, Bahasa Indonesia.

Written communication reduces the complexity of language somewhat, because the words used are more clearly put, and the imprecision of dialect and pronunciation is substantially eliminated. There are two main systems of writing in the world: the Chinese picto-ideographic system (based on characters that graphically represent thoughts and images), and the Egyptian-Semitic-Western system (based on scripts and alphabets, evolved from hieroglyphics, that convey phonetic representations of spoken words). Modern Chinese and Japanese languages are part of the Chinese picto-ideographic system, and they are written from top to bottom and from right to left on the page (and thus books and magazines are read from

what a Westerner would consider back to front). Other languages are part of the Egyptian-Semitic-Western system— even Korean, Thai, and Vietnamese (although related to Chinese as part of the Sino-Tibetan language group, they developed their own alphabets)—and are written from left to right.

The Chinese picto-ideographic system can be compared to a system of symbols. Analogies in English would be $, lb., and %. Because of the representational nature of Chinese characters, the written Chinese language communicates over many dialects. It can also be understood, to some extent, by people who can read a related language. For example, educated Japanese, Koreans, and Vietnamese are fairly able to read Chinese. But Chinese characters have no relation to the way words are pronounced. For example, the word character for "man" is pronounced *jên, nyin, lên, nên,* and *yên* in different spoken dialects. This contrasts with written languages that are based on a phonetic script or alphabet, such as English, in which the written language gives guidance to pronunciation and fewer dialects develop.

Other basic differences in the languages of the Asia-Pacific region are found in the ways words are distinguished and meanings conveyed. In some languages words are given different meanings with varying flexional and grammatical endings, sometimes according to gender, as well as various verb endings. In other languages words are given meaning by their position in a sentence. This is especially true of Chinese, which is based on words of single syllables. English also relies substantially on word position, and syntax, to convey different meanings (e.g., "John sees Mary" versus "Mary sees John").

In spoken communication some languages distinguish words by tone and pitch. Chinese, Thai, and Vietnamese, for example, are tonal languages. So is Burmese (like Chinese, Thai, and Vietnamese, a member of the Sino-Tibetan language group), and linguistics specialists like to use the Burmese word *ma* as an example of tone. Pronounced in five different tones, *ma* means "Help the horse; a mad dog comes!"

Japanese and English are not tonal languages, for the most part, although accent or stress sometimes conveys different meanings. Both Japanese and English are polysyllabic languages (many words contain more than one syllable), but in English words are often identified by accenting certain syllables, whereas in Japanese they normally are not. For example, the name of the Japanese city Yokohama is pronounced by a Japanese without accenting any syllable (but an American would probably accent the third syllable, pronouncing it "Yo-ko-*ha*-ma").

Pronunciation of languages not your native tongue can sometimes be difficult. For instance, neither Chinese nor Japanese has a sound identical to the English *r*, and it is often confused with the English sound *l*. This can lead to mispronunciations such as "lice" for *rice*, or a slightly trilled "herro" for *hello*.

LANGUAGE REFLECTS LIFE

A language often reflects the culture, traditions, and environment of a society. In the Eskimo language, spoken where winter dominates life, there are more than a dozen words for "snow," depending upon whether the snow is hard-packed, soft, crusted, loose, frozen, and so on. By contrast, in the Hawaiian language, spoken where the climate is never extreme, there is no word that precisely means "weather."

In Malay, Thai, and Vietnamese, spoken in cultures that give careful attention to social status, there are numerous words that distinguish the status of a person. For example, in Vietnamese the word for "hello" *(chao)* is always joined with another word (for older man, younger man, older woman, younger woman, girl, boy, and so on) applicable to the person addressed.

Also in Malay, spoken in cultures that emphasize politeness, there are numerous ways to say "no" without offending. For example, in Bahasa Indonesia the word *belum,* meaning "not yet," is frequently used, as in "She is not yet married" (even of a woman ninety years of age), and the phrase *tidak usah* is also common, meaning "not necessary," as in "No, I don't want it."

In Japanese, the language of another polite people, the particle *O* is often affixed to nouns as an indirect honorific of the person addressed, as in *O mizu kudasai,* literally "Honorable water, please" but meaning "Honorable person, please bring water."

In English, the language of individualistic cultures, the word *I* is capitalized in writing, whereas in the languages of many collectivist cultures its equivalent is not.

And in Chinese, the language of a society known for its subtlety and graceful arts, the imagery presented by the written characters is highly picturesque. For example, Chinese characters describe weather as a "one coat day," "two coat day," and so on; a wish for a good journey is "one road tranquil quiet"; and regret over a long absence is "one day not see like three autumns."

Chinese characters for a person's name sometimes (but not always) indicate meaning and sound: the left side of a character indicates meaning, and the right indicates sound, for pronunciation. Also, many Chinese characters present images that are not conveyed by a literal script. For example, the characters for the name Ming show images of the sun and the moon and mean "brilliance" and "light." Because of the significance of Chinese characters for names, when the name of a Chinese person appears in English text, it is often followed in parentheses by the Chinese characters in order to convey the full meaning.

SECOND-LANGUAGE PROBLEMS

It is a great advantage for an international businessperson to be able to speak more than one language. Nonetheless, if communications cannot be held in his or her own first language, significant problems can arise, and the discomfort that one feels when communicating in a second language adds tension and anxiety to a relationship, the reverse of what is needed. When using a second language, you are concerned that you might embarrass yourself by saying something stupid, or might harm yourself or your company by making an error, or might fail to understand correctly what the other person says. Discomfort is especially strong for people away from familiar surroundings (as when traveling overseas) and when speaking (as opposed to writing) in a second language. When writing in a second language, there are again concerns about looking foolish or saying the wrong thing. As a result, people who feel unsure of themselves in communicating in a second language will hesitate to speak or write.

It is often the case, however, that a person can read and write a second language much better than he or she can speak it or understand it when spoken. And sometimes a person understands more in a second language than he or she lets on, using a feigned lack of comprehension to advance a new idea or to gain time to frame an appropriate response.

> **ICD Prevention Tip—Cultural Clues**
>
> *As you become familiar with another language, look for usages that are culture indicators. For example, in the Thai language as in Vietnamese, various forms of address are used depending on the social status, age, and relationship to the speaker of the person addressed. These usages provide clues to the culture and Formality Factor of a country or ethnic group, and will help you in your communications.*

LOWERING THE LANGUAGE BARRIER

Here are five ways to minimize language problems in your Asia-Pacific business communications:

Remember the basic communications guidelines. Especially remember to write and speak clearly and concisely. If you are communicating in writing, use short, declarative sentences and avoid jargon, difficult words, subtle meanings, and humor. If communicating face-to-face or on the telephone, do the same, and speak deliberately and enunciate clearly. (See Chapter 3.)

Put your counterpart at ease. If you, but not your counterpart, are communicating in your first language, try to let your counterpart know that exceptional skill in your language is not expected. Compliment your counterpart's language skills without being patronizing.

Invite your counterpart to keep written responses brief and simple and to keep conversations and meetings short. Apologize for not being able to converse in your counterpart's first language.

Don't play games. If the language used is not your first language, do not risk a relationship by feigning a lack of understanding (for example, to gain time to respond or some other advantage) if you do in fact understand. If the language is your first language, do not consciously use words that will confuse your counterpart or heighten his or her discomfort.

Use translators and interpreters. Have important written communications, such as formal proposals and marketing materials, professionally translated into the language of your counterpart. For meetings, even if conducted in your first language, take an interpreter who can assist in clarifying points of discussion.

Be helpful. In response to written communications and during conversations, do not let a linguistically imperfect comment or statement lie in awkward silence. Help your counterpart to clarify the point. But overlook mistakes that are not important to the matters under discussion.

6

NAMES, TITLES, AND ADDRESSES

Business success depends in large measure upon accuracy and reliability. In business communications, there is no more important place
to start conveying your accuracy and reliability than in the statement
of a counterpart's name, title, and address. This is especially important for your first communication with the counterpart.

In the Asia-Pacific region, names and titles can be especially confusing for the international executive. Even the chief executive of the
United States, President Bill Clinton, despite having plenty of staff
support, made an embarrassing mistake during a state visit to South
Korea in July 1993. Mr. Clinton, at a state dinner, repeatedly referred
incorrectly to the wife of South Korea's President Kim Young-sam as
Mrs. Kim. He was apparently unaware that in Korea a woman keeps
her maiden name. Mr. Kim's wife is Sohn Myong-suk, and is addressed
as Mrs. Sohn.

Sometimes, however, one can be on the receiving end of someone
else's mistake. An Australian executive who returned this book's
survey questionnaire reported that his company once received a profitable piece of business because it was mistaken for another with a
similar name.

This chapter lays out the basic usages in names, titles, and addresses
in each of the countries covered by this book. Use this chapter as a
guide. Then, if you have any concern about the accuracy of a name,
title, or address that you plan to use in a communication, go to considerable lengths to check it out. Your efforts can include telephoning or

sending a fax to someone who will confirm the name and title of the person and give you correct spellings and an accurate address.

AUSTRALIA

In a country that values informality and disdains pretension, you normally need not worry particularly about getting a person's title right or otherwise deferring to rank and status. And the sooner you get on a first-name basis with an Australian, the better your communications will be. However, this is a sensitive, individualistic society, and you do need to get a person's name right, especially the first name, and remember it well.

There is a wide variety of names in Australia. While most are Anglo-Saxon, many originate in Asia and Eastern Europe.

Standard honorifics are used: *Mr., Mrs., Miss,* and, gaining in popularity, *Ms.* Professional honorifics such as *Dr.* are used but often ignored (and standard honorifics used) outside professional circles.

Business titles are normally standard Western ones (e.g., *president, vice president, secretary, treasurer*), and often British (e.g., *chairman, managing director*). The title *manager* is common if the person is not an officer of a company. Responsibilities typically suit a person's title, but it is worth noting that a company secretary in Australia, in keeping with British traditions, often has the rank of a senior officer, in contrast to a company secretary in an American company, whose rank is often one step lower. And a company secretary in Australia or the United States is not to be confused with an office secretary. Office secretaries normally have very low nominal rank but very high practical influence.

Company names often end with *Proprietary Limited* or *Pty. Ltd.,* indicating a private (non-public) corporation (having limited liability). If there is no *Pty.* in the name, the company is probably a public corporation. Less frequently, company names will end in *Corporation* or *Corp.* and *Incorporated* or *Inc.*

> **ICD Prevention Tip— Addresses**
>
> *The postal systems of most countries prefer that the name of an overseas country be written out in capital letters on the envelope, as in "AUSTRALIA" rather than "Australia." Following this practice will help expedite your mail.*

Addresses are typically stated as the number of a *street* or *avenue*, for example, "200 Metropolitan Street." Sometimes a postal box is used for a mailing address, referred to as a "General Post Office Box" or "G.P.O. Box" number. Australia presently uses four-digit postal codes (e.g., 2001), placed after the name of the state. States' names are normally abbreviated, as in *NSW* for New South Wales and *ACT* for Australian Capital Territory (site of the national government). Here is the complete list of standard postal abbreviations of Australian states:

ACT	Australian Capital Territory
NSW	New South Wales
NT	Northern Territory
QLD	Queensland
SA	South Australia
TAS	Tasmania
VIC	Victoria
WA	Western Australia

Letterheads often carry both a street address (to help you find the location) and a postal box number (to use for correspondence). When corresponding, you do not need to use both.

Here are two examples:

Mr. John Smith
President
Apex Consultants Pty. Ltd.
200 Metropolitan Street
Sydney, NSW 2001
AUSTRALIA

Ms. Jane Doe
Managing Director
Condex Corporation
G.P.O. Box 123
Melbourne, VIC 2601
AUSTRALIA

[Note: Examples of names and addresses given in this chapter are fictitious but representative.]

CANADA

Names, titles, and honorifics are a standard mix in Canada. There is a variety of names, coming mostly from England and Europe. French names are prevalent in Québec. And there are now many Asian names, especially in British Columbia and larger cities such as Toronto.

Business titles are a mix of Western and British styles (e.g., *president, vice president, secretary, treasurer, managing director, manager*).

Standard honorifics are used: *Mr., Mrs., Miss,* and *Ms.* Professional honorifics such as *Dr.* are used, but no offense is taken if a standard honorific is used instead.

Company names often end in *Limited* or *Ltd.* (the British style of indicating a corporation's limited liability) and sometimes end in *Corporation, Corp., Incorporated,* or *Inc.* However, *Proprietary* and *Pty.* are not commonly used.

Addresses are typically stated as the number of a street or avenue, for example, "123 Bay Street." A postal box (or post office box), expressed as "P.O. Box," is often used for a business mailing address. Postal codes, placed following "CANADA," are indicated by a combination of six numbers and letters separated in the middle by one space. The names of provinces are normally abbreviated, as in *BC* for British Columbia and *ON* for Ontario. Here is the complete list of standard postal abbreviations of Canadian provinces:

AB	Alberta
BC	British Columbia
MB	Manitoba
NB	New Brunswick
NFLD	Newfoundland
NS	Nova Scotia
NWT	Northwest Territories
ON	Ontario
PEI	Prince Edward Island
PQ	Québec
SK	Saskatchewan
YK	Yukon

ICD Prevention Tip—Addresses

The postal systems of Australia, Canada, and the United States use the standard abbreviations for states and provinces indicated in this chapter. The abbreviations are not required, however, and the sender may spell out the name of the state or province if desired. If you use the abbreviations from outside the country, be sure to include the name of the country addressed (Australia, Canada, or USA). Otherwise, the originating postal service might not recognize the destination.

A company's letterhead often has both a street address (to help you find the location) and a postal box number (to use for correspondence). When writing to the company, you do not need to use both.

Here are two examples:

Mr. John Smith
Treasurer
Futures Limited
123 Bay Street
Vancouver, BC
CANADA V6M 4E7

Mrs. Jane Doe
President
ZNR Corporation
P.O. Box 456
Toronto, ON
CANADA M5X 1B8

CHINA (PEOPLE'S REPUBLIC OF CHINA)

Time magazine's "Man of the Year" in 1978 was Teng Hsiao-p'ing. Its "Man of the Year" in 1985 was Deng Ziaoping. Different men? No, he is one and the same, China's paramount leader. The difference is that an alternative Chinese phonetic alphabet system, the Pinyin system, officially replaced the older Wade-Giles system in China in 1979. Each system enables the Chinese characters of names and places to be expressed in romanized form. The Wade-Giles system is still used in Taiwan.

To add to the confusion for people who do not read or speak Chinese, names written in romanized form often look different than they sound. For example, to an English speaking person, the *-eng* in the names of Deng Xiaoping and China's Premier, Li Peng, should sound like the *-eng* in the English words *length* or *strength*. However, the Chinese sound, to an English speaking person, is actually more like *-ung*, as in the English word *lung*.

When written in romanized form, Chinese names of the same sound are often spelled differently. For example, the Cantonese name Choy (common in Hong Kong) is spelled "Cai" in Pinyin and "Ts'ai" in Wade-Giles. Each sounds like "Choy," to a Westerner, at least. Of course, in foreign settings, people with Chinese names did not change the spelling of their names in 1979. Moreover, and again in foreign settings, a Chinese name may take on a sound that is different from the original Chinese sound but is more easily pronounced. For example, Westerners would not think of pronouncing "Ts'ai" the same as "Choy," so the Western pronunciation might become something like "Sigh" or "Say." Also, they might drop apostrophes (as in *Tsai*) and use different spellings (as in *Li* and *Lee, Wu* and *Woo, Yung* and *Young*).

To help alert you to some of the anomalies of Chinese name spellings, here are a few examples of names that sound the same in Chinese:

Pinyin Letter	Wade-Giles Letter	As in	Name Examples	Name Sound
c	ts'	chip	Choy, Cai, Ts'ai	choy
zh	ch	John	Zhang, Chang	chang
q	ch'	cheek	Qing, Ching	ching
x	hs	she	Xie, Hsieh	shay

Recognizing given and family names in Chinese is also a challenge, but knowledge of a few simple rules can be helpful. A Chinese name is normally composed of three words, each of a single syllable. The basic rule is that the family name comes first. A generational name (indicating the person's generation within the family) often comes next. A given name comes last. When generational names are used, there is normally one for the females in a family and a different one for the males. Thus, in the Chen family, sisters might be named Chen Sao Min and Chen Sao Lu, and brothers might be named Chen Kai Ke and Chen Kai Yu. In addition, generational and given names are sometimes joined, with or without a hyphen, as in Mao Ze-dong and Deng Xiaoping.

But Chinese who deal with Westerners (more often found in Hong Kong, Taiwan, Singapore, or various Western countries than in China) frequently reverse the name order, so that Chen Kai Kee goes by Kee Kai Chen. It is also common for Chinese to go by the initials of their given and generational names, as in K. K. Chen, who would be addressed by family and close friends as K. K. And Chinese who live in Western countries often take a given Western name, using their Chinese given and generational names as middle initials, as in George K. K. Chen.

Titles are important in China, and you should use a person's title in salutations and face to face, if you know it. For example, when addressing a letter to Manager of Production Li Tao Qing, one should say, "Dear Manager Li." Western titles are becoming popular, and you will see titles such as *president, managing director,* and so on. If a person does not have a title, or you do not know it, you should use the standard honorifics: *Mr., Dr., Mrs.,* and *Miss.* The honorific *Ms.* is not yet used in China.

> ### ICD Prevention Tip—Names
>
> *To avoid confusion in listing names of people whose family names often appear first, as in Chinese and Korean cultures, it is helpful to spell family names in capital letters. For example, in a list of people attending an international conference, Chen Kai Kee of Hong Kong can be listed as CHEN Kai Kee.*

Chinese women do not take their husband's names. If married they should be addressed with their title if they have one. If a woman does not have a title, or it is unknown, use *Madame,* or *Mrs.* if the woman is married, or *Miss* if she is unmarried.

Company names in China are in flux. China is rapidly changing from a socialistic, centrally planned economy to one with an expanding, market-driven private sector. Some state-owned industries are being privatized, and others are authorized to undertake private-sector activities and enter into equity joint ventures with foreign companies. State-owned enterprises, in English translation, are normally described by their function, such as the Shanghai Red Flag Manual Vehicle Factory and the Beijing Guanghua Wood Processing Factory. Corporations normally have *Corporation, Inc., Company Limited,* or *Co. Ltd.* at the end of their names, such as the Double Happiness Tyre Industries Corp.

Addresses are normally stated as the number of a road or street (for example, "600 Gu Bei Road"), sometimes with a building identified, and sometimes with only a postal box number used. The province or autonomous region is stated, then the city. (There are twenty-three provinces, five autonomous regions— Tibet is one—and three municipalities: Beijing, Shanghai, and Tianjin. The municipalities are not part of a province or region, so their names appear alone.) China uses a six-digit postal code, normally placed after the country's name. The name China is used, rather than People's Republic of China. The county is not normally identified in the address. Here are two examples:

....
ICD Prevention Tip— Honorifics

If you do not know whether a Chinese woman is married or unmarried, use the honorific Madame *for an older woman and* Miss *for a younger woman. If the woman's age is not apparent, use* Miss.
....

> Mr. Liu Yeh Fan
> Section Manager
> Zhan Jiang Motor Factory
> 600 Gu Bei Road
> Fuzhou, Fujian, CHINA 361005

> Mrs. Kwok Lanye
> Treasurer
> East Trading Co. Ltd.
> P.O. Box 691
> Beijing, CHINA 100044

HONG KONG

Chinese name usages in Hong Kong are the same as described in the section "China," except that many more of them are Westernized, with family names placed last.

Honorifics are the standard ones. For women, *Mrs.* and *Miss* are preferred to *Ms.* A married woman retains her birth name but uses the honorific *Mrs.*

Titles are not as important in Hong Kong as they are in China. Business titles are often in a British style. *Managing director* is a common title. Other Western titles (e.g., *president, vice president,* and so on) are also common.

The standard honorifics will normally do. *Dr.* should be used, if applicable.

Company names are diverse in style, but most end with the British *Limited* or *Ltd.* Subsidiaries of foreign companies often have Hong Kong in their names in parentheses, as in "Trade Consultants (Hong Kong) Ltd."

Addresses normally indicate a building and floor (the floor usually indicated before or after the name of the building and expressed thus: "5/F"). The number and name of a street (often a road) and a district (e.g., "Central") are indicated. Post boxes ("G.P.O." or "P.O.") are used occasionally but not frequently. No postal codes are presently used.

Here are two examples:

Mr. K. K. Chen
Managing Director
Specialties Limited
4/F, Yu To Sang Building
37 Queen's Road, Central
HONG KONG

Mrs. Jing-Mei Tsu
President
Textiles Ltd.
East Point Centre, 12/F
555 Hennessy Road, Causeway Bay
HONG KONG

INDONESIA

There is great diversity of customs and practices when it comes to Indonesian names. Some Indonesians have only one name and no family name. Suharto is President Suharto's only name, for example. Many given names are the first thing a mother sees or thinks of after the birth of a child, so that an Indonesian's name might be that of an object, such as *Payung,* literally "umbrella."

Despite their diversity, citizens of Indonesia are encouraged to take Indonesian names regardless of their ethnic names given at birth. Consequently, it is difficult or impossible to identify the ethnic background of a person by his or her name. For example, a prominent ethnic Chinese Indonesian is named Jusuf Wanandi.

In international business circles, the standard honorifics should be used. *Dr.* and *Professor* should be used where applicable because of the importance accorded education. *Ms.* is accepted but not used frequently.

To speak cordially to an Indonesian who holds a respected position in society (which can be a younger as well as an older person), it is appropriate to address a man as *Bapak* or *Pak* and a woman as *Ibu* or *Bu,* as in *Pak Subroto* or *Bu Saleh.*

Titles are often used in addressing government officials and professional

> ### ICD Prevention Tip—
> ### Honorifics and Titles
>
> *If the person you are addressing is from a country with a moderate to high Formality Factor, and you are unsure of the person's correct honorific and title, err on the side of flattery; use the honorific* Dr. *and the title* vice president *or even* president. *You might be wrong, but you will be forgiven.*

people, as in Minister Noor or Engineer Sjahrir. Otherwise, standard honorifics are used. Business titles, not used in salutations, are normally Western ones (*president, vice president,* and so on). *Manager* is often used if the person is not a company officer.

Company names are normally stated in Bahasa Indonesia or English (or a language of the company's origin) or both. The Indonesian abbreviation *PT* before a company's name, short for *Perseroan Terbatas,* indicates that it is incorporated. Other corporate indicators (e.g., *Inc., Ltd., Corp.*) are also seen.

Addresses normally indicate a building and a street address. In addresses, you will often see the Indonesian word for building *(Wisma),* sometimes with the number of the floor (e.g., *Lantai 5),* and the word for street *(Jalan,* abbreviated as *Jl.).* The street number is placed following the street name. Sometimes, in cities, there is also the name of a district (e.g., *Menteng* or *Kuningan)* or section *(Kaveling,* abbreviated as *Kav.).* Post boxes (expressed as "P.O. Box") are often used in the cities instead of street addresses. A five-digit postal code system is used. The province or island (e.g., Java, Sumatra) is not normally indicated.

Here are two examples of Indonesian addresses:

Dr. Soegiarto
Head of Administration
PT Bukit Baru
Wisma Kosgoro, Lantai 4
Jl. H. R. Rasuna Said, No. 23, Kav. C12
Jakarta 12940
INDONESIA

Mrs. Haryati Hassan
Vice President
PT Service Far East
P.O. Box 224
Bogor 16111
INDONESIA

JAPAN

Japanese name use varies but need not be complicated. Usual Japanese order is to put the family name first and the given name second. However, the Western style of putting family name last is generally used in international business and other dealings outside Japan. Given names are seldom used except by family members and close friends—certainly in a business setting, one should never presume to use a person's given name alone unless specifically invited to do so.

Married women use the family names of their husbands. In fact, Japanese law requires that a couple choose, at the time they are married, the family name they will use. In 1993 a married professional woman sought a judicial order permitting her to use her maiden name in her business and the order was denied.

The first names of Japanese women, incidentally, often end in -ko, as in Michiko and Fukiko. This is a familiar usage, similar to the ending -ie in names of Western women, such as Jackie. By itself, ko means child in Japanese.

Standard Western honorifics (Mr., Mrs., Miss, and Ms.) are used. Dr. and Professor should be used where applicable because of the importance accorded to education. The Japanese honorific *-san* can also be used as a suffix to the family name of a man or woman, as in Mori-san (but then *Mr.* or another honorific should not also be used). In face-to-face meetings with top Japanese officials, you will hear other suffixes such as *-shacho* (company head), *-kacho* (group head), or *-bucho* (division head). However, Westerners should probably stick with the standard honorifics rather than risk appearing awkward or patronizing. (See, in Chapter 3, "Don't Be a Phony.") Also, a standard honorific will avoid a possible mistake in using *-san* when *-shacho* is more appropriate, and vice versa.

Titles are most often Western ones (e.g., *president, vice president,* and so on, for company officers). British titles such as *managing director* are occasionally seen. Nonofficer positions are often stated as "manager of . . ." or "director of. . . ."

Company names sometimes end in *K. K.,* the abbreviation for *kabushiki kaisha,* Japanese words for a corporation, but more often they appear with the typical Western endings: *Corp., Inc.,* and *Ltd.*

Addresses in Japan present a more complex picture, and stories are legion about foreign visitors getting lost in Japanese cities despite having a correct address in hand. The problem is that address numbers relate to the age of the address rather that the linear position of a building on a street. For example, the immediately higher number of two addresses might be in the next block, rather than next door or across the street, because chronologically the address having the higher number was the next building to be constructed in that area. In fact, streets are not named; there are only districts, subdistricts, and numbers. Alternatively, postal boxes are used as addresses, but not as frequently as location addresses.

In practice, a Japanese address normally states (1) the name of the building (often with a floor number), (2) the number of a subdistrict (sometimes the first digit of a hyphenated series, as in "2-4-1," and sometimes with the suffix *-chome*

ICD Prevention Tip— Addresses:

If you are visiting Japan and need to find an address that is unfamiliar to you, take directions written in Japanese that include a map as well as the street number. If the address is an office building, be sure to have the building's name as well as the street number. If you have trouble finding the address, people on the street will help you; however, it is more reliable to ask for directions at a nearby police box.

following a two-number hyphenated series, as in "4-1, 2-*chome*"), (3) the location number ("4-1" in this example), (4) the name of the larger district (e.g., "Marunouchi"), (5) the name of the next larger district or ward (ending in the suffix -*ku,* as in "Chiyoda-ku") or that of an even larger one (ending in the suffix -*shi,* as in "Toyonaka-shi"), and, finally, (6) the name of the city followed by a three-digit postal code. Two examples are

Mr. Maki Haruna
Vice President
Transnational Ltd.
Ryokuchi-Eki Building, 2F
2-4-1 Terauchi, Toyonaka-shi
Osaka 560
JAPAN

Mrs. Michiko Aikawa
Director of Public Relations
Fujimaru K. K.
Kowa Building
4-10, 1-chome, Marunouchi
Chiyoda-ku
Tokyo 100
JAPAN

MALAYSIA

Malaysian names and titles are an adventure for anyone who is unfamiliar with them. A Malay's principal name (not necessarily a family name) is normally placed first, followed by an indication of the father's name. For example, Isa bin Jamari is Isa "the son of" Jamari. A Chinese Malaysian normally places the family name first (as in Li Kuo-shu, whose family name is Li) but sometimes reverses the order if there are frequent dealings with Westerners. Some common Malay names are often abbreviated, for example "Mohd." for Mohamed and "Abd." for Abdul.

The standard Western honorifics (*Mr., Dr., Mrs., Miss,* and *Ms.*) are normally used in international business circles, but professional titles such as *Professor* should be used where applicable.

The various titles of Malaysian royalty and officialdom should also be used where applicable. *Tunku* and *Tengku* are titles of royalty comparable to prince or princess. *Tun, Tan Sri,* and *Dato'* (or *Datuk*) in descending order are titles of high-ranking male officials. *Toh Puan, Puan Sri,* and *Datin* are titles given women or the wives of titled men. *Datin Paduka* is a title given to a woman in her own right. The Malaysian honorifics *Y.B.* and *Y.M.* (abbreviations for Malaysian words comparable to *Sir* or *Your Excellency, Y.M.* being applicable to royalty only) normally precede these titles.

You will sometimes see the word *Haji* in a name (sometimes abbreviated *Hj.*), indicating that the person, a Muslim, has made a pilgrimage to Mecca. You will also see *Encik* and *Cik* (or *Puan* in the case of an older woman), the equivalents of *Mr.* and *Ms.,* respectively, in Bahasa Malaysia. Rather than addressing a Malaysian as *Encik* and *Cik,* however, a Westerner should use a standard Western honorific.

Business titles normally follow British styles as a result of Malaysia's long history as a British colony. Accordingly, *managing director* is a common title. Other Western titles (e.g., *president, vice president,* and so on) are also common.

Company names most often end in the words *Berhad* or *Sendirian Berhad,* abbreviated as *Bhd.* and *Sdn. Bhd.,* the Malaysian words for "corporation" and "private corporation," respectively. However, branch offices of foreign companies use standard Western endings, such as *Ltd.* And the Malaysian word for "company," *syarikat,* is often seen in the names of Malaysian companies.

Malaysian addresses often indicate the name of a building (*wisma* and *banqunan* are Malaysian words for "building"), the floor, and the street (*Jalan,* abbreviated *Jl.* or *Jln.*), frequently without a street number. Alternatively, post office boxes are often used (expressed as "P.O. Box"). A five-digit postal code then precedes the name of the city, which is followed (except for Kuala Lumpur, a federal government territory) by the name of the state. Here are two examples:

> Mr. Abd. Ariffin bin Rahman
> Managing Director
> Kuala Lumpur Antara Berhad
> Wisma Damansara
> Jalan Sultan Hishamuddin
> 50778 Kuala Lumpur
> MALAYSIA

Y.B. Tan Sri Tan Lee Seng
Deputy Executive Director
Apex Malaysian Industries Sendirian Berhad
P.O. Box 1442
47301 Petaling Jaya, Selangor
MALAYSIA

NEW ZEALAND

Most New Zealand names are Anglo-Saxon, but there are many names of Maori and Polynesian derivation. A common New Zealand practice is to use first initials only with names, as in R. L. Brown, often making it difficult to know if the person is male or female.

Standard Western honorifics are used, and they go back a long way in New Zealand history. The story goes that one of the principal Maori chiefs in the early 1800s, Hongi Hika, was presented to King George IV in London as a key ally of the British in their new colony. A carefully rehearsed Hongi said, "How do you do, Mister King George?" And the monarch replied, "How do *you* do, Mister King Hongi?"

The only titles of great consequence in this nation of farmers and ranchers are those of government officials and business executives. Business titles are primarily of British style, with *Director, Managing Director, Manager, Chief Executive,* and *Secretary* having prominence.

Company names are typically Western, with *Limited* or *Company, Ltd.* being the favorite ending.

ICD Prevention Tip—Professions

In most countries, especially Western ones and those with Western traditions, such as Singapore and Malaysia, professionals often use indicators following their names to identify their training or status: Ph.D. *for doctor of philosophy, a high academic degree;* C.P.A. *for certified public accountant;* M.D. *for medical doctor;* Esq. *or Esquire for a lawyer; and, in British Commonwealth countries,* Q.C. *for Queen's Counsel, a senior barrister who represents clients in court. When one of these indicators is used in an address, an honorific is not also used; for example, the person will be addressed as "John Jones, Esq." but not "Mr. John Jones, Esq."*

Business addresses are a simple affair in New Zealand. Often a postal box is preferred, expressed as "P.O. Box" with a number or sometimes simply as "Private Bag" with no number. Street numbers and names are also used. There is sporadic use of postal codes, called "postal zones," of only one or a few digits. Here are two examples:

Mr. B. D. Johnson
Director
Metal Products Ltd.
Private Bag
Auckland 9
NEW ZEALAND

Mrs. L. M. MacGregor
Secretary
International Consultants Limited
15 Taumaru Avenue
Wellington
NEW ZEALAND

PHILIPPINES

Names and usages in the Philippines reflect Spanish and American origins resulting from many decades as a colony or protectorate of Spain and the United States. A number of Asian names are also prevalent, especially those of Chinese, who are active in the business community.

Standard honorifics are used, especially *Dr.,* if applicable, because of the importance to Filipinos of education and professional status.

Titles are important in the Philippines. In salutations and greetings, professionals and senior officials in business and government should be addressed with their titles, as in Professor Montes, Chairman Monsod, Ambassador Mutuc, Engineer Ramos, and Attorney Robinson. In informal settings, or if a title is not known, use a standard honorific.

In business circles Western titles (e.g., *president, vice president,* and so on) are the norm. Company names also follow Western styles, with the typical endings of *Corp., Inc.,* and *Ltd.* Subsidiaries of foreign companies sometimes include *Philippines* or *Phil.* in their names in parentheses, as in "New Zealand Products (Phil.) Ltd."

Business addresses frequently are stated with a postal box followed by capital letters (e.g., *MCPO*) indicating the post office. Alternatively, a street address is given. Names of buildings are not often used. In Manila a section and area of the city are also indicated (e.g., "Pasay City, Makati"), and the city is called "Metro Manila," often abbreviated "M.M." Four-digit postal codes exist but are not faithfully used. Here are two examples:

Ms. Corazon Espino
President
Capital Industries (Phil.) Inc.
345 Alvarado Street, Legaspi Village
Makati, M.M. 1200
PHILIPPINES

Mr. Lee Chung Lim
Production Manager
Philippine Technologies Corporation
1634 Osmeña Boulevard
Cebu City
PHILIPPINES

SINGAPORE

The population of Singapore is mostly ethnic Chinese, and Chinese name usages are the same as described in the "China" section except that many more of them are Westernized, with family names placed last.

Honorifics are the standard ones. For women, *Ms.* is sometimes used but *Mrs.* and *Miss* are preferred. A married woman often retains her birth name but uses the honorific *Mrs.*

Titles are not as important in Singapore as they are in China. The standard honorifics will normally do. *Dr.* should be used, if applicable, because educated people are highly respected.

Business titles are often in a British style as a result of Singapore's having been a British colony. For example, *Managing Director* is a common title. Other Western titles (e.g., *president, vice president,* and so on) are also common.

Company names are diverse in style but, except for branches of foreign companies, most end with the British *Limited* or *Private Limited* (or the abbreviations *Ltd.* or *Pte. Ltd.*) Some are stated in the Malay equivalent *Berhad* or *Sendirian Berhad,* abbreviated as *Bhd.* and *Sdn. Bhd.*

Business addresses in Singapore are most often stated as a street address followed by a number that shows the floor and suite, expressed as in "#02-12" (indicating the second floor, suite 12). The building is sometimes named following the street address. Postal boxes are alternatively used, but not frequently. A four-digit postal code is added after "Singapore." Here are two examples:

Mr. Kin Yong Goh
Managing Director
Travel Associates Pte. Ltd.
400 Orchard Road, #03-02
SINGAPORE 0923

Ms. Ming Cho Tsu
Area Vice President
Southeast Asia Enterprises Limited
250 North Bridge Road
Raffles City Tower
SINGAPORE 0617

SOUTH KOREA (REPUBLIC OF KOREA)

The challenge in communicating with South Koreans is in identifying the right person. It seems that the family name of every person is Lee, Park, or Kim. All the more reason to get the title and address correct! Fortunately, a person's full name is used; initials seldom appear.

South Koreans normally have three names: a family name and two given names. As with Chinese names, the family name usually comes first, although Koreans who are in frequent contact with the international business community sometimes place their family names last, Western style. The best clue to a person's family name is that it often stands alone—the two given names are often hyphenated, as in Park Kang-Hong and Kim Sang-Tai.

Outside their immediate families, Koreans are normally addressed by their family name, often followed by the honorific *sônsaengnim* (pronounced "song-sang-nim"), which means "respected person," or by *sôngsaengnim* alone. However, Westerners and others who are not familiar with the Korean language should use a standard Western honorific (*Mr., Mrs., Miss, or Dr.* as appropriate) with the person's family name. (*Ms.* is seldom used in South Korea.) Titles can also be used, as in Manager Kim or Engineer Park.

Business titles follow Western styles. *President, executive vice president, manager,* and the like are common.

Company names also follow Western styles, often ending in *Co., Ltd., Inc.,* or *Corp.* With large companies, the name sometimes ends with the word *Group.*

South Korean business addresses very often use a postal box, expressed with a letter or name indicating the postal district, as in "C.P.O. Box" or "Yoido P.O. Box." If a postal box is used, a postal code is not needed. Otherwise, as in Japanese addresses, an address indicates the age of the building rather that its linear position on a street. Such addresses show a number, then a subdistrict (ending with the suffix *-dong*), then a larger district (ending with the suffix *-ku* or *-gu*), followed by the name of the city and a three- or six-digit postal code. A building is sometimes identified. Here are two examples:

Mr. Cho Kang-Hong
President
Yukong Company, Ltd.
C.P.O. Box 189
Seoul
REPUBLIC OF KOREA

Mr. Lee Sang-Eung
Manager of Production
Samwhan Industries, Inc.
Aekyung Building
15, Puksong-dong, Chung-ku
Inchon 400-201
REPUBLIC OF KOREA

TAIWAN (REPUBLIC OF CHINA)

Name usages in Taiwan, which has an ethnic Chinese population, are the same as described in the "China" section. The family name normally comes first, although Taiwanese who are in frequent contact with the international business community sometimes place their family names last, Western style. Initials are sometimes used in place of the given and generational names.

In salutations and greetings, titles and standard honorifics are used, as in Manager Lee or Miss Huang. *Ms.* is seldom used in Taiwan. A married woman often retains her birth name but uses the honorific *Mrs.*

Business titles in international circles are primarily Western ones, such as *chairman, president, managing director, manager,* and so on.

Company names also follow Western styles, often ending in *Corp., Inc., Co. Ltd.,* and so on.

Business addresses in Taiwan normally state a floor (as in "5F"), the street address (streets are often called "roads"), and the city. The name of the building is sometimes but not often stated. Postal boxes are occasionally used. There are postal codes, but they are not faithfully used. In Taipei, a huge city with some very long roads, it is sometimes important to indicate whether the road address is north, south, east, or west, and to include the section number of the city. Here are two examples:

Mr. Chen Li Meng
President
Tatung Cement Corporation
5F, 95 Chung Shan North Road, Sec. 2
Taipei
TAIWAN, ROC

Mrs. S. M. Chow
Manager, Administrative Services
Sincere Trading Co., Ltd.
10F, Lotus Building
136 Jen Ai Road, Section 3
Taipei 10628
TAIWAN, ROC

THAILAND

Name usages in Thailand are quite unique. They are the reverse of the Chinese and Korean practice of placing family names first and addressing people by their family names. In Thailand, family names are placed last, and people are addressed by their given names.

Few Thais used family names until the 1920s, when King Rama VI decreed that they should. All Thais now have family names (placed last in sequence, Western style), but they invariably go by their given names and consider it odd to be addressed by the family name. Consequently, you should address Thais by their first names even in formal circumstances, and you should not be surprised if a Thai addresses you by your first name.

The standard honorific of Thailand is *Khun* (pronounced "koon"), as in Khun Amnuay, used for men and women in place of *Mr., Mrs., Miss,* or *Dr.* However, Westerners and others who are not familiar with the Thai language should normally use a standard Western honorific with the person's first name. Titles are seldom used in greetings and salutations. Thais are not addressed, for example, as Vice President Kaset or Engineer Prasong.

Business titles are normally the Western variety, (e.g., *chairman, president, managing director, manager,* and so on), as are company names (ending, for example, in *Limited, Corp., Inc.*).

Business addresses in Thailand do not follow a set pattern. Street addresses (a street is often called a "road") are the most common, sometimes with the name of a building and a floor number. Alternatively, a postal box number may be used. A five-digit postal code is normally stated. Here are two examples:

Mr. Sunthorn Chulasai
Vice President
Thammasat Limited
Central Plaza Building, 3rd Floor
1693 Phaloyothin Road
Bangkok 10900
THAILAND

Mr. Siri Chantem
Manager, Financial Planning
Pacific Rim Credit Corp.
Bangkok Bank Building—14th Floor
333 Silom Road
Bangkok 10500
THAILAND

UNITED STATES OF AMERICA

Names in the United States vary too much to warrant specific discussion here. Those of ethnic origin are often easily recognized, unless translation from a phonetic pronunciation has given an odd result. For example, in one instance, the family name of a Japanese man named Yagi was written by a U.S. immigration officer generations ago as Yaki, and descendants continue to use this accidental spelling.

Chinese and Korean family names, of course, are placed last, Western style. And many people with foreign names change them to something that sounds or looks Western. The United States, after all, is a nation of immigrants who have traditionally sought to blend with others in their adopted home. This tradition has been less strong in recent years, as many people have sought to preserve their national and ethnic roots, but it continues nonetheless.

Standard Western honorifics (*Mr., Mrs., Ms., Miss,* and *Dr.*) are used in greetings and salutations, but titles are not used except in a professional context (e.g., "Professor Smith"). Some academics and professionals, who have advanced degrees that entitle them to be addressed with the honorific *Dr.,* feel slighted if addressed as *Mr. or Ms.,* but they seldom admit to this.

Business titles are the Western variety (e.g., *chairman, president, vice president, managing director, manager,* and so on), as are company names (ending, for example, in *Corp., Inc., Limited*). *Chief Executive Officer,* or *CEO,* has become a popular business title for the heads of organizations in recent years and has produced a number of offspring, such as *Chief Financial Officer, Chief Operating Officer,* and *Chief Legal Officer. Managing Director* is another business title of recent popularity. *Vice President* comes in many styles, generally to indicate the level of the position (normally, in descending order, *Executive Vice*

President, Senior Vice President, Vice President, Assistant Vice President), and is often combined with a phrase indicating the person's responsibilities (for example, *Vice President, Marketing; Vice President, Asia Pacific Operations;* and *Vice President and Chief Financial Officer*).

Business addresses in the United States are normally a street address (often followed by a suite number), the city, state, and postal code (zip number). The suite number can be important if the address has many separate offices. Postal boxes (expressed as "P.O. Box" and sometimes "P.O. Drawer") are often used as alternatives to a street address. Building names are indicated occasionally. The names of states are typically identified by two capital letters (e.g., *NY* for New York, *CA* for California). The complete list of standard postal abbreviations of U.S. states is

AL	Alabama
AK	Alaska
AZ	Arizona
AR	Arkansas
CA	California
CO	Colorado
CT	Connecticut
DE	Delaware
DC	District of Columbia
FL	Florida
GA	Georgia
HI	Hawaii
ID	Idaho
IL	Illinois
IN	Indiana
IA	Iowa
KS	Kansas
KY	Kentucky
LA	Louisiana
ME	Maine
MD	Maryland
MA	Massachusetts
MI	Michigan
MN	Minnesota
MS	Mississippi

MO	Missouri
MT	Montana
NE	Nebraska
NV	Nevada
NH	New Hampshire
NJ	New Jersey
NM	New Mexico
NY	New York
NC	North Carolina
ND	North Dakota
OH	Ohio
OK	Oklahoma
OR	Oregon
PA	Pennsylvania
RI	Rhode Island
SC	South Carolina
SD	South Dakota
TN	Tennessee
TX	Texas
UT	Utah
VT	Vermont
VA	Virginia
WA	Washington
WV	West Virginia
WI	Wisconsin
WY	Wyoming

Postal codes in the United States are five digits with an extender of four digits (e.g., 94104-1309). The extender identifies a more specific location (which is sometimes the postal box number). Using the four-digit extender is optional but entitles a domestic sender to a lower postage rate for bulk mailings and, in some cases, speedier delivery.

Here are two examples:

Ms. Norma L. Johnston
Chief Operations Officer
Tefledden, Inc.
Three Bush Street, Suite 630
San Francisco, CA 94104
USA

Mr. Charles C. C. Chang
Senior Vice President
Polynomenclature Corporation
1234 Avenue of the Americas, Suite 100
New York, NY 10022-0100
USA

VIETNAM (SOCIALIST REPUBLIC OF VIETNAM)

As in Chinese and Korean cultures, family names in Vietnam are placed first, but, as in Thailand, Vietnamese are normally addressed by their given names. Vietnamese men usually have three names, the family name followed two given names; a man named Tran Van Duc, whose family name is Tran, would be addressed as Duc or Mr. Duc. Vietnamese women normally have four names, the family name followed by three given names (but only two are normally used by Vietnamese women who live in Western countries). A woman named Nguyên Thi Ngoc Lan, whose family name is Nguyên, would be addressed as Lan or Miss (or Mrs.) Lan. Popular middle names are Van for men and Thi for women. Married women do not take their husbands' family names.

Honorifics are normally not used by Vietnamese except in international circles, where the standard honorifics (*Mr., Mrs., Miss, Madame,* and *Dr.*) are common. Titles are not used in addressing Vietnamese unless the person is a professor or has a military or governmental title.

Western business titles (e.g., *president, vice president, treasurer, manager*) are seen, as are company names ending in *Corp., Inc., Limited.* A number of military titles are used by people in government.

Business addresses in Vietnam are typically a street address that consists of a number and the name of the street, often without the word *Street*. In Ho Chi Minh City, the street address is followed by a district number (sometimes expressed with the Vietnamese word for district, *quan*, as in "Quan 2" or "Q2"). Postal codes are not used. Here are two examples:

Mr. Nguyên Van Dung
President
Nguyên Energy Company
105 Hai Ba Trung, District 1
Ho Chi Minh City
SOCIALIST REPUBLIC OF VIETNAM

Mrs. Pham Thi Kim Chi
Secretary
Pham Services Corporation
11 Ba Trieu Street
Hanoi
SOCIALIST REPUBLIC OF VIETNAM

7

LETTER PERFECT

FEW BUSINESSPEOPLE FAIL TO APPRECIATE a fine letter. For a thoughtful moment, a reader will admire its neat appearance or its artistic letterhead, or hold it to the light to see the watermark of its high-quality stationery. In that instant, such a letter will reflect well on its writer. If what is written there is well stated, the writer will capture the reader's attention under the most favorable circumstances.

In interviews and in responses to survey questionnaires for this book, Asia-Pacific executives—especially Asians—stressed the importance of an attractive, well-presented letter in writing to counterparts on whom they want to make a favorable impression. The importance assigned to this varies, largely in keeping with the Formality Factor, (see Chapter 3). For example, the Japanese, who place great emphasis on style and precision, assign greater importance to an attractive, neat letter than do Americans, who tend to be casual about such things. Yet even Americans, and others who are low on the Formality Factor scale, appreciate the importance of a fine letter.

Executives repeatedly recommended that first contacts with an Asia-Pacific counterpart be made by letter, delivered by mail or courier, instead of by fax or telephone (for more information on the fax, see Chapter 8). They also recommended that important documents and materials intended to convey an impression of integrity and quality—such as contracts and marketing materials—be sent by mail or courier instead of fax. In the case of contracts and other important business documents, a courier service will also afford a degree of security and guarantee of safe, trackable delivery that regular mail services may not offer.

When time constraints dictate that important letters or materials be sent by fax—that is, when mail or even courier delivery would arrive too late—it is nevertheless advisable to send them by mail or courier following the fax transmission. Indeed, when communicating by fax to someone having a high Formality Factor, it is often a good idea to send "hard copy" by mail even when the communication is routine. This may seem redundant and unnecessary, but to many—especially Japanese—it is an indication of commendable diligence. Also, in countries that have strong bureaucratic traditions and elaborate filing systems—and this includes most Asian countries—"hard copy" originals are considered very important.

THE ASIA-PACIFIC BUSINESS LETTER

Business letter styles in the Asia-Pacific region are as diverse as the region itself, but they are strongly influenced by three factors:

- ▲ **Formality Factor.** The higher the Formality Factor, the more formal the letter style (see Chapter 3).
- ▲ **Stage of Relationship.** The newer the relationship, the more formal the letter needs to be.
- ▲ **Addressee's Status.** The higher the status of the addressee, the shorter and more formal the letter should be.

While this is not a book on how to write a good business letter, I will mention a few basic letter-writing rules.

Before composing a letter, give careful thought to the following:

- ▲ *Purpose of the letter.* Have a clear idea of your reasons for sending the letter. If a complex strategy or relationship exists in relation to the addressee, have it well in mind before composing the letter. Even if the letter is an introduction to a new relationship, have a strategy for developing the relationship.

▲ *The reader.* Know as much as possible about the person or persons who will read the letter. This will enable you to "connect" well with the reader, to use words and address subjects that are of interest to him or her.

▲ *What you want to accomplish.* Have a clear idea of what you expect the letter to accomplish. Business readers are impatient, action-oriented types. With clearly focused expectations, you will be able to phrase more precisely what action you are requesting of the reader and what will happen next.

The basic business letter–writing rules are true to business activities around the world. They are as follows:

▲ *Be concise.* Asia-Pacific executives whom I interviewed or who responded to the survey for this book repeatedly emphasized that business communications—letters, faxes, telephone conversations—needed to be concise and to the point.

▲ *Use ordinary words and short, simple, clear, direct sentences.* Avoid jargon, slang, idioms, and fancy words. Write sentences that are short and direct—noun, verb, object. Avoid modifying and conditional clauses wherever possible. Avoid uncommon verb forms.

▲ *Be positive and courteous.* When you see a negative word (e.g., *no, not, never*), give a moment's thought to how the sentence might be phrased in a positive way. Also, be polite and considerate in your expressions.

▲ *Personalize your letter.* Add one or more references of a personal nature (e.g., recalling a recent visit or sending best wishes for a holiday) so that the reader will feel the communication is direct. It will help to review prior correspondence with the reader before writing and to visualize the reader as you write.

The structure of a business letter can normally follow a fairly set pattern. Here is a standard structure:

▲ *State the subject, purpose, and background.* After any appropriate personal remark, mention why you are writing the letter. State its purpose and the general subject matter. Refer to any pertinent background.

▲ *Next state what you want or state your response.* Say what you are asking or, if your letter is a response, what you have concluded.

▲ *Then give your reasons.* Explain why you need or want what you have asked for, or explain the reasons for the response you gave. Set forth any relevant supporting information.

▲ *Finally, state what happens next.* Say what you will do to follow up on your request or response. Even if there is nothing further to be done, promise to stay in touch. Do not leave the reader to wonder, Where do we go from here?

Writing the Asia-Pacific business letter calls for all of the preceding advice and more. An Asia-Pacific business writer should assess the three letter-writing factors at the beginning of this section and then apply the following additional rules:

▲ *Work especially hard at being clear, concise, and positive.* Language differences make clarity, concision, and a positive approach important, especially when the language used is the first language of the writer but not of the reader. A writer using his or her first language is too often insensitive to the difficulty of understanding writing that is not in the reader's first language.

▲ *Start with polite greetings.* Begin by offering good wishes, hopes that the reader is in good health, that the weather is good, that business is prospering, that the reader's family is well. Convey grateful thanks for a recent act of generosity or thoughtfulness by the reader. Allude to a past event that you enjoyed with the reader. Apologize for any oversight on your part or any inadequacy of your, or your company's, efforts.

▲ *Convey no bad news at the start.* Do not commence your letter with any negative news. For example, do not say something like "I regret to inform you . . ." in the first sentence or even the first paragraph.

▲ *Make your points with bullets or in outline form.* Points that are presented in abbreviated outline form tend to be more easily understood than those made in run-on sentences or even paragraphs. In addition, this form of presentation invokes a writing discipline that promotes simpler, more direct expression. In outline format, writers normally omit unnecessary descriptive words and clauses and complex grammar.

▲ *Close with pleasant thoughts.* Conclude with a final short paragraph or phrase that graciously conveys your wishes for the reader's continued good health and prosperity, and—especially—your appreciation for your valued relationship with the reader.

▲ *Indicate copies to key players.* Unless your letter contains sensitive information or negative statements, send copies to people known to have key roles relating to the matters discussed, including people in the reader's organization. This assists the communication process, especially in Asian organizations. Care must be exercised, however, to avoid putting the addressee on the spot.

A FEW DETAILS

The survey questionnaire that I sent to Asia-Pacific executives in the course of doing research for this book included a number of questions about the use of stationery and other details of written communications. Here are a few key points, gleaned from survey responses, to bear in mind:

Stationery size. While businesses in the United States and Canada normally use stationery with dimensions of 8½ by 11 inches, businesses in the rest of the Asia-Pacific region normally use stationery known as "A4," measuring about 8¼ by 11½ inches. The difference sometimes affects an addressee who uses a different size stationery than that of the sender. For example, file folders and envelopes on the receiving end might not fit, and a fax sent on A4 may spill onto two sheets of 8½ by 11 inch paper. Also, if A4 letterhead has printing at the very top and very bottom, something might be cut off in photocopies using shorter paper.

Stationery color. Most Asia-Pacific executives have a clear preference for white stationery of good quality. A few preferred an off-white stationery, such as beige or ivory.

Letterheads. Some executives prefer letterheads with office addresses and other information only at the top of the page. Others prefer their address or other information (such as addresses of affiliated offices) at the bottom of the page. Various reasons are cited, some executives wanting "vital" address information at the top, where it can easily be noted, and others wanting such "distracting detail" at the bottom. If your letterhead design sets forth your address on a single line, consider using bullets to indicate line breaks.

Here, with my comments, are a few examples of letterheads used around the Asia-Pacific region.

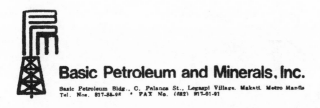

Basic Petroleum and Minerals, Inc.

Basic Petroleum Bldg., C. Palanca St., Legaspi Village. Makati. Metro Manila
Tel. Nos. 817-88-98 • FAX No. (632) 817-01-91

Basic Petroleum's letterhead utilizes an artful logo that combines the initials of its name with the image of an oil-drilling rig, indicating its activities. All address and telecommunications information is conveniently set forth at the top of the page, including the name of its building. The address information is on one line, as are those of Business Advisory and Swire Transtech on the following pages. This presents a clean look from a design standpoint, although a person unfamiliar with local addresses would be advised to check locally (or in Chapter 6 of this book) to be sure of the correct break points for stating the address on more than one line—say, on an envelope.

BUSINESS ADVISORY INDONESIA

The Business Advisory Indonesia letterhead has the company's name and logo by itself at the top, and its address (including the name of the building, Kuningan Plaza) and telecommunications information at the bottom. The address information is on the one line, assuming some familiarity with Indonesian address layout. The phrase "P. T. Yasa Monindo Perdana" is the corporate name of the firm in the Indonesian language, Bahasa Indonesia.

P.T. YASA MONINDO PERDANA, KUNINGAN PLAZA N. TOWER SUITE 304, JL. H.R. RASUNA SAID KAV. C 11 - 14, JAKARTA 12940, INDONESIA

TELEX 62151 AIRFAS IA, PHONE 5207696, 5207689, FAX.   5202557

**Business
Strategies
International**

David L. James
President

44 Montgomery Street, Suite 500
San Francisco, California 94104
Telephone: (415) 955-2744
Fax: (415) 397-6309

The officers of Business Strategies International use letterheads that include their own name. I prefer letterhead like this, that has all of the communications information at the top, where it can be readily seen and is less likely to be deleted if photocopied.

INTERNATIONAL PUBLIC RELATIONS PTY. LTD.

ACN 004 928 652

IPR is part of the worldwide Shandwick Group with 104 offices in 23 countries including: London Glasgow Paris Madrid Brussels Bonn Zurich Rome The Hague Ottawa
Vancouver New York Boston Washington Chicago Los Angeles Atlanta Hong Kong Jakarta Singapore Bangkok Beijing Kuala Lumpur Tokyo Seoul Auckland Wellington

The letterhead of IPR uses a double globe logo printed in gold above its name. Its affiliation with the Shandwick Group is mentioned below its name, as is its Australian Company Number (ACN)—all Australian companies are required to have such a number (individuals have a Tax File Number) and to indicate it on business correspondence and other papers. At the bottom of the letterhead, IPR sets forth communications information for each of its seven offices, enabling the same letterhead and design image to be used throughout the organization. The telephone codes that are shown are for internal use in Australia (see "Country and City Telephone Codes" in the Resource Files for more information on these).

ADELAIDE	BRISBANE	CANBERRA	HOBART	MELBOURNE	PERTH	SYDNEY
17 Rundle St	41 Leopard St	35 Kennedy St	119 Sandy Bay Rd	33 Walsh St	22 Charles St	55 Falcon St
Kent Town	Kangaroo Point	Kingston	Sandy Bay	West Melbourne	South Perth	Crows Nest
SA 5067	QLD 4169	ACT 2604	TAS 7005	VIC 3003	WA 6151	NSW 2065
Ph (08) 363 3088	Ph (07) 391 8955	Ph (06) 239 6600	Ph (002) 23 3966	Ph (03) 329 9333	Ph (09) 474 2544	Ph (02) 968 0999
Fax (08) 362 2256	Fax (07) 391 8314	Fax (06) 239 6565	Fax (002) 23 3593	Fax (03) 329 7996	Fax (09) 474 1928	Fax (02) 956 5683

LADNER DOWNS
BARRISTERS & SOLICITORS

PETER A. MANSON, Q.C.

900 WATERFRONT CENTRE
200 BURRARD STREET
P.O. BOX 48600
VANCOUVER, CANADA V7X 1T2
TELEPHONE (604) 687-5744
FAX (604) 687-1415

DIRECT LINE (604) 640-4158

Ladner Downs sets forth its affiliations at the bottom and its communications information at the top of its letterhead, together with the name and direct telephone number of the barrister or solicitor using the letterhead. The name and suite number of the building where its offices are located are clearly set forth, with both street address and post office box to indicate location and mailing address.

OSLER RENAULT LADNER

London • Paris • Hong Kong • New York

OSLER RENAULT LADNER IS AN INTERNATIONAL PARTNERSHIP OF OSLER, HOSKIN & HARCOURT, OGILVY RENAULT AND LADNER DOWNS

Swire House, 14, Ichibancho, Chiyoda-ku, Tokyo 102 Japan   Tel. 03-3230-9200   Fax. 03-3221-7957   ⊠ The Swire Group

Swire Transtech uses a clear name logo and sets forth its communications information on a single line. For information on usual line breaks in Japanese addresses, see Chapter 6. Swire Transtech's affiliation with the larger Swire Group is also clearly set forth (note the complementary design of the entities' logos). Local telephone and fax prefixes are used. (See "Country and City Telephone Codes" in the Resource Files for more information on these.)

U B S International
A Division of Unison International

San Francisco   Shanghai   Beijing

友升大樓系統國際公司

UBS International sets forth its address and telecommunications information at the bottom of its letter paper, enabling it to be used by all three of its offices. The Chinese characters on the right-hand side, which make the document familiar in the largely Chinese-speaking region where the company operates, say, "Unison Building Systems International Company," as UBS is known in China.

SAN FRANCISCO AREA
651 Gateway Boulevard, Suite 880
South San Francisco CA 94080 USA
Phone: (415) 877-0780
Fax: (415) 742-0828
Telex: 6504154303 MCI UW

SHANGHAI
Jinjiang Hotel Ste. 531-3
Shanghai, China 200020
Phone: 2582582 ext. 5312
Direct: 4330626   2535644
Telex: 33385 UNISH CN
Fax: 4330626

BEIJING
31/F Unit 5, Jing Guang Centre
Beijing 100026 China
Phone: 501-3388 ext. 31051, 31052
Direct: 501-3080, 501-3083
Telex: 210496 UNIBJ CN
Fax: 5016528

Company logos. There is a strong liking for company logos throughout the Asia-Pacific region. Logos are seen as adding to a company's identity. Asians whose languages are based wholly or in part on ideograms (i.e., Chinese, Koreans, and Japanese) are especially fond of logos.

Dates. Only Americans and Canadians customarily write a date with the month first (as in January 1, 1995). Asia-Pacific people write the day first, then the month.

> **ICD Prevention Tip—Style**
>
> *In writing dates, there is no need to adopt a usage that is not your own, but you should be careful when making abbreviations; 2/8/95 could be understood as either February 8 or August 2, 1995.*

Format. There is no consistent practice by Asia-Pacific executives in using either the indented or block style of paragraph format. Follow your personal preference.

Salutations. As mentioned in Chapter 6, it is important in greetings and salutations not only that you use a person's name (rather than a generic such as *Sir* or *Madam* or *Ladies and Gentlemen*) but also that you use the name correctly. With most Asians, you should use a person's family name unless he or she indicates that you should use the given name. See Chapter 6 for guidance on honorifics and titles that might be used in salutations.

Handwritten Salutation and Close. It is a British practice, sometimes observed in former British colonies such as Malaysia, Singapore, and New Zealand, that a personal letter be typewritten, sometimes with the addressee's name and address at the lower left, but with the writer's salutation, close, and signature all handwritten.

Complimentary close. All the standard complimentary closes are used in the Asia-Pacific region: "Very truly yours," "Respectfully,"

> **ICD Prevention Tip—Honorifics**
>
> *Sometimes it is difficult to know whether the person to whom you are writing is a man or a woman, for instance, when the person's given name is unfamiliar to you or you have only initials. In these cases, use the honorific Dr., as in "Dr. Chou." You will be forgiven if you are wrong.*

"Sincerely," "Yours sincerely," "Cordially," "Best regards," and various others. The choice is a matter of personal preference. You should use a complimentary close that suits you and the Formality Factor of your communication. In writing to Asians with a high Formality Factor, "Sincerely" is an excellent complimentary close because it reflects a valued personal characteristic, sincerity.

Signing agents. Some business letters are signed "for" the writer by a secretary or assistant. Others have a notation at the bottom saying, "Dictated but not read." These are not good practices for the Asia-Pacific region because they convey, perhaps unintentionally, that the writer does not take full responsibility for the communication. To some extent they imply disrespect for the reader and for the writing itself.

Signatures. Most Asia-Pacific executives prefer to sign their letters in black ink. Some, especially Koreans, like blue ink. Other colors do not appear to be used. Indeed, it is very bad luck for a Korean's name to be written in red, because in Korea a red mark through a person's name indicates his or her death.

EXAMPLES

Here are four sample letters that illustrate some of the points made in this book. The senders, addressees, and subject matter of these letters are fictitious, but the style of each is representative. The sender dates each letter with the day of the month first, international style, and the letters are sent by mail, courier, and fax for the various reasons mentioned in the introduction to each. For more about faxes, and postal and courier services, see the next two chapters.

▲ ▲ ▲

"Formally Introduced"

The following letter is typical of one that might be sent to a person and organization with a high Formality Factor at the outset of a relationship. An introduction has been arranged. The letter identifies the sender's organization and capabilities and encloses a brochure. It is precise about the purpose of the requested appointment and arrangements to follow up. It is respectful and pleasant, and closes with hope for developing a mutually beneficial relationship. The letter and enclosure are sent by courier. No fax is sent.

ASIA-PACIFIC TECHNOLOGIES CORPORATION

Robert B. Bellcast, President

56 Montgomery Street
San Francisco, California 94104
Telephone 415-987-6543
Fax 415-987-6521

17 March 1995

By Courier

Mr. Cho Kang-Hong
President
Yukong Company, Ltd.
C.P.O. Box 189
Seoul
REPUBLIC OF KOREA

Dear Mr. Cho:

My company and I are grateful for this opportunity to send you our most respectful greetings. We hope that you have now received the letter of United States Senator William Brown dated 3 March 1995 introducing my company and me.

The purpose of this letter is to request an appointment to meet with you or one or more of your executives during the week of 20 April 1995, when two of my colleagues and I will be visiting Seoul. We would like to tell you about our products and services and describe to you how they can assist you in your business.

Asia-Pacific Technologies is a recognized leader in the manufacture of computer hardware. Enclosed is a brochure describing our company and its products and services.

I look forward to hearing from you whether a meeting will be possible during my visit to Seoul, and I look forward with anticipation to the prospect of developing a mutually beneficial relationship between our two companies. My assistant, Mr. Frederick Jones, will telephone your office on Monday, 27 March 1995, to ask if you have any questions concerning our visit.

Sincerely yours,

Robert B. Bellcast
President

Enclosure
cc: U.S. Senator William Brown

"Asian Polite"

This sample letter is typical of one that might be sent to a person with a high Formality Factor whose culture values politeness. The sender and addressee have an established relationship, but the sender does not use Mr. Haruna's first name in the salutation. A contract number is mentioned before the salutation, for specific reference. The letter opens with pleasantries (references to weather and shared events are popular for Japanese) and presents a problem only after making a positive, but perhaps not entirely accurate, statement (the "tracking bars . . . are performing well"). Points are made with bullets to enhance clarity. A request is made in clear terms, and a response is requested by a certain date. There is an apology for any inconvenience. The letter closes with a pleasantry and with appreciation for a continuing relationship. The original of the letter is sent by mail. Because there is a time constraint and the parties have an established relationship, a copy is sent by fax (see Chapter 8 for further details).

ASIA-PACIFIC TECHNOLOGIES CORPORATION

Robert B. Bellcast, President　　　　　　　　　　　56 Montgomery Street
San Francisco, California 94104
Telephone 415-987-6543
Fax 415-987-6521

17 March 1995

Mr. Maki Haruna
Vice President
Transnational Ltd.
Ryokuchi-Eki Building, 2F
2-4-1 Terauchi, Toyonaka-shi
Osaka 560
JAPAN

<u>Contract No. 45678</u>

Dear Mr. Haruna:

I hope you are well and that the cold winds of winter in Osaka will soon give way to the pleasures of a warm springtime. I have happy memories of your visit to San Francisco last September, when we were able to enjoy a game of golf together in perfect weather.

I am writing to report the following:

- The tracking bars that we purchased from your company are performing well.
- Unfortunately, two of the tracking bars have developed a hum that might adversely affect sound reproduction.

Because of this development, we make the following request:

- Please arrange for your representative to come to our plant in San Francisco to assess the cause of the hum and to make appropriate suggestions to us.

We apologize for any inconvenience that our request causes you. Please contact us by 31 March 1995 to advise us if your representative will be able to visit our plant.

I hope that your business is prospering. We appreciate our relationship with you, and we look forward to strengthening it further in the future.

Sincerely,

Robert B. Bellcast
President

Original of letter sent by mail.
Copy by fax (to 81-6-3456-7890).

"Business Direct"

The following sample letter is an appropriate communication to someone with a moderate Formality Factor with whom the sender has an established relationship. It is especially appropriate for an addressee who values efficiency in communications, such as a person from Hong Kong, Singapore, or Taiwan. It comes quickly to the point and is precise in its request, with a response date mentioned, but it does not omit opening and closing pleasantries. References to good health, prospering business, and family well-being are particularly fitting when writing to an ethnic Chinese. The sender knows, by the way, that the addressee places her family name last, Western style. A copy of the letter is sent by fax.

ASIA-PACIFIC TECHNOLOGIES CORPORATION

Robert B. Bellcast, President
56 Montgomery Street
San Francisco, California 94104
Telephone 415-987-6543
Fax 415-987-6521

17 March 1995

Mrs. Jing-Mei Tsu
President
Containers Ltd.
8/F, 10 Duddell Street, Central
HONG KONG

Dear Mrs. Tsu:

I hope this letter finds you in good health with prospering business.

We need your proposal for the supply of shipping containers for our 1996 tracking bars by 1 September 1995.

Please advise me by fax by 15 May 1995, whether you will be able to submit your proposal by that date.

With kindest regards to you and your family,

Yours truly,

Robert B. Bellcast
President

Copy of letter by fax (to 852-865-1234).

"Informally Yours"

This last sample letter is representative of one that might be sent to a person with a low Formality Factor—or to someone from an individualist culture—with whom the sender has an established relationship. It is informal and somewhat casual in tone, evidencing an apparent friendship between sender and addressee. However, the sender's request is clearly stated, as is a response time. Regards are sent to the addressee's wife, Mary. The letter is sent by courier for special handling of its enclosures.

ASIA-PACIFIC TECHNOLOGIES CORPORATION

Robert B. Bellcast, President

56 Montgomery Street
San Francisco, California 94104
Telephone 415-987-6543
Fax 415-987-6521

17 March 1995

By Courier

Mr. John Smith
President
Apex Consultants Pty. Ltd.
200 Metropolitan Street
Sydney, NSW 2001
AUSTRALIA

Dear Jack:

Thanks for your help on the Baker Project, mate!

Could you handle another assignment for us? Enclosed are the marketing materials of one of our customers, Maximus Limited. Maximus wants our help in designing a disk drive that could be a smashing success in Australia. We could use your analysis and recommendations.

Let me know by 1 May whether this is a job you would like to undertake. Also, at that time, give me a rough estimate of what your fee and expenses would be.

Best wishes to Mary.

Sincerely,

Robert B. Bellcast
President

Enclosure

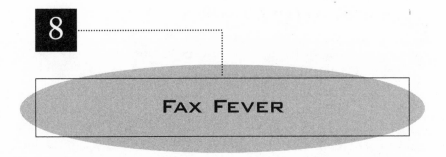

8

FAX FEVER

THE STARTLING STATISTIC THAT EMERGED from the survey I conducted in researching this book was that a majority of Asia-Pacific executives now send most of their written communications by fax. To be precise, 68 percent of the executives who responded to the survey said that 50 percent or more of their written communications go by fax rather than by mail or courier. And *fax*, by the way—verb or noun—is now the global word of choice, rather than its parent *facsimile*, or cousins *telecopy* and *telefax*.

One executive who was interviewed for this book complained that the fax had degraded the quality of business life. It used to be, he said, that he could send off a business letter to a client and have at least a week to attend to other business before having to deal with the matter again. Now, with faxing, the client is back in his face the next day with some new request or suggestion. Too many businesspeople "fax first and think later," he claims. He's grateful for additional business activity, but he thinks that there is too much "undisciplined overcommunication."

Other Asia-Pacific executives are wholly enthusiastic about the fax. They hail the increased productivity and ease of communicating that it brings to their businesses. One executive, based in Shanghai, also claims that the fax is dramatically changing patterns of communication in China. There, a written communication from one organization to another traditionally travels down the sender's bureaucracy and up the addressee's bureaucracy to reach its destination. Lately, more and more communications are traveling directly by fax from sender to addressee.

LEARNING TO LOVE THE FAX

At the beginning of the national leaders' session of the Asia Pacific Economic Cooperation organization in Seattle in November 1993, attended by most of the leaders of the major Asia-Pacific nations, President Fidel Ramos of the Philippines quipped, "I hope we will all exchange fax machine numbers!" The speed with which fax machines have entered our lives is breathtaking. Several factors account for this.

First, telecommunications technology is expanding globally at a lightning pace. Satellite transponders and telephone lines now reach even the most remote village. Second, fax equipment and transmission are affordable for many, in businesses and even homes. Fax transmissions sometimes cost even less than postage, at least compared with domestic mail. Third, graphic designs and Asian-language script and ideograms transmit as easily as typeface. Handwriting and drawings can be clearly transmitted. In Tokyo, where finding the office location of your next appointment can be especially frustrating, a favorite use of the fax is in transmitting street maps and handwritten directions. Fourth, speed of delivery substantially enhances productivity. Efficiency experts have long pointed out that productivity is improved if you attend to a task immediately rather than put it off. With fax capabilities, one often says to a counterpart, "I'll send it to you by fax right now." Indeed, many workers have fax transmission capabilities in their computer workstations; they can create a letter or document and send it by fax without even printing it out and feeding it to a fax machine. And some organizations offer automated "fax back" services: you can telephone their automated "voice mail" with a Touch-Tone telephone, enter a code that designates the information you want, then enter your fax number, and in a few minutes you will receive a fax containing what you requested. (For more about telephone voice mail, see Chapter 10, and for more about "fax back" services, see Chapter 11, "Networking Opportunities.")

But the fax is not yet a complete threat to the fine letter. Here are some of its problems, and some suggested solutions and tips.

Fax problem: Insubstantial appearance. Letitia Baldrige, author of *The New Complete Guide to Executive Manners,* recently commented that a fax is "slimy and unattractive." Manufacturers of fax machines are now producing "plain paper" machines that do not require the thermal paper that is so "slimy" and insubstantial. However, a fax transmission under the best of circumstances is less crisp than a type-written letter and may appear slightly fuzzy. Also, if the telephonic connection is not clear, the transmission can be unreadable.

ICD Prevention—Clarity: *There is nothing you can do to improve the recipient's fax machine, but you can make certain that the document you transmit is clear and distinct. Your letterhead and logo should be defined and sharp. Use a typeface, or font, that is slightly larger than what you normally use. If the document has colors, be sure that they transmit well. Dark colors normally transmit well, but light colors do not. Some letterheads have special colors, such as gold or silver, that also do not transmit well. Black is normally the best bet. Use a black pen for signatures and other markings.*

Fax problem: Confidentiality. A fax cannot be sealed in a personally addressed envelope at the sender's end and marked "personal and confidential, to be opened by addressee only." It emerges from a fax machine at the other end for all to see, at least all those who will handle it.

ICD Prevention—Alert the Other Party: *If your fax is confidential, be sure that the addressee knows it is coming and can make appropriate arrangements for receiving it. He or she might want to stand at the fax machine as it is received. If there is a substantial time zone difference between you, program your fax to transmit at a prearranged time. A fax can be programmed to transmit from New York City at 8:00 P.M. and be received at 9:00 A.M. in Hong Kong.*

Problems arise when the recipient's fax machine is not located nearby. Some companies like to use a central fax facility to coordinate the function better, similar to a "mail room." However, for efficiency and confidentiality, it is better to have one or more fax machines, with independent telephone lines, located in each department.

Although a warning to unauthorized people affords little real protection, your fax can carry a statement similar to the following:

> *"Confidentiality. This message and any accompanying documents are intended only for the person or entity to whom addressed and may contain information that is confidential and privileged. Confidentiality and privilege are not lost by their having been received by the wrong person. If you are not the intended recipient or the person responsible to deliver it to the intended recipient, please notify us by telephone and return this fax to us by mail. Any distribution, reproduction, or other use of this fax by an unintended recipient is prohibited."*

Fax problem: Confirming receipt. Even though a sender's fax machine today can sense electronically whether the fax was received at the other end, a sender still has a gnawing concern that it might not have gone through. Perhaps we are not yet comfortable with the technology. (Many of us live in countries where we have come to trust the postal system; after we send a letter, we do not give much thought to whether it is received. We seldom ask for a return receipt.) Or perhaps there is something about the immediacy of a fax that makes us concerned about its being received. Since receipt is just moments or hours away, we do not turn our minds to other matters. The question lingers: Did it go through?

ICD Prevention—Follow Up: *Ask the recipient to telephone you or send a fax confirming receipt. If you do not want to put the recipient to the trouble or expense of doing that, you can telephone to ask if it was received. And if you do not wish to appear so neurotic, invent a reason to telephone the recipient— for example, to clarify a point in the fax. If you are the recipient, be sure to acknowledge the receipt of a fax in your next communication to its sender.*

Fax problem: Transmission and reception difficulties. Busy signals are a growing problem as fax usage and telecommunications expand. Machines are busy. Lines are busy, especially in underdeveloped countries. Static or interference is sometimes a problem.

ICD Prevention—Timing and Features: *Send faxes during the recipient's nonbusiness hours. If connecting lines are busy, or if the recipient tells you that the fax was not received clearly because of static, ask an international operator to assist in routing the call and obtaining a clear connection. Also, make certain that your fax machine has an automatic redial feature (most do).*

For incoming faxes, have your fax machine serviced regularly and be certain that it always has an adequate supply of paper. Don't wait for the paper to run out. (Another approach is to use a fax machine that has a "memory" that will hold a fax until the paper supply is replenished and then print it out.) Also, to combat busy signals at your end, have more than one fax machine, each with a separate telephone line, and program each line to "hunt" or "roll over" to one of the other lines if it is busy.

Fax problem: Unsolicited marketing materials. Aggressive marketers of goods and services are now faxing their materials to potential and existing customers, tying up the recipients' fax machines and depleting their supplies of fax paper. Telecommunications companies make it possible for these marketers to transmit faxes ("broadcast" them) to hundreds of fax machines simultaneously.

ICD Prevention—Be Selective: *Be cautious in publishing and listing your fax number. If your organization has several fax numbers, publish and list only one, and give the others selectively to your important business connections. Also, when you receive an unwanted solicitation, contact the organization that sent it and ask them to remove your name and number from their fax list. They will do so.*

▲ ▲ ▲

MORE ICD PREVENTION TIPS

Fax equipment. The principal choices in fax equipment are (1) personal computers with software and modems that enable you to send and receive faxes directly from and to the computer screen, printing out hard copy only when needed, (2) "plain paper" fax machines, and (3) thermal paper fax machines. There are advantages and disadvantages to each. Computer faxing is efficient and saves paper, but with most systems the computer must be turned on at all times in order to receive incoming faxes. Also, if you want to fax something that was not generated or received on the computer, you must first "scan" it into the computer (a text scanner is yet another piece of equipment). A "plain paper" fax machine avoids the "slimy paper" problem referred to earlier; a thermal paper fax machine is usually less expensive and less bulky, but its paper feels insubstantial and is difficult to handle, and often yellows or fades over time—not ideal for file copies. Moreover, most thermal paper is too thin to be refaxed, and a coating on the paper can damage the transmitting parts of the machine. Generally, you must photocopy the fax onto plain paper in order to retransmit it.

ICD Prevention: *If cost is not a consideration, it is best to have both a computer fax and a "plain paper" fax machine. That way you will have the efficiency of the computer for sending and receiving faxes without hard copy and the ability to send faxes of hard copy materials that are not generated on the computer. If cost is a consideration, you will find that a thermal paper fax machine is adequate, the only inconvenience being those occasions when you* want to retransmit a fax that you received on the machine, and that a photo-copy will have to be made for filing purposes.

Cost savings. Telecommunications companies provide reduced rates for communications during low usage hours. These rates often do not apply during business hours at the origin or destination of a call, so it is not always possible to save on office telephone calls. It is possible, however, to schedule fax transmissions during reduced rate hours. You do not need to stay late at the office to take advantage of the savings, or send your faxes from your home. Computer fax software and most fax machines can be programmed to transmit a fax at a set time, like an alarm clock.

ICD Prevention: *Ask your telecommunications company for the hours of the lowest rates for calls to the country you plan to fax. (For example, AT&T's lowest standard rates for calls from California to Hong Kong fall between 11:00 P.M. and 10:00 A.M., California time.) Send your fax during those hours or set up your computer or fax machine to transmit it automatically at an appropriate time in your absence.*

Fax paper. Many businesses now send faxes directly from the computer, omitting paper altogether. However, if you use a fax machine, it is not necessary to use letterhead on expensive stationery for communications that will only leave your office by fax. You can save your expensive stationery for communications sent by mail or courier. (See Chapters 3 and 7.) In addition, you need to be aware of two transmission problems. First, your expensive stationery, or other documents sent by fax, might not fax clearly if printed on paper that is not entirely white or if the print is shaded or light. Second, anything printed on dark paper might take longer to transmit (sending more electronic data) and might be unrecognizable at the other end, because the machine couldn't distinguish the print from the paper.

ICD Prevention: *Use plain white paper for fax machine transmissions. Inexpensive paper can be used. For letters, have your letterhead printed in black ink on plain white paper. (See the accompanying box "Designs for the Times" on p. 206.)*

Names and addresses. The postal service will not be delivering your fax. The important things are the name and title of the addressee and the name of the addressee's company.

ICD Prevention: *A fax should be the essence of efficiency and simplicity. Forget about street addresses, postal boxes, and postal codes. But be sure to get names and titles right. These, with the person's department, organization, city, and country, should be enough.*

Marginal notes. Some executives will respond to a fax by making marginal notes on it and faxing it back to the sender. This is efficient, since a new fax is not prepared. It is also clear (assuming the marginal note is readable), since the response can be compared directly with the original message.

ICD Prevention: *Marginal notes by the fax recipient are acceptable if relations with the sender are informal and comfortable and the Formality Factor is low. If there is a high Formality Factor, however, avoid this practice, as it might give an impression of disrespect for the sender's communication.*

Fax forms and cover sheets. In the beginning, there was the cover sheet, announcing somewhat self-importantly that a communication of a certain number of pages, "including the cover sheet," would follow. Many businesses use cover sheets and fax forms to set forth basic transmission information, such as the addressee's fax number and the sender's telephone number in case of a transmission problem. A fax form is useful if it improves efficiency, for example, by printing information that would otherwise need to be typed. It is also useful for short messages that can be included on the cover sheet itself. However, if it is used as a cover sheet for a letter or other document that already bears your letterhead and other relevant information, it wastes a page of transmission time.

ICD Prevention: *Omit cover sheets that add nothing to the communication. Like a letter, your fax at the outset can state the name of the addressee, the fax number, and the number of pages transmitted. (See the following sample fax under "Efficiently Formal.") Your letterhead will indicate your telephone number in case the transmission is garbled. If you like to use a confidentiality warning, it can be set forth as a footnote on the first page of your fax.*

Here, with my comments, are a few examples of fax forms and cover sheets used around the Asia-Pacific region.

BUSINESS ADVISORY INDONESIA

		FAX Transmission		

To   :

Fax   :
Location :

From :

Tel   : (62-21) 520-7696 / 7689
Fax   : (62-21) 520-2557

Date :
Time :

Page   :

The Business Advisory fax form is based on its letterhead, formatted for insertion of relevant fax imformation.

P.T. YASA MONINDO PERDANA, KUNINGAN PLAZA N. TOWER SUITE 304, JL. H.R. RASUNA SAID KAV. C 11 - 14, JAKARTA 12940, INDONESIA

TELEX 62151 AIRFAS IA, PHONE 5207696, 5207689, FAX.   5202557

**INTERNATIONAL
PUBLIC RELATIONS PTY LTD**
(INCORPORATED IN VICTORIA). A.C.N. 004 928 652

FACSIMILE FORM

TO_____   FROM_____

COMPANY_____   FAX No (06) 239.6565

LOCATION_____   NO OF PAGES ATTACHED _____

FAX No _____   DATE_____ TIME_____

If you do not receive all pages clearly please telephone (06) 239.6600

MESSAGE

Fax forms used by IPR vary from the company's standard letterhead (see Chapter 7). Each carries relevant faxing information, but is specific to each of its several offices. This one is used by its Canberra (Kingston) office. While the globe logo is printed in gold on the company's letterhead, on the fax form it is reproduced in black and white, for clearer transmission.

35a Kennedy Street, Kingston ACT   PO Box 4205, Kingston ACT 2604 Australia

Phone (06) 239 6600. Fax (06) 239 6565

LADNER DOWNS
BARRISTERS & SOLICITORS

900 WATERFRONT CENTRE
200 BURRARD STREET
P.O. BOX 48600
VANCOUVER, CANADA V7X 1T2
TELEPHONE (604) 687-5744
FAX (604) 687-1415

WE INTEND THIS FAX MESSAGE ONLY FOR THE PERSON OR ENTITY NAMED BELOW. THIS MESSAGE MAY CONTAIN INFORMATION THAT IS PRIVILEGED, CONFIDENTIAL OR EXEMPT FROM DISCLOSURE UNDER APPLICABLE LAW. IF YOU ARE NOT THE ADDRESSEE OR AN EMPLOYEE OR AGENT RESPONSIBLE FOR DELIVERING THIS MESSAGE TO THE ADDRESSEE, PLEASE NOTIFY US IMMEDIATELY BY TELEPHONE AND RETURN THIS DOCUMENT TO US AT OUR EXPENSE AT THE ADDRESS NOTED ABOVE. ANY DISSEMINATION OR COPYING OF THIS MESSAGE BY ANYONE OTHER THAN THE ADDRESSEE IS STRICTLY PROHIBITED.

TO: FAX NO.:

ATTN: LOCATION:

FROM: PETER A. MANSON, Q.C.   DATE:

NUMBER OF PAGES (INCLUDING COVER PAGE):

IF YOU DO NOT RECEIVE A CLEAR COPY OR THE CORRECT NUMBER OF PAGES PLEASE CALL (604) 687-5744, LOCAL .

[X] Originals will not be sent   [ ] Originals will be sent under separate cover

MESSAGE:

The fax form used by Ladner Downs is formatted for insertion of relevant fax information, and sets forth a confidentiality warning at the top.

OSLER RENAULT LADNER
London • Paris • Hong Kong • New York
OSLER RENAULT LADNER IS AN INTERNATIONAL PARTNERSHIP OF OSLER, HOSKIN & HARCOURT, OGILVY RENAULT AND LADNER DOWNS

Swire House, 14, Ichibancho, Chiyoda-ku, Tokyo 102 Japan Tel. 03-3230-9200   Fax. 03-3221-7957   ◾️ The Swire Group

SWIRE TRANSTECH LIMITED

Fax: 813-3221-7957   Tel: 813-3230-9200

FAX MESSAGE

To: _____   Date: _____

Attn.: _____   Fax No.. _____

Re: _____   No. of pages: _____
                                 (Including this page)

From: _____

Message:

> *Swire Transtech fax form utilizes its letterhead, for-
> matted for insertion of fax information. Note the
> fax and telephone codes: this form is specifically
> designed for transmission outside Japan. (See
> "Country and City Telephone Codes" in the Resource
> Files for further guidelines.)*

* If you do not receive all the pages, please inform the above.

ASIA-PACIFIC BUSINESS FAX EXAMPLES

The following three examples indicate the wide variety of fax usages in the Asia-Pacific region. As with the sample letters in Chapter 7, the senders, addressees, and subject matter are fictitious but the style of each is representative. Each fax is dated with the day of the month first, international style. Three senders are indicated to illustrate different transmission usages. Only one of the senders uses a cover sheet. None of the transmissions will also be sent by mail or courier; hence, detailed postal addresses are not used.

▲ ▲ ▲

"Efficiently Formal"

The following fax takes care of the business at hand formally but efficiently. A single page is transmitted on the sender's letterhead. The parties correspond with each other frequently, but the relationship is formal even though the Formality Factor of each person's country is low. Since this is a fax, the addressee's full postal address is not used, but it does include his title and the name of his organization.

ASIA-PACIFIC TECHNOLOGIES CORPORATION

Robert B. Bellcast, President 56 Montgomery Street
San Francisco, California 94104
Telephone 415-987-6543
Fax 415-987-6521

22 March 1995

Mr. Robert Townsend
Executive Vice President
Royal Columbia Bank
Vancouver, BC
CANADA

Fax No.: 852-865-1234   One Page Transmitted

Dear Mr. Townsend:

We again need your assistance on short notice in arranging a letter of credit for our Canadian subsidiary, Asia-Pacific Technologies (Canada) Ltd., in connection with the purchase of a large order of tracking bars to be shipped from Osaka, Japan.

The president of our subsidiary, Mr. Daniel Westphal, will telephone your office tomorrow to supply you with the details.

Thank you for your assistance in this matter.

Very truly yours,

Robert B. Bellcast
President

cc: Mr. Daniel Westphal (by fax)

▲ ▲ ▲

"Confidentially Covered"

The sample fax that follows uses a cover sheet that sets forth a brief message identifying, and requesting comments on, a nine-page attachment. (The attachment is not included in this illustration.) The cover sheet form uses a format that is easily completed. It also sets forth the firm's standard confidentiality clause at the base. (See "Fax problem: Confidentiality" on p. 191.) The original of the draft contract was not also sent by mail or courier; when final contracts are prepared, they will be sent by courier.

GLADNER & ORR
Attorneys at Law
Nine Embarcadero Center
San Francisco, California 94111
Telephone: 415-987-9780

FAX TRANSMISSION

To:	Ms. Corazon Espino	Fax No.:	63-2-897-0196
Organization:	Capital Industries (Phil.)	Location:	Makati, M. Manila
From:	Fernando Mendozo, Esq.	No. of Pages:	Ten (Including this page)
Date:	22 March 1995		

If you do not receive all pages clearly, please telephone 415-987-9783

MESSAGE:

Dear Ms. Espino:

Pursuant to the contract negotiations held last month in Manila, attached to this fax cover sheet is the draft of a nine-page contract for the purchase of four metal stamping machines from Apex United. I believe the interests of Capital Industries will be well protected by this contract as drafted. Please let me have your questions and comments by fax at your early convenience.

Sincerely yours,

Fernando Mendozo

CONFIDENTIALITY. This message and any accompanying documents are intended only for the person or entity to whom addressed and may contain information that is confidential and privileged. Confidentiality and privilege are not lost by their having been received by the wrong person. If you are not the intended recipient or the person responsible to deliver it to the intended recipient, please notify us by telephone and return this fax to us by mail. Any distribution, reproduction, or other use of this fax by an unintended recipient is prohibited.

▲ ▲ ▲

"Timely Connections"

This last sample fax sets up explicit arrangements for a telephone call that the sender hopes to place two days hence. There is an intervening day for the addressee or his secretary to notify the sender of a problem with the suggested time. A fax form serves the purpose well.

TATUNG CEMENT CORPORATION

5F, 95 Chung Shan North Road, Section 2   Telephone: 886-2-799-2900
Taipei, Taiwan, R.O.C.   Fax: 886-2-799-2911

FAX TRANSMISSION

To: Mr. Steven Brown, V.P.   Fax No.:   1-312-876-7196

Organization: CMF Corp.   Location: Chicago, U.S.A.

From: Chen Li Meng, President   No. of Pages: One
                                               (Including this page)
Date: 21 March 1995

If problems with this transmission, please telephone 886-2-799-2915

MESSAGE:

Dear Mr. Brown:

I need to speak with you about your invitation to bid on the supply of
cement and other building materials for the new Taipei-Taichung highway
project. I will telephone you at 9:00 a.m. your time on 23 March 1995. (It will
be the evening of the 24th for me, and I will telephone you from my home.)
If this is not a convenient time for you, please fax me beforehand with a suggested alternative time and date. I believe our conversation will require
about twenty minutes. Please have our recent correspondence at hand when
I telephone.

                                   Sincerely yours,

                                   Chen Li Meng
                                   President

Designs for the Times

Spokane, Washington, may seem to be on the edge, rather than in the heart, of the Asia-Pacific region, but Kroma International, Inc., a graphic arts and printing company located there, is surely on the leading edge of designs for Asia-Pacific communications. In 1993 Kroma was asked by Kemph Technology & Investment Company of Idaho Falls, Idaho, to design a logo that would give the company a contemporary international image. Kemph is a diversified company that specializes in joint ventures of Chinese and United States companies engaged in agriculture and food processing, construction, and energy generation.

"In designing a logo for Kemph's letterhead, business cards, and brochure, we took into consideration that Kemph would often send communications by fax," says Kroma's Creative Director, Karen Shea. "Kemph's original logo did not fax well because it consisted of silver lettering on a dark background. So we designed a special fax letterhead with their logo in black ink on white paper."

BEFORE   AFTER

"Kemph saves money by using the special fax letterhead, which is less expensive than their regular letterhead," says Shea. "Also, the new logo can easily be digitized for communications faxed directly from a computer and modem."

9

POSTAL AND COURIER SERVICES

Tʜᴇʀᴇ ɪs ᴀ ɢʀᴏᴡɪɴɢ ɴᴜᴍʙᴇʀ ᴏғ ᴏᴘᴛɪᴏɴs for the physical delivery of your communications. During the last two decades, private courier companies have found a strong and expanding market for fast delivery of documents and packages. Government postal services, losing market share to courier companies in these more profitable segments of their operations, have responded in part by expanding their services to meet the competition and in part by limiting the activities of private courier companies in order to protect their postal systems. In the United States, for example, only *urgent* letters may be sent by courier; hence, the prominently displayed word *urgent* on courier envelopes. But restrictions on courier companies are not aggressively monitored and enforced. Also, bureaucratic inefficiencies and inadequate financing continue to hamper the competitive response of postal systems.

This chapter gives an update on the offerings of postal and courier services and, when you consult with the agencies and companies that provide these services, will help you select the right services for you.

POSTAL SERVICES

The Mail Must Go Through

One of the most colorful episodes in U.S. history was that of the Pony Express, a system of mail delivery by riders on horseback that operated between St. Joseph, Missouri, and Sacramento, California, between April 1860 and October 1861. The riders carried pouches of mail on galloping horses, changing horses at relay stations along the way, and passing the pouches to fresh riders after several hours of continuous riding. A distance of 1,838 miles was covered in about ten days. Customers were charged five dollars per half ounce of their communications. The first advertisement for Pony Express riders appeared in a San Francisco newspaper:

WANTED

Young, Skinny, Wiry Fellows, not over 18.
Must be expert riders, willing to risk death daily.
Orphans preferred. Wages $25 a week.

The Pony Express was a private postal enterprise whose sponsors hoped to obtain a profitable mail contract and government subsidy. At its height, it utilized 190 relay stations, 500 horses, and 80 riders. Its stations were from seven to twenty miles apart. Its riders rode nonstop, changing horses six to eight times en route. After resting they galloped back to their point of departure with new pouches. One of these young riders was "Buffalo Bill" Cody, who later became a famous frontier scout and showman.

The Pony Express was, however, never a commercial success, and it ceased operation with the completion of transcontinental telegraph lines. The telegraph provided a faster and less expensive means of communication.

Postal services have come a long way since the days of the Pony Express. In the Asia-Pacific region, they are the most important networks of domestic communications. Internationally in the region, where they compete with telecommunications and private delivery services, they continue to be a significant link in an increasingly complex web of communications.

Asia-Pacific businesspeople who use the international mails normally need to give thought to only three things:

▲ Enclosing the communication in a sturdy envelope or wrapping. (This point is not as obvious as it might appear. Many envelopes and wrapping that look adequate at origin tear in transit because the paper quality is poor.)

▲ Addressing the envelope or package properly. See Chapter 6 for some guidance.
▲ Affixing the proper postage.

However, people who send materials other than correspondence sometimes need to do more than this. They need to be sure that what they send by mail will not be returned or delayed as a result of postal requirements on the receiving end.

Lengthy regulations govern the postal system of every country in the Asia-Pacific region. For each country there are lists of materials and subject matter that are prohibited or restricted. In addition, a customs declaration is often required for packages, and duty must be paid for certain items upon delivery.

Materials typically prohibited from the mails include dangerous and hazardous goods (firearms, radioactive materials, and so on), items that might contain pests or disease (food, biological substances, and the like), and money (including bonds and negotiable instruments). Items such as these are normally transmitted in other ways, under license or by special handling.

Here is a sampling (by no means representative or complete) of postal prohibitions and restrictions set forth in manuals that are available from postal services around the Asia-Pacific region; many of the prohibitions and restrictions set forth here reflect applicable national policies.

> ### ICD Prevention Tip— Postal Regulations
>
> *Improperly sent letters and packages can cause the recipient considerable inconvenience and expense. Be sure that you (or the mail department of your company) are up-to-date on international mail regulations, have a current set of international mail manuals and guides, and have a general understanding of how postal services operate overseas. Manuals and guides are normally made available by a country's postal service without charge; in the United States, you should keep on hand a current issue of the U.S. Postal Service's "International Mail Manual."*

▲ In Australia, goods bearing the name "Anzac" and goods produced in prisons or by convict labor are prohibited from the mails. Prison and convict goods are also prohibited in Canada.
▲ Reptile skins are prohibited in Australia and New Zealand, and ivory is prohibited in Canada.

- ▲ China prohibits books, films, photographs, and other materials that could do "political, economic, cultural, or moral harm to the People's Republic of China."
- ▲ Indonesia prohibits "Chinese products" and books and periodicals printed in any Indonesian language outside Indonesia, except approved educational books.
- ▲ Malaysia prohibits pornographic materials.
- ▲ The Philippines prohibits "coffee in any form."
- ▲ The Philippines, Singapore, South Korea, and Thailand prohibit "communist materials."
- ▲ Singapore prohibits "lotteries and advertisements concerning lotteries."
- ▲ Taiwan prohibits "anti-government documents," and Australia and Singapore prohibit seditious literature.
- ▲ Vietnam prohibits "invisible ink, codes, ciphers, symbols or other types of secret correspondence, and shorthand notes."

In What Condition?

Recently an American business executive posted to Jakarta could not understand why mail to his company's post office box arrived sporadically and very late. And some items that he knew had been mailed to him from the United States never appeared. After investigation it was discovered that the postal codes for Jakarta post offices had been reorganized and the American's mail often sat in the wrong post office until it was occasionally discovered and forwarded to the proper one. In one instance, during the rainy season in Indonesia, the American received a large quantity of mail that was completely soaked.

Mail delivery problems are not confined to less developed countries. The same American received an envelope from the U.S. Postal Service enclosing a letter addressed to him that had been virtually destroyed. A note from the Postal Service apologized and explained that modern mail handling machinery is sometimes jammed by a piece of improperly prepared mail, causing damage to the offending piece and to properly prepared mail as well.

And When?

Delivery times are another issue. Domestic mail within a large country can take anywhere from a couple of days to a couple of weeks under the best conditions. Some large cities, such as New York

City, are notorious as delivery bottlenecks. Others, such as Singapore, are models of efficiency. In Shanghai there are normally two mail deliveries a day; if a letter is posted to another address in Shanghai by 8:00 A.M., it will be delivered that afternoon.

International delivery times are normally a function of the efficiency of the originating country's postal service. International mail is delivered directly to designated receiving centers of the destination country. If the originating service organizes and transfers the mail properly to the destination service, delivery will normally be timely.

Modern technology holds promise for increasing mail delivery efficiency. The United States and a few other countries are starting to use "delivery bar code sorters" in handling domestic mail. Bar codes on mail are those short vertical lines of varying height imprinted immediately above or below an address. They are used mostly by commerical organizations to obtain lower postage rates, but they also tend to assure faster delivery in any event. (Delivery bar code sorters can sort about 30,000 letters an hour.) Governments are beginning to work together to establish international standards for bar codes and bar code sorters. Within a few years, it is expected that mail with delivery bar codes will be automatically sorted in both the country of origin and the country of destination, resulting in improved delivery times.

> **ICD Prevention Tip—Bar Codes**
>
> *To speed delivery of mail deposited to the United States Postal System for domestic U.S. delivery, it is possible to use word-processing software that automatically imprints bar codes on address labels. Several software products are available. One is a "mail-list management" application called MailWorks by CompuWorks. In addition, a number of popular word-processing applications, including WordPerfect and Microsoft Word, apply delivery bar codes to envelopes.*

To Serve the Public

While governments offer some postal services that are intended to maintain the more profitable segments of their businesses (such as the U.S. Postal Service's Express Mail), they also offer vital services on which the bulk of the population depends. One of the most important functions of postal services in many Asia-Pacific countries is transmitting money for the general population. Personal checking and credit card systems are uncommon in many of these countries, and government-owned postal services fill this need. People who want to send money to a relative in a distant city or town, or who want to pay for something that is delivered to them through the postal service C.O.D. (collect on delivery), do so with cash at the local post office. In these countries post offices serve as a public banking system. In addition, post offices are sometimes combined with telecommunications centers, especially in small villages where there may be only one telephone line. In remote areas the post office is often the center of social activity.

COURIER SERVICES

The major international courier companies operating in the Asia-Pacific region—DHL Worldwide Express, Federal Express, TNT Express Worldwide, and UPS Worldwide Express—provide a sophisticated array of communication services. DHL (the letters are the first letters of the last names of its three founders, Adrian Dalsey, Larry Hillblom, and Robert Lynn) has the most extensive network in the region, but Federal Express is the largest worldwide, and each is a substantial organization. (For contact information for these courier services companies, see the Resource File, "Useful Contacts and Sources of Information.")

Each of these couriers serves all the countries covered in this book and at least 180 countries worldwide. They operate extensive networks of warehouses, receiving and dispatching offices, customs clearance facilities, and consolidation and sorting centers. They own and charter fleets of vehicles and aircraft. In most countries they own and operate their centers and facilities. In some countries, they operate through joint ventures and alliances with local courier organizations. For example, DHL serves 73,000 destinations in 208 countries and territories with a fleet of 149 aircraft, their 28,000 employees handling more than 71 million shipments a year. Federal Express has 464 aircraft, 31,000 vehicles, and more than 94,000 employees.

Rates vary but are competitive. Here are the principal services that courier companies provide:

Express delivery. Envelopes and packages are picked up and delivered door to door in most cities of the region in one to three days, and sometimes overnight. Hong Kong, Singapore, and Sydney are the major hubs and sorting centers. Satellite and wireless computer linkages are able to track the whereabouts and status of most shipments on a twenty-four-hour basis.

Packages of dutiable items clear customs rapidly. Before their arrival DHL and Federal Express electronically transmit shipping data and documents to their offices and brokers at their destinations so that the customs-clearing process can begin early.

Air freight. Each courier also transports freight, dutiable goods, and materials requiring special handling.

Shipping systems. For high-volume shipping customers, DHL and Federal Express provide the computer hardware, software, installation, and training that enable a shipper to produce its own shipping labels, shipping documents, and reports. These systems allow a company to keep track of its shipments and better manage its shipping schedules.

Remail. Companies that have a high volume of nondutiable mail, such as direct marketers who send out catalogues and financial services companies who mail financial statements and reports, can save up to half of the cost of public postal service mailings by using the "remail" services of private couriers. Typically, the courier picks up the customer's unsorted mail in boxes or bags, sorts the mail, and delivers it into the appropriate domestic mail streams of the addressees. DHL does its initial sorting in the Netherlands and Federal Express in Denmark. TNT does its initial sorting at origin.

> **ICD Prevention Tip—Remail**
>
> *Remail is not only for those who regularly send materials by international bulk mail. Consider using remail services anytime you anticipate making a large mailing.*

Faxing. DHL and Federal Express offer fax services to speed delivery of documents to people at distant locations who do not have fax equipment. A customer can fax or deliver a document to the courier, who in turn will transmit it to an office near the addressee's location. There, hard copy will be produced, and the document will be physically delivered or locally mailed to the addressee in an envelope. A single fax can be transmitted to multiple addressees.

TELECOMMUNICATIONS COMPANIES

Companies such as AT&T and MCI provide faxing services, similar to those of couriers, for the physical delivery of documents (see the Resource File "Useful Contacts and Sources of Information" for details). Normally, however, their services do not include door-to-door delivery. Rather, the faxes are placed in the local mail stream.

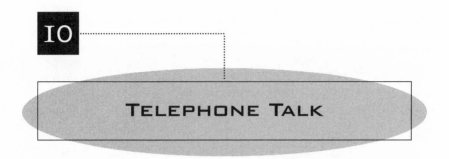

10

TELEPHONE TALK

POOR CONNECTIONS

An American executive who was interviewed for this book said that a few years ago he was surprised that the telephone connections between the United States and Asia were so poor in a westerly direction. Frequently, after he reached an Asian on the telephone and could hear him well, the Asian would say, "Sorry, this is a very poor connection," and hang up. If he placed the call again, the Asian would not be available. But after a time the American realized that his Asian counterpart was using this excuse to indicate that he did not want to speak on the telephone or continue a phone conversation.

Whether because of "poor connections" like these or something else, the telephone has its limitations in international business communications in the Asia-Pacific region. International telephone usage has not kept pace with advances in telecommunications technology there. One reason is that some Asia-Pacific countries are not yet "well wired." Underdeveloped countries in particular are deficient in telecommunications infrastructure—switching stations and telephone lines. In all countries of the region, the licensing process is controlled by government bureaucracies that are sometimes slow to act. Further, in many countries provision and servicing of telecommunications equipment is in the hands of government-owned organizations that are often inefficient.

Let's take a look at the extent to which the countries covered in this book are "wired."

Country	Population (in millions)	Main telephone lines per 100 population	Number of fax machines (1993 estimates)	Number of cellular phones (1993 estimates)
Australia	17.5	47.10	600,000	639,000
Canada	27.4	58.91	500,000	1,150,000
China	1,175.7	0.98	89,271	160,000
Hong Kong	5.8	48.62	172,168	288,000
Indonesia	191.2	0.78	32,000	35,000
Japan	123.4	46.73	500,000	2,300,000
Malaysia	18.8	11.13	46,000	240,000
New Zealand	3.4	44.99	40,000	94,000
The Philippines	64.3	1.03	10,000	60,000
Singapore	2.8	41.60	40,000	110,000
South Korea	43.7	36.34	250,000	349,000
Taiwan	20.8	35.66	200,000	430,000
Thailand	57.8	3.10	10,000	333,000
United States	255.0	56.49	6,000,000	13,000,000
Vietnam	69.5	.29	5,000	none

Sources: International Telecommunication Union and U.S. Department of Commerce

While this table does not accurately reflect business usage, and population size accounts for vast differences in "lines per 100 population," several countries (for example, China, Indonesia, the Philippines, Thailand, and Vietnam) can be seen as lagging in telecommunications.

But there are other reasons why international telephone usage in the region has not kept pace with technological advances.

▲ *Language differences.* It is sometimes difficult to understand another person over the telephone, especially if that person is speaking a language that is not your first language. For example, while many Asians can read and write English well, it is more difficult for them to understand spoken English, even under favorable circumstances. Over the telephone the listener is unable to see the gestures and eye and mouth movements that assist understanding.

▲ *Accents and dialects.* Even if the parties speak the same language, accents and dialects can impair understanding. Again, the inability to see gestures and eye and mouth movements diminishes comprehension.

▲ *One-dimensional.* With only the voice to work with, the speaker cannot convey meaning as well as when face to face with the listener. This is especially inhibiting to Asians, who rely more heavily than Westerners do on subtlety in communications. (See Chapter 3, "Set up a personal meeting if possible.") The Japanese, in particular, are fond of "belly language," various movements, gestures, positions, and other body language that add dimension and weight to the spoken word and sometimes convey strong meaning without words.

▲ *Cultural discomforts.* Asians place such a premium on personal relations that they tend to be uncomfortable in using the telephone. Japanese, when making a request to a counterpart on the telephone instead of writing a letter or arranging a meeting, will often say, "I am sorry to ask this by telephone, but. . . ."

▲ *Time zones.* What international executive has not been frustrated by time zones? Or—worse—has not been awakened in the middle of the night by an overseas caller who failed to consider time zone differences or calculate them correctly?

Time zones are no problem for businesses in the same or adjacent zones, even if separated by thousands of miles in a north-south direction. For example, there is no problem for calls between Tokyo, Seoul, Jakarta, Manila, Hong Kong, and Beijing, nor for calls between Vancouver, Seattle, San Francisco, and Los Angeles. But calls between Asia and North America present a significant time zone problem. (See the "Asia-Pacific Time Zone Table" in Resource Files.)

Time differences are complicated by "daylight savings time," the practice of some countries to extend daylight hours, for enjoyment and work, by setting clocks ahead one hour in the springtime and back one hour in the fall. (The saying "Spring forward, fall back" often helps people remember the direction of the settings.) The changes of time are normally carried out on the first Sunday of April and the last Sunday of October. Of the Asia-Pacific countries featured in this book, six use daylight savings time: Australia (except for Queensland), Canada, New Zealand, the Philippines, South Korea, and the United States (except for of Hawaii, Arizona, and certain local regions). Australia and New Zealand, being in the Southern Hemisphere with their seasons the opposite of those in the Northern Hemisphere, set their clocks back when others are set forward, and vice versa. The remaining nine countries in this book remain on standard time throughout the year.

The most that can be said for east-west time zones in telephone usage is that they extend your business day. That's the good news and the bad news: a convenience and a curse. The convenience is that, early in your day, you can catch people to the east of you while they are still in their offices; and, late in your day, you can catch people to the west of you as they arrive at their offices. The curse is that you might find little respite from your business.

▲ *Connecting with the person you call.* First there is the problem of having the correct telephone number for the person you wish to call. Although government trade offices, chambers of commerce, business associations, and some private publishers publish telephone directories for overseas use, these directories are sometimes out of date or do not have the listings you want. Further, telephone company information services are expensive to reach from overseas and sometimes do not have operators who speak your language.

Second, there is sometimes the problem of first speaking with the secretary or assistant or household staff of the person you want to reach and finding it difficult or impossible to com-

---

**ICD Prevention Tip—
Telephone Numbers**

Are you missing a digit? Maybe yes, maybe no. In most modern telephone systems, a local number normally has seven digits (following the country code and the city or area code). However, Tokyo's local numbers now have eight digits. And in many cities and countries where systems are in the process of upgrading, there are both six-digit numbers and seven-digit numbers. See also the discussion of "Country and City Telephone Codes" in the Resource Files.

---

municate because of language differences. Also, sometimes the person you speak with first is overprotective of the boss or wants to handle the call him- or herself.

Third, there is the problem of being connected to the wrong person, perhaps someone with the same name. In countries such as Korea, with so many people of the same name, this can be a real problem.

Fourth, there is "voice mail," the automated telephone answering systems that assist in handling incoming telephone calls. These are telephonic software systems that enable the caller to hold for an operator, be transferred to one or more destinations within a company, or leave a message. Normally recorded prompts ask the caller to enter selections on a Touch-Tone telephone (a telephone with a keypad that generates electronic signals, standard in many businesses in the region) or hold for an operator. For callers who do not have Touch-Tone telephones, some systems now have voice-recognition capability for simple commands such as "yes" and "no" and certain numbers. Voice mail improves efficiency and lowers personnel costs for companies that use it, but it can be extremely annoying, expensive, and confusing for outside callers, especially long-distance callers. Voice mail is now ubiquitous in the United States. It is also becoming popular in Canada and Australia. However, it is seldom found elsewhere in the Asia-Pacific region. In Asian countries, largely because of cultural resistance to its impersonal nature, it is not likely to become popular anytime soon. Consequently, an overseas caller from Asia who is connected with voice mail is apt to be frustrated and possibly offended.

Finally, there are telephone-answering systems that merely request the caller to leave a message. These are less likely than voice mail systems to frustrate an overseas caller, but they might cause an unwanted expense if the caller hoped to do more than leave a message.

▲ *Expense.* The cost of overseas telephone communications today is remarkably low compared with what it was just a few years ago, and the major international telephone companies offer a wide range of discounts. However, telecommunication expenses can mount rapidly. Compared with fax transmissions, the expense of a long telephone call can be substantial. And a long call will not be cost-effective if the parties fail to come to the point quickly.

GOOD CONNECTIONS

There are a number of things that Asia-Pacific executives can do to improve the efficiency of overseas telephone calls. Consider the following:

▲ *Plan your calls.* The best way to ensure a successful overseas telephone call is to plan ahead. Prepare detailed notes for the points you wish to cover so that the purpose of the call will be accomplished thoroughly and efficiently. Also, keep a chart handy that tells you the time zone difference between you and the person you plan to call. Your secretary can assist with this. If you are on the road, a digital wristwatch or personal computer that gives you local times in various cities is also helpful. Executives who responded to the survey for this book generally said that they preferred to receive overseas calls during the mid-morning or early afternoon of their business day.

▲ *Fax first, call later.* Send a fax to the person you intend to call, stating the time you will call and asking the person to fax you back if a different time would be more convenient. Allow enough time for the person to respond before you make the call. To be safe, state in your fax the telephone number you intend to use when you make your call.

▲ *Good manners: Call direct.* A number of executives who were interviewed for this book or who responded to the survey expressed annoyance with callers whose secretaries "got them on the line" before the caller got on. Frequently, these executives would be on "hold" while the caller came to the line. The impression conveyed was that the caller's time was more important than that of the person called. This practice is a serious breach of good manners, especially in the view of Asians. If you are the caller, handle the call yourself, or have your secretary get the other person's secretary on the line and then handle the call yourself.

▲ *Good Manners: Avoid the speakerphone.* Executives who were interviewed for this book or responded to the survey were also critical of people who use speakerphones without an apparent need to do so. These executives say they can tell when a speakerphone is being used on the other end. If it is, they want to know who else is in the room to hear the conversation. And since the reception is never quite as clear, they want to know why the other party does not use the handset.

   Unless there is a good reason to use a speakerphone, as, for example, if two or more people in the room need to participate in a telephone conversation, or if you need two hands free, you should avoid using one. If you do need to use a speakerphone, you should immediately explain the need to the other party to the call, state who else is in the room, and obtain the other party's consent to the use.

▲ *Speak clearly.* Remember to enunciate clearly and speak deliberately, especially if the first language of the other person is not your own. Also, if your first languages are different, try to avoid slang, jargon, and idiomatic expressions.

▲ *Be cost conscious.* If you place the call, be polite but come to the point of your call quickly. Even though you will pay for the call, you are taking time from the other person. If you receive the call (or the other person will be charged for the call), be especially careful not to ramble or unnecessarily prolong the conversation. And if you place your call at a time that takes advantage of low rates offered by your telecommunications company (see "Cost Savings" in Chapter 8), be certain that the time is during normal business hours at the call's destination.

▲ *Avoid voice mail.* If your company uses voice mail, consider giving your Asia-Pacific counterparts telephone numbers that will reach you directly. Also, review the selection messages that your voice mail offers to determine whether they can be easily understood by a person who speaks a different first language. Finally, keep the voice mail selections few so that a caller who does not have a Touch-Tone phone or who wants to speak with a live operator does not have to wait through a lengthy string of choices. For example, if there are several choices, one of the first should enable the caller to speak to an operator.

▲ *Maintain your collection of telephone numbers.* You or your secretary should be diligent in maintaining up-to-date files of telephone and fax numbers. Numbers should be collected from letterheads and business cards that you receive, and from other sources, and entered in your file system. Computers now make this task much easier than in the past, and make it possible for you to carry your files with you when you travel. (See Chapter 14 for more about address files and traveling with computer notebooks.) Also, obtain telephone directories that you might need from trade offices, chambers of commerce, business associations, and others, and replace them with updated editions on a regular basis.

▲ *Telecommunications at home.* Make sure you are well set up to place and receive overseas telephone calls at home. You should have international direct dialing if it is available. You should also take advantage of any discounts that your telephone company may offer for overseas calls or calls to certain countries. A second telephone line for a fax machine at home, if possible, is also a good idea.

▲ *Telecommunications on the road.* Depending on how you do your business and where you live, a cellular telephone, if available, might be worth the expense. Some executives are away from their offices for long periods of time and cannot be easily reached. Some live in large cities and spend hours commuting or stuck in traffic. In Jakarta or Bangkok, for example, a person can be stuck in traffic for two hours or more while traveling as little as three miles to an appointment.

Also, wireless systems, such as pagers, "palmtop computers," and "personal digital assistants," now send lengthy messages and have international connections to Canada, Hong Kong, Singapore, and the United States. For more on telecommunications away from the office, see Chapter 14.

▲ *Phone cards.* Be sure that you have an appropriate phone card or telephone credit card with you at all times, especially if you are traveling overseas. In most Asia-Pacific countries today there are telephones in hotels, airports, and many public places that take credit cards and telephone debit cards. The debit cards are commonly referred to as *phone cards,* or sometimes as *stored-value cards.* They are electronically programmed with values that diminish as calls are made, when they are placed in telephone stations that accept them, or they set forth an identification number that the caller enters on a Touch-Tone telephone to access a stored value of telephone time. Phone cards are thrown away when used up, although some are now printed with commemorative designs and text and are saved as collectors' items, like postage stamps and baseball cards. Where they are used, you can purchase phone cards in hotels, stores, and other public places in various denominations (such as five, ten, or twenty dollars). Telephone credit cards, on the other hand, charge the cost of the call to the caller's account. At some telephone stations, the card is inserted into the telephone and its account number is automatically entered; otherwise, the caller enters the number on the telephone's Touch-Tone number pad or gives it to an operator. Before leaving on a trip, make certain that your telephone credit card can be used where you will be, and make other arrangements if it cannot. (For more about phone cards and telecommunications when traveling, see Chapter 14.)

TELECONFERENCING AND VIDEOCONFERENCING

Telecommunications companies will help you connect people at several locations around the world to a single telephone conference call. Typically, the call is scheduled for a set time, the conference operator calls each party in advance and holds each on the line while others are connected, a roll call is then held, and the conference proceeds. Parties to the call speak through a handset, or with a speakerphone at a location where several participate. Conference calls are useful for corporate board meetings, financial closings, and various transactions that must be carried out simultaneously with participants at various locations.

But teleconferencing is not an ideal means of communicating in the Asia-Pacific region for several reasons. First, there are the Asian "cultural discomforts" previously discussed. Second, it is not always possible to know whether each party to the conference hears everything that is said or has an opportunity to speak at appropriate times. Third, the identity of each speaker is not always clear unless the person identifies himself or herself with each statement made. Fourth, the acoustic quality of a call connected to more than two locations, and when speakerphones are used, is often poor.

In some countries, teleconferencing services are provided by independent specialists as well as international telecommunications companies. In the United States, for example, dozens of small firms provide teleconferencing services linked through international lines. One such firm, Aloha Conferencing Services, Inc., located in Honolulu, Hawaii, finds that its location at the center of the Pacific Ocean facilitates the scheduling of Asia-Pacific connections and often gives customers a cost advantage.

Videoconferencing is provided in a few countries, but it is expensive and inconvenient. Participants must normally go to a studio for such conferences. A few multinational corporations have their own facilities, but cost-effective use of this means of communication lies several years in the future. One alternative that is now available is the transmission of digital video images by video cameras mounted on the top of computer monitors. The cameras transmit images of a person at one computer terminal to the screen of another terminal. Two or more people at separate terminals can communicate by voice, and see images of the others in a

> ### ICD Prevention Tip— Conference Calls
>
> *When arranging telephone conference calls, try to limit the number of locations that are connected and to use handsets instead of speakerphones. Also, when deciding to arrange a conference call, ask your telecommunications company whether the call will be transmitted by satellite, cable lines, or fiber-optic lines. Fiber-optic lines provide the clearest transmission. Satellite connections sometimes produce brief echoes or delays.*

section of the computer screen, while working on a document that is also displayed on the screen. While the technology is new and expensive, and requires fiber-optic digital transmission for best results, it provides a glimpse of things to come.

FUTURE TALK

Despite the constraints to international telephone usage mentioned at the outset of this chapter, the future holds much promise for the telephone in the Asia-Pacific region. Telecommunications infrastructure will make the telephone more available. Cellular telephone usage will increase dramatically. Cultural and language impediments to effective telephone communication will gradually diminish. Video telephones will someday be affordable to businesses and will do much to overcome cultural and language impediments. In due course, videoconferencing will become cost-effective and will add an important new dimension to telecommunications.

II

ON THE
INFORMATION HIGHWAY

THE NEXT STEP UP

Scott McNealy, chairman and chief executive of Sun Microsystems Inc., a U.S. computer systems company, took his notebook computer with him on a two-week business trip through eight Asian countries in 1993. Each business day he connected his notebook computer (a Hewlett-Packard OmniBook) through a telephone jack to Sun's local area network (LAN) and browsed through 150 to 200 electronic mail messages posted to him. "This way, I'm able to keep up with the office chatter and memoranda," says McNealy. "Of course, my managers hate it. It means they can never get away from me now."

Dean Ho, chairman and president of UBS International, a division of Unison International Corporation, a Shanghai-based advisory services company, takes his laptop with him on his frequent business trips throughout China. Ho says, "I'm never out of touch with my office. And I send and receive faxes and messages just by connecting my laptop to a telephone line."

McNealy, Ho, and many other Asia-Pacific executives have taken the next step up in international communications. They use personal computers—in their offices and homes and on the road—to communicate with others over telephone lines and cellular connections. They communicate with their companies' local area networks (linkages of computer stations within a company, referred to as LANs, or sometimes, if geographically extensive, as WANs, for wide area networks);

with customers, suppliers, and third parties; and with extensive data-bases and other resources on the Internet, the so-called information highway.

Network communication in business is still relatively new in the Asia-Pacific region, but it holds immense promise for enhancing economic activity in the region. Governments in the region need to provide the infrastructure, resources, and licensing to promote network communication. Businesspeople need to start communicating in this medium if they are not already doing so. If they do not, they will be left in the dust by those who do.

THE TELEX REMEMBERED

In 1987 an overseas visitor to the representative office of the State of Illinois in Tokyo noticed a telex machine against one wall. The visitor asked the director of the office for his telex number for future communications. (The number was not on the director's business card.) The director replied, "Oh, we never use the telex anymore. We only use the fax."

Nonetheless, the telex is in active use in many countries throughout the Asia-Pacific region. There are over 200,000 telex subscribers in the region exclusive of the United States and Canada, and over 1.5 million subscribers worldwide in over 200 countries. Telex usage is especially strong in underdeveloped countries, where more sophisticated telecommunications technology is not yet available.

The telex is a precursor to network communications. It enables users to exchange messages electronically either "on-line" or, with the help of a telecommunications company, on a "store and retrieve" basis. That is, a telex message can be sent to its destination immediately and the recipient can respond immediately, or it can be held by the telecommunications company for retrieval by the addressee at a later time. An important advantage of the telex is confirmation of receipt. With its "answer-back" message, the sender knows that the telex is going through to the intended addressee.

NETWORKING OPPORTUNITIES

The principal business use of network communication is something akin to the telex: electronic messaging, called e-mail. Normally e-mail is used within a single organization or group of linked organizations—through the organization's LAN or WAN. Thus, the geographically dispersed plants and offices of McNealy's Sun Microsystems are linked to a WAN that shares Sun's messages and data. For example, a person in one department can send an e-mail message to one or more persons or departments within the system. The message is stored in the system for retrieval by those to whom it is sent. Those to whom it is *not* sent cannot retrieve it even though they are part of the system. When a Sun employee turns on a personal computer (PC) that is linked to the WAN, any messages addressed to the employee can be retrieved, sometimes with a password to assure confidentiality. The employee will scroll through them, printing out those for which hard copy is needed, saving others on the PC, and deleting those that do not need to be retained.

Similar electronic messages can be sent over telephone links to customers, suppliers, and other third parties who have the necessary computer systems to receive them. "Folders" of electronic messages or information can be stored in an e-mail system for retrieval by designated persons. For example, technical information applicable to one of a company's products can be stored in a "folder" that can be retrieved only by customers who have bought the product. Telecommunications companies, such as AT&T, MCI Corporation, Sprint, and Fujitsu Ltd., provide various services that facilitate external communications like these.

> ## ICD Prevention Tip—E-Mail
>
> *Despite the immediate transmission of e-mail, one of its disadvantages is that a busy or traveling executive might fail to check his or her e-mail messages. Businesspeople who send and receive e-mail need to remind themselves to turn on their PCs and modems to check for their messages, and sometimes they need to advise an e-mail addressee by telephone or fax that a message has been, or will be, transmitted.*

Also, electronic data interchange messages (called EDIs) can be used to transmit information within an organization or between unrelated parties in standardized formats. For example, formatted spreadsheets, reports, and purchase orders can be transmitted, revised or completed by the recipient, and then retransmitted to the sender. In addition, EDI files can contain a seller's product catalogues and offerings; customers can review these on their own PCs and then immediately transmit orders to the seller. Applications such as these expand simple e-mail messaging directly to the active conduct of business.

Telecommunications companies also offer enhanced fax services. For example, a fax that you want to send to a list of up to 1,000 addressees can be "broadcast" simultaneously to each. The appearance of a "broadcast" fax is exceptionally good; graphics, logos, letterheads, and signatures are clearly reproduced in a digitized transmission. Telecommunications companies also offer "storage and retrieval" of faxes much as they do for e-mail. If you are traveling, you can arrange for faxes sent to you to be stored in the system until you retrieve them electronically with your laptop. Another service is the "fax catalogue," sometimes referred to as a "fax back" service. A person with a fax machine can telephone a company's fax catalogue and, by entering index code numbers and the number of the fax machine, receive a fax of the requested information.

The Export Hotline in the United States is an example of a fax-back service. Anyone with a fax machine (even in another country), after registering by telephoning 1-800-872-9767 (or, from outside the U.S., 1-617-248-9387), can receive, without charge, one or more of over 4,500 market information reports, covering seventy-eight countries and fifty industries. The information is collected from more than a hundred different sources, and is on an extensive database. There is also a useful directory of firms offering products and services.

In addition, numerous public and private organizations offer access to computer databases through direct telephone line connections or over a series of telecommunications linkages known as the Internet. A person can sit in front of a PC and scroll through library catalogues, read and copy articles from periodicals, review recent government reports and research studies, obtain the text of legal decisions, view electronic bulletin boards, participate in on-line forums, and acquire copious quantities of information and data on innumerable subjects.

THE INTERNET

Most global network communications and databases are carried on the Internet. This complex web of telecommunications linkages, often referred to as the "information highway," was created by the U.S. government in the 1960s to enable Department of Defense researchers at widely scattered universities to share scientific information. It grew rapidly. Universities and businesses expanded the Internet simply by tapping into one of its arteries via an electronic telephone link, following standard international telecommunications protocols. Telecommunications companies provided others with "gateways" to the Internet, enabling virtually anyone with a PC and a telephone line to connect and navigate through interlocking telecommunications networks around the world.

Because the Internet is unregulated, its precise contours are an enigma. No one keeps track of who and what is on the system. It is estimated that at least 30 million people and organizations in more than ninety countries currently use the Internet, and one million users are added each month. Many of the users subscribe to "on-line" services that provide to their subscribers computer software that enables them to access the Internet and navigate through its offerings. CompuServe, Prodigy, America Online, and Dow Jones News/Retrieval are several of the organizations that offer these "gateway" services throughout the Asia-Pacific region. Normally subscribers pay monthly fees and hourly on-line charges. When one is on-line, much Internet data is free or can be purchased from the database owner. (For contact information for Internet database services companies, see the Resource File, "Useful Contacts and Sources of Information.")

The problem for users of the Internet is navigating through its undisciplined maze of offerings and searching for the information they want. The on-line services provide assistance for this, and undoubtedly the problem will ease as their software becomes more sophisticated and "user friendly," notwithstanding the growing size and complexity of the Internet.

BEYOND THE INTERNET

The networking opportunities described earlier in this chapter—local and wide area networks (LANs and WANs), e-mail, electronic data interchange (EDI), enhanced faxing—go beyond the database resources of the Internet, and they are provided by several telecommunications companies that operate in a number of Asia-Pacific countries. These include AT&T's Easylink Services, MCI Mail, NEC's PC-VAN, Sprint's The Most, and Fujitsu's Nifty-Serve.

Many businesses find that the comprehensive management services provided by these companies offer the best solution to their telecommunications needs. Nanci Kelley, assistant to an executive of Capital Investments of Hawaii, Inc., communicates throughout the Asia-Pacific region with the help of AT&T's Easylink Services. Kelley sends and receives e-mail messages, faxes, and spreadsheets directly from her PC workstation in Honolulu. "I seldom print out hard copies. One keystroke and a fax is sent, and there's never a paper jam!" she says. "Clients and others have our AT&T e-mail code number. But we also have confidential passwords that prevent unauthorized persons from obtaining access to our private communications."

Businesses that use electronic data transmission extensively, such as large multinational companies, often lease telephone lines for their exclusive use ("dedicated connections") and manage their own WANs and Internet access systems. A company that believes it may find communications advantages in a WAN and in linking to the Internet should explore the various options available with several telecommunications service providers.

CASTING THE NET

Resources and facilities for network communications exist globally, but networking remains a distant goal for many Asia-Pacific businesses.

To network beyond its own offices, a business needs one or more PCs, modems, telecommunications and networking software, and one or more telephone lines. Modems are devices that permit one computer to communicate with another through a telephone line. Software translates computer data into usable forms of information and routes the information as directed. Unless a business has its own network management system, it also needs the services of a telecommunications company to manage transmissions to and from third parties. In addition, there must be an adequate telecommunications infrastructure. Sufficient telephone lines and switching stations must exist, and government regulators must have authorized telecommunications companies to provide network management services to those who require them.

The United States presently leads other Asia-Pacific countries in the use of network communications. If you walk into virtually any business office in the United States, you will see a computer on someone's desk—sometimes on every desk in sight, including those of managers and top officers. In the United States there are 42 PCs used in business for every 100 workers, and 56 of every 100 PCs in use are connected to LANs, enabling workers to network within the organization and often with outside parties. In Japan, the next leading country in network communications, there are only 10 PCs used in business for every 100 workers, and only 14 of every 100 PCs are connected to LANs.

LIMITING FACTORS AND HOW TO OVERCOME THEM

Stepping up to network communications in the Asia-Pacific region, however, requires more than hardware, software, and telecommunications services. It takes cultural adaptation of the kind discussed earlier in this book. Here are the two major obstacles to Asia-Pacific networking, along with some suggestions.

Network problem: Cultural discomfort. As with the telephone, Asians tend to be uncomfortable with communications that are not face to face. They value personal relations so highly that they often consider it disrespectful not to communicate in person. In the ranking of communications media, the face-to-face meeting is best, then comes a formal letter after an introduction, next comes a fax, and finally—in a tie for last place—comes an electronic message or a telephone call. Moreover, Asians rely heavily on subtlety in communications. They consider it highly important, if possible, to be able to read another person's full meaning by observing his or her expressions and body language. Accordingly, they have a preference for face-to-face communications. (See Chapter 3, "Set up a personal meeting if possible.")

ICD Prevention—Relationships: *Depending on an Asian's Formality Factor and experience with network communicating, Westerners should suggest network communications to the Asian only after a relationship is established. Do not expect networking to be effective at the outset.*

Network problem: Language incompatibilities. Although PC hardware and transmission protocols for network communications are essentially uniform, networking software is presently mostly in English. Moreover, word-processing systems in English and Asian languages are quite different, and different keyboards are used. Word processing in Asian languages tends to be more complex than in English. Microsoft Corporation, in developing word processing in Japanese for its Windows applications, invented a system for generating more than 2,000 written characters from two phonetic Japanese alphabets. Because of these differences, a PC cannot easily be used for communicating in more than one language. And since the English language has dominated the development and usage of network communicating to date, PCs dedicated to English-language usage are normally required for international networking.

ICD Prevention—Consider Setup Costs: *Before English-speaking businesspeople pressure their Asian colleagues to step up to network communicating, they should carefully inquire whether these colleagues are willing to invest in the software and personnel needed to utilize a networking system on a consistent basis. They should also consider whether telex would be a more successful means of networking with certain colleagues.*

12

TRANSLATING YOUR MESSAGE

SOME YEARS AGO AN EXECUTIVE of an American manufacturing company needed to confer with the company's Japanese joint venture partner about plans for the manufacture of a new product. Following good Asia-Pacific communications practices, the executive planned for a face-to-face meeting with his counterpart and sent a telex suggesting arrangements. In the telex he said, "We wonder if you would prepare an agenda for our meeting." In Tokyo the telex was routinely translated into Japanese and given to the counterpart. Unfortunately, the translator used the Japanese word *gimon* (meaning "doubt") for the English word *wonder,* and the sentence became "We *doubt* that you would prepare an agenda for our meeting." This was taken by the counterpart to be an outrageous insult. He abruptly canceled the meeting, and for some time thereafter the joint venture was on shaky ground.

Even seasoned Asia-Pacific communicators sometimes stumble over a mistranslated word, an inadvertent but potential ICD pitfall. Stories of translation errors abound, and they range from the humorous to the catastrophic. People to whom they occur often do not know whether to laugh or cry. In China, billboards for Coca-Cola intending to say "Enjoy Coke" in Chinese, once said "Feel Coke." Not precisely the message intended. And a Japanese executive stated to me that an American once presented him with a translated business card indicating, in Japanese, that the American was dead.

A MAJOR INDUSTRY

With the dynamic expansion of international communications in the last two decades, demand for translation services has grown immensely. Translation services worldwide are now a $20 billion industry. And approximately one-half of these services are performed in Asia.

Translating occurs in both written and spoken form. People who perform written translations are normally referred to as "translators," and people who perform spoken translations are referred to as "interpreters." Interpreters are used widely in meetings where the participants speak different languages.

Because English is a common international business language, translators are seldom employed on a full-time basis by companies that operate primarily in the English language. On the other hand, companies that operate primarily in a different language often employ translators full-time. This is frequently the case in Japan and South Korea, at least in larger companies. Elsewhere in Asia, in smaller companies, and in Western countries, translation services are obtained from firms and individuals who provide them on a contract basis.

WHEN TO USE A WRITTEN TRANSLATION

Since most international businesspeople in the Asia-Pacific region use or understand the English language, written communications can normally be in English. However, if English is not one's first language, it might be necessary to translate communications—those that need to be sent in English and those that are received in English. In addition, English-speaking people will need to consider when a communication should be translated into the first language of the person who will read it.

> **ICD Prevention Tip—Communications Practices**
>
> *Do an "audit" of your written communications to counterparts in countries where a different first language is spoken to see if translations would have made them more effective. Assess the hypothetical cost of appropriate translation services, and do a cost-benefit analysis of your communications practices.*

Generally, the need for a written translation of a communication that is not in the reader's first language depends upon three factors:

- ▲ The importance of the communication.
- ▲ The language ability of the reader in the language used in the communication.
- ▲ The reader's motivation to understand something that is not in his or her first language.

Accordingly, with formal proposals, contracts, minutes of meetings, and other important communications, it is common to send the communication together with a translation. This is the case if the translation itself may have legal significance, or if the ability of the reader is weak in the language of the communication. Also, solicitations and brochures may be prepared in the language of intended readers and sent with a brief cover letter in the sender's first language. Day-to-day business communications, between people in an established relationship who have different first languages, are normally in only one language, the one that works most efficiently in the relationship, often the language of the person who has no capability in the other language. However, until a problem appears, many will initiate and continue communications in their own language because they are more comfortable in doing so and it avoids the expense of translations.

TRANSLATION AS AN ART FORM

Translating is a specialty that requires enormous skill. The range of ability of translators and interpreters is wide. Moreover, the risks are substantial, because the client cannot easily evaluate the product—the client does not understand the translation. Even with a working knowledge of the language into which a communication is translated, the client might miss errors of idiom and style.

Literal and verbatim translations are seldom enough. For example, in translating a letter from English to Japanese, a skilled translator will use new words, phrases, and concepts that will change the tone of the letter to be more polite and formal. Also, in translating contracts from an Asian language into English, translators will often add material that is not in the original contract. Asian contracts, relying more on the relationship than the written word, are typically very basic, referring to the subject matter, price, delivery or performance dates, and little else. To make them appear more acceptable in English, translators will add various "boilerplate" provisions, such as force majeure clauses, that are tacitly understood in the Asian language.

BLAME THE TRANSLATOR

One advantage of translations is that a misunderstanding can often be blamed on the translator or interpreter, even if the fault lies elsewhere. This is a popular ploy of businesspeople who communicate in a language that is not their first. It is a humorous Asia-Pacific anecdote that when these people receive a response indicating disagreement with a proposal that was sent earlier, they send a fax saying, "New translation follows!" and then they send a revised proposal that will be more acceptable.

ICD Prevention Tip—Translation Review

Asia-Pacific businesspeople should review carefully the work of translators, especially when legal, marketing, and other important materials are involved. Ask the translator what he or she may have added to the translation in order to clarify meaning and to review with you any concerns about interpretation. The addition of "boilerplate" provisions to the translation of a legal contract can be useful but is not a safe practice; the effect of such additions should be reviewed with legal counsel in each instance.

INTERPRETERS

Business executives around the Asia-Pacific region highly recommend that a company include an interpreter on its team when its executives attend important meetings with people who speak a different first language, even meetings that will be conducted in the company's own first language. An interpreter can advise the company on the best way to present certain issues and can assist in clarifying points of discussion.

The role of an interpreter in business meetings is different from that of one who does simultaneous or sequential translations of speeches, as at forums such as the United Nations. In business meetings, the interpreter normally follows the discussions but translates only when asked to explain a point or amplify a statement.

Interpreters can be arranged for telephone calls and teleconferences through your own translation service or that of a telecommunications company. In the United States, for example, AT&T provides interpreters in more than 140 languages at any hour of the day or night. The best arrangement, of course, is to schedule in advance the services of an interpreter whose capabilities are known to you.

GETTING HELP

Translators and interpreters can be employed full-time, engaged on an hourly basis, or hired to complete a specific assignment. Firms providing translation services are found in every major city of the Asia-Pacific region. These firms normally operate as agents, supplying clients with the right translator or interpreter for each assignment. Translators and interpreters frequently work out of their own homes on a freelance basis. Documents for written translation, and the translations when completed, are often delivered by fax or messenger. See the Resource File "Useful Contacts and Sources of Information" for a listing of associations that can be helpful in identifying firms and individuals who provide translation and interpreter services.

In an age of high technology, it would seem that computer software would lighten the burdens of time and expense in producing written translations. Unfortunately, the task is so complex that little progress has been made in designing software for computer-assisted translations. Differences in idiom, style, vocabulary, and grammar substantially complicate the computerized analysis of language and the mechanical substitution of words, phrases, and sentences. While some software exists, and is used in about 3 percent of written translations, it produces elementary and inaccurate translations. Translators who have access to this software often prefer to prepare their translations—sentence by sentence and passage by passage—without its help.

One company, NaviSoft, is working on translation software that might be more reliable. The methodology of one of its projects is multilingual data search and retrieval. Another aims to design software that will translate English into what linguistics specialists call "deep language" or "deep understanding," a fundamental form of language which can be decoded by electronic means and designed for electronic purposes. Once computer-based deep language is designed, it will be possible to translate one spoken or written language into another through a deep language "interface." That is, the language being translated will be converted into deep language, and the deep language translation will then be translated into the local language desired.

Unfortunately, it is estimated that these computer-based translation projects will not be completed until the year 2000, and even then their translations probably will be only 80 percent accurate. Thus, translators and interpreters seem to be assured of steady employment for a long time to come. Asia-Pacific businesspeople are encouraged to make use of their skills. Because of the inherent problems of language translation, however, businesspeople should exercise care in the selection of translators and interpreters and should review their work on a continuing basis.

13

COMMUNICATING YOUR SALES PITCH

IF THE PURPOSE OF A COMMUNICATION IS to sell a product or service, you may need to be especially sensitive to the cultural distinctions and preferences of the Asia-Pacific country in which you want to make the sale. In international marketing, firms in many countries make the mistake of assuming that what appeals in their culture will appeal elsewhere. To the contrary, however, cultural differences deeply affect the way people perceive things. This applies not only to a particular product or service itself but also to how a product or service is advertised, presented, and promoted.

ADVERTISING

A few years ago, the U.S. consumer products firm Procter & Gamble ran television ads in Japan comparing its Pampers diapers to "Brand X." Procter & Gamble aimed to show that Pampers were superior to "Brand X." But Japanese viewers focused rather on the fact that the ads showed "Brand X" to be inferior to Pampers, and they did not like the put-down. The ads "bombed." Hidenori Shimano, an advertising executive with the Los Angeles–based advertising joint venture Dentsu/Young and Rubicam, points out that the hard-edged, comparative advertising common in the United States is considered insulting in Japan. "You should never attack a competitor," he says. "Even if you have evidence that your product is better, Japanese people don't like that kind of advertising—it's impolite."

Advertising campaigns for Western goods and services in Asia sometimes fail to capture consumer attention because they are too direct in their appeals or are too boastful. Western advertising directors sometimes select themes and ideas for these campaigns that do not take into account the impor-

tance to Asians of subtlety, indirection, and modesty. Often an idiomatic or humorous expression creeps into the advertising that makes sense to the Westerner but completely escapes an Asian. Even worse, sometimes these campaigns employ sexual imagery or some other device that is genuinely offensive to Asians.

Such advertising lapses occur on both sides of the cultural street. A few years ago, Nissan Motors mounted a television advertising campaign in the United States for its then new Infiniti automobile. The campaign started with a series of beautifully filmed scenes of running water, forests, and other natural subjects, each concluding simply with the word *Infiniti*. The ads were Asian in their quiet elegance and subtlety and were much admired by advertising professionals. However, the final assessment was that they were ineffective with the American viewing public. Early sales in the United States were disappointing. A more direct approach would probably have been better.

In advertising messages, Asia-Pacific executives who were interviewed for this book indicated that quality, value, and service are the most important themes to communicate. Asian executives ranked these three themes in the following order of importance: service, quality, value. To them, superior service reflects a seller's continuing commitment to a buyer and an established relationship between them, matters that are highly valued in their collectivist societies. Western executives, on the other hand, ranked the three themes in this order: value, quality, service. To these executives, who are more profit-minded and not as concerned with relationships, value deserves the greatest emphasis.

PRESENTATION

The presentation of products and materials also has cultural implications, whether it is the packaging of a product for shipment, the formatting of a proposal, or the display of marketing information in a folder.

If a visitor to Japan walks into almost any department store in Tokyo, he or she will be impressed with how beautifully the merchandise is displayed and packaged. Even in produce markets in residential areas, fruit is not in a jumble. Instead, it is carefully—even artistically—arranged in matching sizes, shapes, and colors. When asked recently what is the most common failing of foreign companies in introducing products to Japan, the head of a large Japanese trading company quickly responded, "It's amazing how often you see poor packaging," explaining that foreigners often don't make allowances for the Japanese obsession with harmony and precision.

> ### ICD Prevention Tip—
> ### Proposals and Packaging
>
> *When preparing a proposal or designing packaging for a product, give thought to the culture, style, and Formality Factor of the recipient. You might well use different approaches in presenting or packaging the same proposal or product for people from different cultures or countries.*

On the other hand, highly meticulous or stylized packaging and presentations might appear fussy or frivolous in other cultures. For example, many Hong Kong shopkeepers place greater emphasis on having a wide variety of merchandise in shops that might appear crowded and confusing to a Japanese but inviting to local Chinese and many of their foreign customers.

SALES BROCHURES

As with advertising, sales brochures need to be designed and written with the cultural background of the target audience in mind. It is not good enough—at least, it is not as good as it could be—to send the same brochure to people throughout the Asia-Pacific region, even if it has been translated into the appropriate languages. In describing capabilities, brochures should cite success or experience relevant to the target audience. If you are selling a product in Indonesia, do not cite its success in withstanding corrosion in the dry, cold climate of Wyoming. If you are selling market research services in New Zealand, do not cite experience in Japan.

> **ICD Prevention Tip—Brochures**
>
> *You might not have the right successes or experience to cite in a brochure directed to a particular audience. If so, it is better to generalize in your brochure and present your specific capabilities in face-to-face meetings.*

Brochures also need to conform to local usages. Throughout most of the region, weights and measures should be stated in metrics. In the United States, where metrics have been slow to catch on, they should be stated in traditional units. For a convenient conversion table, see Resource Files, "Measurement Conversion Table."

DIRECT MARKETING

Selling consumer products and services directly through catalogues, by telephone ("telemarketing"), over television ("home shopping networks"), or door to door is very big business throughout the world. In the United States, telemarketers make over 15 million telephone calls a week, and home shopping television programs are viewed in over 50 million households. In Japan, 17 million pieces of direct marketing mail are delivered every month. In Guangdong Province, China, Avon Products is highly successful in door-to-door sales.

In the Asia-Pacific region, direct marketing is more active in Western countries than in Asian countries. There are several reasons for this:

▲ Mailing costs tend to be lower in Western countries. Rates are generally lower, and there are deeper discounts for bulk mail.

▲ In Western countries, mailing lists for direct marketing are derived largely from magazine subscription lists, and publishers sell their lists to direct marketers. In Asian countries, most periodicals are sold on newsstands and in stores. Mailing lists in Asian countries consist largely of "compiled lists" (derived from directories and other available sources) and "response lists" (derived from responses to various mailings). Western marketers tend to buy lists; Asian marketers tend to compile their own.

▲ Where Asian mailing lists can be purchased, they cost two to three times as much as lists purchased for a Western country.

▲ Asians are often reluctant to compile direct marketing lists, and hesitant to conduct direct marketing activities, because they feel a strong commitment to their customers, including their customers' right to privacy. They are also reluctant to sell mailing lists because they feel doing so may breach a customer's confidence.

Yet direct marketing is expanding in Asian countries. Catalogue sales are presently the most successful form of direct marketing because they are the least intrusive on the customer. Direct marketers normally prepare catalogues in the language of the country where they are distributed. Western companies are able to use English-language catalogues in Hong Kong, Singapore, the Philippines, and Malaysia. In other countries, such as China, Taiwan, South Korea, and Japan, they use translated catalogues, but they often retain some English phrases and descriptions to enhance the foreign appeal of their offerings.

> **ICD Prevention Tip—Mailing Lists**
>
> *If you are building a response list, include in your communications a form that can be returned to you by fax with the information needed. People who have fax machines often prefer to use them instead of the postal service.*

According to James Thornton, managing director of Mailing Lists (Asia) Ltd. in Hong Kong, Indonesia and the Philippines are currently the most responsive markets in the region for direct marketing in the English language. Thailand is also very responsive, and Malaysia is somewhat responsive. Japan, Korea, and Taiwan are generally not responsive because they are "local language markets." Hong Kong and Singapore are probably the least responsive markets. China is presently inaccessible to international direct marketing because payment cannot be made in foreign currency.

One Asia-Pacific direct marketing success story is that of Austad's, a supplier of golf equipment and accessories based in Sioux Falls, South Dakota. Austad's distributes a Japanese-language catalogue in Japan and an English-language catalogue elsewhere in the region. Orders from Japan are taken by a representative in Tokyo, who relays them every evening by fax to South Dakota. Orders from customers elsewhere are received directly by mail, fax, or telephone. Austad's is enjoying a growing market in the region, especially in Japan. According to Austad's Wayne Steinhauer, Japan's direct marketing industry is about $12 billion per year and has a growth rate of about 12 percent.

Telemarketing is hindered in some Asia-Pacific countries by inadequate telecommunications facilities. The intrusive nature of telemarketing is also a problem in Asian societies, especially in Japan. The Japanese solution to this problem is to use only women as telemarketing operators. The soft, deferential voice of a Japanese woman is found to be more effective than the voice of a man, no matter how polite and engaging he is. In contrast, men are frequently employed as telemarketers in Western countries and, depending on the product being sold, are generally seen to be as effective as women.

International direct marketing is generally hindered by product warehousing and distribution problems. Customers who purchase products by catalogue or telephone are willing to accept some delay in receiving an item, but if a similar product can be purchased at a local store, even at a higher price, they are often not willing to order a product that will require weeks for delivery from overseas. A common issue for direct marketers is whether to warehouse inventory in the country of sale (to provide prompt delivery) or to ship by air from overseas sources.

Payment is another problem for Asia-Pacific direct marketers. In many Asian countries it is customary to pay for goods and services in cash. A person who buys an expensive new automobile will often deliver to the seller a briefcase loaded with money. Direct marketers must therefore

> **ICD Prevention Tip—Deliveries in Asia**
>
> *If feasible, because of the Asian emphasis on service, you should warehouse products that are destined for Asian buyers in the country of sale or nearby. In this way, delays in delivery time will be minimized.*

often develop elaborate and cumbersome arrangements for the payment for and delivery of their products. Even Japan is still largely a cash currency economy, and most products sold there by direct marketing are delivered C.O.D., collect on delivery.

Toll-free telephone response numbers are common domestically in North America and Japan but not elsewhere in the region. These numbers use a standard prefix (for example, in the United States, "800," as in 800-987-6543) that permits a telephone call to be charged to the recipient rather than the caller. Toll-free numbers have proven highly effective in sales promotion and customer relations, and they have proliferated in North America in recent years. International toll-free response numbers can also be set up, but normally they are not practical because of differences in languages and east-west time zones.

> **ICD Prevention Tip— Local Representatives**
>
> *To facilitate customers' orders, payment, delivery of products, after-sale service, and all manner of customer communications, consider having local representatives for your direct marketing activities. To identify candidates for local representation, contact one or more of the direct marketing associations listed in the "Useful Contacts and Sources of Information" section of the Resource Files.*

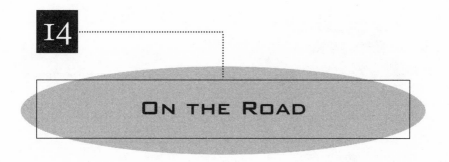

14

ON THE ROAD

ASIA-PACIFIC EXECUTIVES who were interviewed for this book repeatedly emphasized the importance of face-to-face meetings in building relationships and improving communications among businesspeople and organizations in the region. The executives often told of instances in which a proposal or a project languished, with the other organization failing to take anticipated steps to move it forward, until a meeting was held to review its status. In one case, where an American and a Singaporean organization were cosponsoring an international conference in Singapore, arrangements for the conference lagged badly despite frequent telephone and fax communications between the two organizations. Then, in frustration and with growing concern, the executive director of the American organization visited Singapore to help plan the event. The meeting was productive and entirely upbeat. Everything went smoothly from that time on.

This chapter deals with Asia-Pacific business communications "on the road." It discusses preparations for an overseas trip, means of facilitating your work and communications while you are overseas, conduct that is appropriate or inappropriate in certain countries, and various means of assuring the success of your trip.

PREPARATIONS

Check the travel guides. If you are not fully familiar with your destination, a travel guide is a good source of the information you will need: entry requirements, import restrictions on gifts that you might carry, city maps, local transportation services, tipping practices, hotels and restaurants, and activities that are available for visitors during non-business hours.

Get up-to-date. Prepare for more than just the business you expect to transact during your trip. Get up-to-date on other transactions between your organization and the organizations you plan to visit. Learn what you can about their current activities and interests. If you have personal relationships with people you will visit, refresh your knowledge of their interests, the names of their family members, and your most recent contacts with them, such as a luncheon or previous visit. Also, get up-to-date on the current social and political issues of the countries you plan to visit.

Appointments. The importance of introductions was discussed in Chapter 3. This chapter assumes that you have arranged any introductions needed for the appointments you will have during your overseas trip.

The survey and interviews of Asia-Pacific executives conducted for this book indicate that most executives prefer to have at least a week's advance notice to arrange a meeting. The higher the Formality Factor, the more advance notice seems appropriate. Japanese, for example, expect that a request for an appointment will be made in writing, with considerable formality (preferably with an agenda for the meeting), and well in advance. And it seems that South Koreans are reluctant to set a specific date and time for a meeting until they know that you are in the country. Australians, on the other hand, are often willing to arrange a meeting on short notice, on the telephone, from near or afar.

If an executive with whom you want to meet does not wish to see you, the response to your request for an appointment will normally be that the timing of your visit is inconvenient. If you persist with your request, even allowing considerable flexibility in your own availability, you may be given an appointment with a lesser official. It is unlikely that a courteous request for an appointment, made with sufficient notice and a personal introduction, will be flatly denied. Of course, much depends upon how busy the people with whom the meeting is requested are and how interested they might be in meeting with you. To arrange appointments with people who are busy, who do not know you well, or who may see no immediate benefit from a meeting with you, it often helps to request a *short* meeting and to offer a wide range of options for the date and time.

Be careful not to overload your appointment schedule. Build in plenty of time between appoint-

ICD Prevention Tip—Appointments

If a particular appointment will be difficult to arrange, let that be the first one you request and build other appointments around it. Also, if the people with whom you want to meet would be uncomfortable if they knew that you would make a special trip to see them or would accommodate your own schedule to theirs (or if you do not want them to know that you are willing to do so), say that you will be in their city "on other business" and would like to call on them for a short visit.

ments so that last-minute changes can be accommodated and you can arrive for each appointment on time. Traffic problems are severe in many Asia-Pacific cities, and transportation often takes longer than expected when the surroundings are unfamiliar.

Also, if your trip will involve significant travel time and time zone changes, build in one or two days of rest after arrival before commencing any serious business. Some years ago an Australian solicitor flew from Sydney to New York City to attend important business negotiations in which he was expected to advise his American clients on Australian law. He was unable to depart Sydney early enough for any rest in New York before the negotiations, although he did sleep a bit during his flight. During the negotiations, conducted when it was the middle of the night by his unadjusted body clock, he was simply unable to keep his eyes open. It became a humorous routine that when the solicitor's clients needed his advice on a point, he would be poked awake, the point explained, and the advice rendered. To avoid such embarrassment, consult the Time Zone and Flight Time tables in the Resource Files.

ICD Prevention Tip—
Jet Lag

If jet lag might be a problem, plan to arrive at your destination on a Saturday so that you will be well rested when appointments commence on Monday.

Business cards. Check your supply of business cards so that you will not be caught short. Business cards are very important in the Asia-Pacific region, especially in Asian countries, and an executive who admits that he or she has run out of cards is an embarrassment to all.

Business cards are treated with great respect in the Asia-Pacific region. To Asians especially, they reflect the dignity and importance of a person and the person's organization. They are often carried in a special case in one's coat pocket, where they stay neat and clean. They should not be carried where they will become soiled or crumpled, or in a place from which they cannot easily be produced. See "Meetings" for more about the presentation of business cards.

It is often a good idea to arrange to have your cards translated and printed on one side in the language of the country to be visited. While English may generally suffice, the country's own language is particularly recommended for China, Japan, South Korea, Taiwan, Thailand, and Vietnam. You should arrange for the translation and printing of your business cards long before a trip. Although cards can be printed quickly and inexpensively in an overseas city after your arrival there (your hotel could assist you in finding a translator and printer), you might be able to obtain better printing and a more accurate translation at your home base. If your home is in or near a large city, you will easily find printing and translating firms that can provide these services. If not, you will need to obtain the cards from firms elsewhere, but you can order and

ICD Prevention Tip—
Business Card Cases

Plan to use a carrying case for your business cards, and carry it in a breast pocket. Do not carry them in your wallet; many Asians consider this to be an awkward and crude practice.

review proofs of the cards by telephone and fax. Your efforts might cost you several hundred dollars, but it will be a worthwhile investment. Moreover, unless you change the name or location of your business, the costs will be a one-time expense.

In translating business cards to another language, some businesspeople prefer that the name of their company be translated, to assist with pronunciation and meaning in the other language; others prefer that it not be, because it serves as the company's global identity. (See the cards of Mr. Ho, Mr. Kuniyoshi, Dr. Koo, and the author in the accompanying examples.) One's name and address, however, are translated in order to assist with pronunciation. Consideration may also have to be given to the local significance of certain words. In having my card translated into Chinese, I stipulated the Mandarin dialect, but the translation came back with characters that were used in Cantonese for the word *Montgomery* in my address. I was informed by the Taiwanese official who checked the proof of the translation that the Cantonese version originated in Hong Kong with reference to British Field Marshal Montgomery and is not normally used outside Hong Kong. The translation was revised using characters for Mandarin.

> ### ICD Prevention Tip—
> ### Business Card Translations
>
> *Be sure to specify the dialect to be used in the translation of your business card. A translation in a Cantonese dialect is appropriate for Hong Kong; the Mandarin dialect is needed for China and Taiwan. Consult your translator or a local contact to see whether dialect or local use of language should be considered. While written languages as used in a business context usually do not reflect dialect, regional usages may be important.*

Some executives use business cards that have two languages on the same side. See, for instance, the cards of Mr. Hung and Ms. Ba (using Chinese and English) in the following examples. Note that this style permits Ms. Ba to set forth, on the reverse side, information about her firm's overseas offices as well.

Presentation—horizontal or vertical—is another business card issue. (See the cards of Mr. Ho, Mr. Kuniyoshi, Dr. Koo, and the author in the accompanying examples.) The Chinese, Japanese, and Korean languages are often written in vertical columns that read from top down and right to left (instead of across and left to right). While most people who normally read a language in a vertical presentation are not confused by a horizontal left-right presentation, some businesspeople prefer that their card's translation be presented vertically rather than horizontally in order to avoid any possible misinterpretation. (Compare the cards of Dr. Koo and Mr. Ho.) If two languages are used on the translated side of a card (as they are with Mr. Kuniyoshi's and the author's cards), a consistent (horizontal) presentation is usually adopted.

Logos often appear on Asia-Pacific business cards if the person's organization has one. Titles are especially important and should be stated clearly. If you have positions in different organizations, you might need more than one card. However, in Taiwan and Hong Kong it is customary to indicate positions with other organizations on one card, the card of your primary organization, (for example, Dr. Koo adopts this style with the additional reference to his position as an adviser to the California Department of Commerce). Academic degrees should be indicated, if appropriate to your work or helpful in suggesting a proper honorific (for example, *Ph.D.* indicates that the person should be addressed as "Dr."). For cards used in those less developed Asian countries where educators are held in high regard

> **ICD Prevention Tip—
> Business Card Titles**
>
> *If your title does not clearly indicate your responsibilities, add a phrase that does. It is especially important in Asian collectivist cultures that one's status in an organization be clearly understood.*

(such as China, Indonesia, and Thailand) academic degrees are indicated even if they have no relevance to your work.

Apart from size, which is quite uniform throughout the region, business cards come in all sorts of styles and qualities. Some are printed on thick paper, some on thin, some on white stock, some on colored stock—although the standard color is usually white. Wide varieties of typefaces are also used, and while some cards are engraved, some have standard print, and others have raised type.

However, in selecting a business card, you should not stint on quality. Use expensive paper and an expensive printing process. Stick with a white heavy stock (a thicker paper will convey substance and quality) and black printing ink, except for any colors associated with your logo. Expensive touches, such as engraved printing, gold edging, or embossing, will also be appreciated (raised print, however, is now recognized to be inexpensive). However, of paramount consideration should be that the typeface be clearly readable and the card carry concisely as much useful information as possible.

On the following pages are a few examples of business cards of Asia-Pacific executives, including the ones referred to earlier.

Oscar C. de Venecia
Chairman & President

Basic Petroleum and Minerals, Inc.
Basic Petroleum Bldg., C. Palanca St.,
Legaspi Village. Makati, Metro Manila, Philippines
Tels. 817-33-29 ; 817-85-96 * FAX (632) 817-01-91

BUSINESS
ADVISORY
INDONESIA

James W. Castle

Kuningan Plaza, Suite 304 North ● Jl. H.R. Rasuna Said C11 – 14 ● Jakarta 12940, Indonesia
Phone : 5207696, 5207689 ● Telex : 62151 AIRFAS IA ● Fax : 5202557

Both these cards follow the basic design of their companies' letterheads, although Mr. de Venecia's address is expressed here on more than one line. Mr. de Venecia's card is embossed with his company logo.

Business Strategies International

David L. James
President

44 Montgomery Street, Suite 500
San Francisco, CA 94104
Telephone: (415) 955-2744
Fax: (415) 397-6309
E-mail: bsi@crl.com

Business Strategies International

戴維德 L. 詹姆斯
總裁

美國加州舊金山蒙哥馬利街44號500室
郵區號碼: 94104
電話: (415) 955-2744
傳眞: (415) 397-6309
E-mail: bsi@crl.com

Business Strategies International

デイビッド・L・ジェイムズ
社長

〒94104 カリフォルニア州サンフランシスコ市
モンゴメリー通り44番地500号室
電話: (415) 955-2744
ファックス: (415)397-6309
電子メール: bsi@crl.com

The name of the firm is not translated into either Chinese or Japanese; I prefer to emphasize its global identity. The Chinese and Japanese translations are presented horizontally to be consistent with the presentation of the firm's name. Note that my e-mail address is also given; this is a growing practice.

George Kerr
SENIOR CONSULTANT

International Public Relations Pty Ltd
35a Kennedy Street, Kingston ACT 2604
PO Box 4205, Kingston ACT 2604

Telephone:
Bus: (06) 239 6600
Mobile: 018 748 153
Facsimile: (06) 239 6565
AH: (06) 295 6993

Mr. Kerr gives his mobile and after-hours ("AH") telephone numbers as well as his office and fax numbers. After-hours numbers in Australia are sometimes direct office numbers for use after a switchboard closes; sometimes they are home telephone numbers and should be used advisedly.

PETER A. MANSON, Q.C.
Direct line (604) 640-4158

LADNER DOWNS
BARRISTERS & SOLICITORS

900 Waterfront Centre, 200 Burrard Street, P.O. Box 48600
Vancouver, Canada V7X 1T2 Fax (604) 687-1415 Telephone (604) 687-5744

OSLER RENAULT LADNER
London   •   Paris   •   Hong Kong   •   New York
An International Partnership

The "Q.C." following Mr. Manson's name indicates that he is a "Queen's Counsel," that is, a barrister who appears in Canadian courts on behalf of clients. His card indicates his direct telephone number as well as his firm's address and communications information. It also indicates the name, nature, and locations of its affiliate, Osler Renault Ladner.

INTERNATIONAL STRATEGIC ALLIANCES, INC.

Dr. George P. Koo

Managing Director
Advisor, Dept. of Commerce
State of California

1265 Montecito Avenue   Tel: 415-969-1671
Suite 109   Fax: 415-969-1673
Mountain View, CA 94043

Affiliates in Hong Kong, Osaka, Shanghai, Taipei & Tokyo

跨國策略聯盟公司
加州政府商業部顧問

總裁

顧

屏

山

Dr. Koo indicates his academic title (a Ph.D.), highly valued in Asia. He also lists his position as an adviser to the California Department of Commerce. (It is common practice in Taiwan and Hong Kong to list other relevant positions.) Locations of affiliates are also listed.

哈佛企業管理顧問公司
HARVARD MANAGEMENT SERVICES, INC.

突破 雜誌
BREAKTHROUGH

管理雜誌
MANAGEMENT MAGAZINE

總經理

洪 良 浩
Frank L. Hung

5F. NO. 220
Ta-Tung Road, Sec. 3
Hsichih, Taipei, Taiwan

汐止行政中心：台北縣汐止鎮大同路三段220號5樓
電　話：(02)648-5828　　傳　眞：(02)648-4666
分機：121

Both Mr. Hung and Ms. Ba use a vertical format with both Chinese and English on the same side of the card. Consistent with Taiwan practice, Mr. Hung shows his connection with more than one organization, three in this case. Stylized typography is used for the Chinese names of Mr. Hung's businesses. Overseas offices are listed on the other side of Ms. Ba's card.

CT & D Group
中央貿開關聯企業

華盛海外開發公司
WARSON OVERSEAS
Development Co. (Taiwan)

總 經 理

巴 大 文
Frances D. Ba
Executive Director

台北市忠孝西路1段4號18樓
18th Fl., No. 4, Sec. 1, Chung Hsiao W. Rd.
Taipei (100), Taiwan, R.O.C.
Tel: 886-2-311-9933 Fax: 886-2-388-1116

Overseas Offices

Hong Kong: Rm. 101–102, 43rd Fl.,
Office Tower Convention Plaza
1 Harbour Road, Wanchai, Hong Kong
Tel: 852-824-3036, 824-3098
Fax: 852-824-3182

U.S.A.: 2nd Fl., 105 Wall Street, P.O. Box 669
Madison, CT 06443, U.S.A.
Tel: 1-203-245-3739
Fax: 1-203-245-3741

Vietnam: Xa Tan Thuan Dong
Huyen Nha Be, T.P. HCM, SRV
Tel: 848-728-410/7
Fax: 848-725-580

Agents:

Japan Rise Architects & Planners, Inc.
Contact Person: Mr. Shunsuke Takahashi
Tel: 81-3-5992-1881
Fax: 81-3-5992-1884

Thailand MUST Corp. Ltd.
Contact Person: Mr. Santi Ho
Tel: 662-233-1388, 233-4932
Fax: 662-236-6946

Ryoji Kuniyoshi
President & C E O

Swire Transtech Limited
Swire House
14, Ichibancho, Chiyoda-ku, Tokyo 102
Tel. (03) 3230-9200   Fax. (03) 3221-7957

代表取締役社長

國　吉　良　治

スワイヤ トランステック株式会社
東京都千代田区一番町 14　スワイヤ ハウス　〒102
電話 : 03-3230-9200　FAX : 03-3221-7957

The Japanese side of Mr. Kuniyoshi's card retains the English name logo of his firm. Presentation of Japanese characters is horizontal rather than vertical, consistent with the name logo and the presentation in English on the other side of the card.

DEAN T. W. HO
Chairman and President

UBS International
A Division of Unison International

SAN FRANCISCO AREA
651 Gateway Bouleverd, Suite 880
South San Francisco CA 94080 USA
Phone: (415) 877-0780
Fax: (415) 742-0828
Telex: 6504154303 MCIUW

SHANGHAI
Jinjiang Hotel Ste. 5313
Shanghai, China 200020
Phone: 2582582 Ext. 5313
Direct: 4729579, 4722551
Fax: 4729579

BEIJING
31/F., Unit 5, Jing Guang Centre,
Beijing 100026 China
Phone: 501-3388 Ext. 31051, 31052
Direct: 501-3080, 501-3083
Telex: 210496 UNIBJ CN
Fax: 5016528

友升大樓系統國際公司
友升國際公司之分公司

何　志　華
董事長兼總栽

中國上海市錦江飯店5313室
電話：2582582分樓：5313
電傳：33385 UNSIH CN
直綫電話：4729579, 4722551
傳眞：4729579
郵政編碼：200020

中國北京市朝陽區呼家樓
京廣中心31樓5號室
電話：501-3388分機：31051或31052
直綫電話：501-3080, 501-3083
電傳：210496 UNIBJ CN
傳眞：5016528

The English side of Mr. Ho's card gives communication information for the offices of UBS International in San Francisco, Shanghai, and Beijing. The Chinese side gives this information only for Shanghai and Beijing.

Itinerary. It is easy to mix things up or mislay information during a trip, especially if one is jet-lagged or in a rush. To guard against this, have a detailed itinerary of your trip prepared. It should include the dates and times of your flight reservations (with flight numbers and seat assignments), your hotel reservations, and your scheduled appointments. The names, addresses, and telephone and fax numbers of your hotels and the people you will meet should also be included. The itinerary should be left with people at your office and at home who may need to contact you during your trip.

Address files. In addition to the information supplied by your itinerary, carry ample files containing the addresses and telephone and fax numbers of others you might need to contact during your trip, whether they be people in the destination city, at home, or elsewhere. In the destination city, it is often difficult to obtain telephone information assistance. (See "Destination Tips.") Portable computers (including "palmtop" computers and "personal digital assistants") are now ideal for carrying address information on trips.

Telephone credit cards. Carry your international telephone credit card with you and take a few minutes before you leave on your trip to make sure you understand how it can be used for direct dialing at your destination. International telecommunications companies have different access codes in each country. For example, to access an AT&T operator in Thailand, one must dial 001-999-111; an MCI operator, 001-999-1-2001; or a Sprint operator, 001-999-13-877. (The hyphens in these numbers are used by the companies to facilitate reading them; they are not entered in dialing.) Hotels and some public telephone offices at your destination will have these numbers, but it is well for you to have yours with you for calls made from other locations. (See also "Telephones" under "Destination Tips.")

Letterhead. Take several sheets of your letterhead with you in case you need to prepare letters.

Computer equipment. If you take a portable computer with you, consider the following measures before you leave and throughout your trip:

- ▲ Load your computer with any files that you will need during your trip. Make certain that all computer files are up-to-date.
- ▲ Guard your computer against theft. Do not leave it unattended in airport terminals or elsewhere. Better yet, carry it inside another bag.
- ▲ Make sure that your computer has enough of a battery charge to power up for guards at airport security checkpoints, to demonstrate that it is indeed a computer. With global terrorism on the increase, airport security personnel take few chances. To ensure that a computer does not contain a bomb or electronic triggering device, security personnel often require that it be turned on and its software program appear on its screen.
- ▲ You can let your computer pass through security X-ray machines. It will not be harmed, and data and files stored on the hard disk will not be erased. However, data on computer "floppy" disks can be erased; it is best to pass your "floppies" around the X ray, letting airport security personnel inspect them visually.
- ▲ Take voltage converters and electrical outlet adapters that will enable you to use available power supplies en route and at your destination. Hotels often can provide these, but it is better to take your own.
- ▲ If you use your computer with a modem to tap into telecommunications networks, take telephone jack adapters and "inline" couplers that will permit you to connect to the telephone line of your hotel room or a local office. Some hotels have jacks that permit this easily, but many do not. In some cities there are public telephones with jacks for modem connections. If you are a determined telecommunicator, you might also take a small screwdriver and a portable phone jack with wires attached for clipping into phone lines.

Cellular phones and pagers. It might be possible for you to use a cellular phone or pager in the countries you will visit. But rather than take your own cellular phone with you, which would require you to register the phone and obtain a local access number, you should rent one in each country you visit. Check with a country's embassy or consulate for further information, or with its leading telecommunications company. Pagers presently have limited international use but, like cellular phones, can often be arranged for paging from your local office during a visit.

Audiovisual equipment. If you plan on making presentations during your trip that will require audiovisual equipment, it is best to arrange in advance for the equipment to be provided at the other end. There might be power supply incompatibilities or other problems that would make your own equipment inoperable.

If you plan to use a videocassette recording in a presentation, check well in advance to be sure that a player will accept the format of your tape. It might be necessary for you to have your tape converted or to arrange for equipment that will be compatible.

Interpreters. If you will need an interpreter in a city, reserve one before you leave on the trip.

Business gifts and entertaining. Gift giving is important in many of the countries of the Asia-Pacific region. This is especially true in Asian countries, because of the significance of interpersonal relationships in their cultures. Depending on the country you will visit and the nature of your business there,

> **ICD Prevention Tip—Entertaining**
>
> *When you host a dinner or banquet during an overseas trip, let your hotel or your local business representative help you with the arrangements. The guest list and seating arrangements should be considered as carefully as the selection of a restaurant. For dinners with more than about six guests, a set menu—arranged beforehand with the help of your local advisers— is recommended.*

you may want to take a number of appropriate gifts for the people you will see. Here are the countries in which gifts are especially appropriate, ranked in order of greater significance of gifts:

1. Japan
2. South Korea
3. Thailand
4. Vietnam
5. Indonesia
6. Malaysia
7. The Philippines
8. China
9. Taiwan
10. Hong Kong
11. Singapore

The omission of Western countries from the list does not mean that gifts are inappropriate there. It merely means that gift giving in business is not a common practice. Gift giving is normally limited to occasional gifts to major customers, usually once a year at Christmas or when a customer celebrates some milestone. Most Western businesspeople feel somewhat awkward in giving gifts and reciprocating, not knowing what to do or when to do it, worried that the gesture might be inadequate or misinterpreted. However, business entertaining, at lunch or dinner, and sometimes at a social event with spouses, is common.

The placement of Chinese cultures at the end of the list is not because gift giving is unimportant in those countries but because business *entertaining* is considered more appropriate than a gift. It is often desirable for a visitor to host a dinner—or even a large banquet—for a business counterpart, sometimes in reciprocation for a dinner or banquet previously hosted by the counterpart.

The best business gifts are those that are pertinent to a relationship or transaction and can be identified with the giver's organization or home. Generally, appropriateness and thoughtfulness are much more important than value. Lavish gifts should normally be avoided because they place too great a burden of obligation on the recipient. Here are some examples of successful gifts:

▲ Audiotapes or compact discs of famous orchestras or recording stars (if playback systems of the country you visit are compatible)

▲ Books, especially albums with photographs of scenes from your country or region

▲ Business magazine subscriptions from your country

▲ Calendars with scenes from your country or region

▲ Coffee mugs with logos

▲ Coin sets or postage stamp sets from your country

▲ Golf balls with your company logo

- ▲ Items produced by your company
- ▲ Name-brand items from manufacturers noted for quality products
- ▲ Packets of postcards with scenes from your country or region
- ▲ Pens, desk sets, paperweights, and memo pads with your company logo
- ▲ T-shirts with emblems from your country
- ▲ Wines or whiskeys (although not for Muslims)

If you are taking gifts with you, do not wrap them ahead of time. Customs officials may ask you to unwrap them. Rather, carry the wrapping paper separately and wrap them at your destination. Alternatively, your hotel may be able to do the wrapping for you (gift wrapping is a common hotel service in Japan, for example), and you will have the comfort of knowing that the wrapping will conform to local tastes. Wrapping customs, and the significance of the color of wrapping paper, vary from country to country. The general rule is that wrapping should be neat and simple, and that plain white or dark colors should be avoided. For customs of presenting gifts, see "Meetings."

> **ICD Prevention Tip—Logos**
>
> *Use your company's logo on gifts whenever possible. It will remind your counterpart that your company values its relationship with him or her. A personal identification between you and your counterpart is the key to successful gift giving.*

Here are a few culture-specific tips on gift giving:

- ▲ In Chinese cultures, do not give clocks as gifts (the word for *clock* in Chinese sounds like a word relating to funerals, and they are symbols of bad luck).
- ▲ Do not give whiskey or other forms of liquor to Muslims. This applies primarily in Indonesia and Malaysia.
- ▲ Gifts indicating the number 4, or a gift of four of something, are unlucky in Chinese cultures, South Korea, and Japan. The number 13 is unlucky in all Asia-Pacific countries. For more on lucky numbers, see Chapter 3.
- ▲ Knives and scissors symbolize severance of relationships in some cultures. This does not seem to apply to letter openers and desk sets, however.

▲ Gifts that might carry romantic connotations should be avoided in Asian cultures.

Clothing. Take clothing that is appropriate for the climate you will be visiting, and plan to dress on the conservative side for business meetings, especially in Asian countries. In Asian cultures, too much informality can indicate a lack of respect for the people you visit, their organizations, and the matters to be discussed.

Money. Take with you some of the currency of the countries you will visit if possible. Although most destination airports have currency exchange booths (and some of them, such as Singapore's, are open twenty-four hours a day), you will find it convenient to have enough local currency with you to handle local transportation and tips until you are settled in your hotel. In addition, take small denominations of an international currency, such as some U.S. one-dollar bills, for tips and small payments when you do not have the proper amount in local currency.

Also, before you depart, determine what your cash requirements will be and whether there will be adequate resources for cash in the countries you will visit. Many establishments in less developed countries do not accept credit cards or personal checks.

DESTINATION TIPS

Business centers. Check out the business center resources of your hotel. Many offer secretarial help, photocopying, conference rooms, fax machines, and computer facilities. Also, many cities have public business centers and secretarial firms that provide such services, and you might have a local representative who can arrange the assistance you need. To find a public business center or secretarial firm, ask your hotel or local representative to assist you, or consult the yellow pages of the local telephone directory (the commercial listings organized by business category). Business centers are normally listed under "Secretarial Services."

If you have a computer with you but not a printer, you might be able to print out files directly from your computer to a business center printer. Or you might be able to use a floppy disk to transfer files to the center's computer and printer. If you have a computer and modem that enable you to send faxes, but you cannot find a compatible printer, fax by modem the files you want to print to your hotel's business center (or management office if it does

not have a business center), and make copies of the fax. The fax copies may be an acceptable substitute.

Local transportation. Normally taxis are the best way to get around in a destination city. However, if you plan on visiting a number of offices on a tight schedule, or plan trips to locations outside the city, it is sometimes better to hire a car and driver for the day. Your hotel can make these arrangements.

Take with you the addresses of the places you will visit and show them to your driver. The addresses should be written in the country's first language, something your hotel can help with. Also take with you a card showing your hotel's address in the local language. It will help to assure a speedy and direct return.

When entering a taxi, check to see if there is a working meter. If not, negotiate a fare before you start out, or use a different taxi.

Telephones. Many Asia-Pacific countries have public telephones that accept debit phone cards as well as coins. The phone cards can normally be purchased at hotels, post offices, and newsstands. You should consider purchasing one on arrival if you will be in the country for more than a few days. For more about phone cards, see Chapter 10, "Good Connections."

Be aware that each country has its own code for initiating international calls. The direct dial codes are listed in the Resource Files, "Country and City Telephone Codes" table. If you are unsure about how to make a direct dial call, consult the dialing instructions section of the local telephone book or speak to a telephone operator.

Obtaining telephone assistance in a foreign country can be a problem, especially if you do not speak the first language of the country. However, many countries have telephone information operators who speak other languages, although often they are available only during business hours. Most helpful will be the operators of your hotel. In addition, your country's embassy, consulate, or trade office, and the trade and tourist offices of the country you are visiting, can help you find numbers and addresses that you need. Also, international telecommunications companies often have operators who are skilled in a number of languages. And you will often find that there are English-language telephone directories, especially yellow pages directories, available in most of the principal cities of the region, even in countries where English is not the first language.

> ### ICD Prevention Tip—
> ### Public Fax Machines
>
> *In addition to public telephones in airports, hotels, and other public places, there are sometimes public fax machines that will send and receive faxes, normally with the use of standard credit cards. These fax machines are sometimes more convenient than other alternatives, and afford greater confidentiality, since you send the fax yourself. However, be sure to check first the cost of this service: as with many such services, including public telephones available on some air planes, the price for "convenience" can be high.*

MEETINGS

Who attends. The nature and place of a meeting will determine who attends. If it is a first meeting for the parties, it is common in Asian countries—because relationships are so important—for the person who introduced them to attend the meeting. This person acts as a facilitator, undertaking to get the relationship off to a good start.

In meetings between people whose relationship is already established, each side will bring whoever is deemed necessary to the purpose of the meeting. Asians tend to bring more people to meetings than do Westerners, because of their collectivist cultures and consultative decision-making practices. In important meetings where there are language differences, each side will often have an interpreter on its team. Even in informal meetings, someone who speaks both languages will often be included.

In some meetings it might not be clear to one side who is the senior person on the other side. If there is a language difference, the senior person is not necessarily the one who does most of the talking. That person might merely be the person who speaks your language best.

Greetings. Although Japanese normally greet each other only with a bow, and Thais normally only with the *wai* (a gesture made with palms together and fingers up, at the chest or higher, and with a slight bow), the normal greeting in Asia-Pacific business circles is the handshake, often combined with a slight bow. Westerners tend to shake hands with a firm grip and Asians with a soft one.

Business cards. Unless you are meeting with people you already know, you should present your business card immediately after a greeting. In Asian countries, cards are presented with a degree of ceremony. In meetings with people having a high Formality Factor, you should present your card with two hands, holding it so that it faces the person to whom it is presented. On taking the card of another, you should study it for a moment and give a nod of appreciation or make an appropriate comment.

Your card should never be flipped across a table to another person, and neither your own card nor the card of another should be treated casually. These would be

---

**ICD Prevention Tip—
Business Cards**

Collect as many business cards as you can. When you return to your home office, use them to add to or correct your name and address files.

---

signs of disrespect. It is common in Asia-Pacific meetings to place the business cards you are given on a table in front of you, separately displayed. In a large meeting, there may be several cards lined up in front of each participant.

Seating. The host should indicate where people should sit. If you are a guest, you should avoid taking a spot at the head of a table unless the host suggests it. Also, steer clear of a chair with a telephone or some other special arrangement near it; that may well be the host's chair.

The Japanese are meticulous about seating arrangements. Normally there is a rectangular table for a meeting. Guests are placed on one side of the table, facing the door to the room, and the hosts sit opposite. The most senior person on each side sits in the middle, with others of lesser rank seated in descending order. The host's junior "gopher" (a person who goes for things, runs errands, or takes messages) sits nearest the door. Elsewhere, seating arrangements do not receive as much attention, but it is common to give a guest a place of honor and a position that will show off the host's offices to best advantage.

Conversation. Some social conversation before getting down to business is a must in the Asia-Pacific region, especially when some of the participants are from Asian collectivist cultures. Westerners should follow the lead of Asians.

Subjects that may seem quite personal to Westerners—family life, standards of living, age and religion—are common and appropriate in conversations with Asians. Subjects that involve politics and national policies, however, are sensitive with Asians, who tend to be nationalistic and supportive of their governments, at least in conversations with foreigners. Westerners, on the other hand, enjoy conversation about political issues and are usually happy to express their views, which are often critical of their governments. See Chapter 3, "Continuing Communications."

Westerners and Asians alike enjoy conversation about sports, travel, international affairs, food, entertainment, and bargain shopping. Do not be impatient with such conversation. It will enhance the business discussions that follow.

Gift presentation. Gifts are often presented at meetings with the implied "hope that this friendship will last." If there will be a series of meetings, often a small gift is presented at the first meeting and a larger gift at the close of the final meeting.

In Asian countries, gifts should be presented and received with both hands and never in an offhand manner. Normally, a gift is not opened in the presence of the giver because it might not be appropriate or might be too lavish and embarrass the recipient or others present. Therefore, you should not insist that your presents to others be opened, and you should put aside the gifts that you receive unless the presenters repeatedly insist that you open them immediately.

Conclusions. As a meeting concludes, it is always good to close with the promise of a continuing and strengthening relationship. If the meeting does not conclude with a set of tasks to be performed by each side, you should nonetheless undertake to send your counterparts something of interest or of value to them and to keep in close touch.

ON YOUR RETURN

As soon as practical after you return to your home base, communicate with the people and organizations that you met with during your trip, unless you have already done so during your return. Your communications can attend to any business issues that remained open following your meetings. More important, however, they should express your appreciation for the courtesies and time extended to you during your visit, especially any entertainment, gifts, or social amenities, and should convey your hope for a continued and valued relationship.

Finally, if you took a computer with you on your trip, you should remember to transfer to your office computer files any data that were changed or added during the trip. You should also add to your office files any new names, addresses, and telephone or fax numbers—or corrections to existing ones—that you collected.

Resource Files

ICD TROUBLESHOOTING GUIDE

This troubleshooting guide sets forth a number of common International Communications Disorder problems encountered by Asia-Pacific executives. It suggests what might be done to solve them, and refers you to the sections of this book that provide specific answers and further discussion.

COMMUNICATIONS IN GENERAL

ICD Problem	Possible Cause or Concern	ICD Solution	Reference
You do not have a contact at the organization you are approaching.	Communication might be overlooked or misdirected.	Contact the organization by fax/telephone and request appropriate name.	Chapters 3 and 6
You are unsure of a person's family name, spelling, title and honorific.	Possible slight to addressee, or misdirection.	Understand the culture's name placement; contact the other organization for advice.	Chapters 3 and 6
You need to make a very good first impression.	Important business at issue, or high Formality Factor of other party.	Arrange for an introduction; send a letter and brochure by courier.	Chapter 3

ICD Problem	Possible Cause or Concern	ICD Solution	Reference
You need the address/telephone/fax number of another party.	Arranging first contacts.	Seek assistance from trade groups, government trade offices.	Chapters 3 and 10
Not enough time to send a letter, and the relationship is new or the Formality Factor of the other party is high.	Fax would appear too informal.	Fax and send letter by mail/courier, indicating in the fax that original is en route.	Chapters 3, 7, and 8
Fax contains highly confidential information.	Fax could be read by unauthorized people.	Advise addressee by telephone or fax when confidential fax will be transmitted; addressee or assistant can wait at fax station.	Chapter 8
Particular need to avoid misunderstanding in written/telephone communication.	Language differences.	Use straightforward language or clear, deliberate speech; arrange for translator/interpreter.	Chapters 3, 7, 10, and 12
Disappointing or negative news to be conveyed to addressee with high Formality Factor.	Potential embarrassment to the addressee or others, possibly damaging business relationship.	Arrange a face-to-face meeting. If not possible, couch the communication in positive terms.	Chapter 3

ICD Problem	Possible Cause or Concern	ICD Solution	Reference
No response received to letter or fax.	(1) Wrong address. (2) Your letter/fax ignored cultural protocol or style. (3) Mail or transmission error.	Recheck address information and try again; if a new contact, arrange an introduction and try again; send the letter by courier.	Chapters 3, 6, 7, and 8
A communication from a counterpart indicates a misunderstanding.	Language differences; your earlier communication was unclear.	Send a new, clear written communication to uncover and correct the source of the misunderstanding; possibly consult an interpreter.	Chapters 3, 5, 7, and 12
Your communications are being referred to a junior executive.	Failure to observe protocol or rank.	Ask an introducer or a senior executive in your organization to write a senior executive of the other organization, and copy to the junior executive.	Chapters 2, 3, and 7
Counterparts frequently ask questions about your organization and your responsibilities or title.	Your organization and its activities are complex or unclear, or your status and authority are unclear.	Take time to describe your organization and your responsibilities.	Chapters 2, 3, and 14

ICD Problem	Possible Cause or Concern	ICD Solution	Reference
Your counterpart complains that your fax or telephone lines are often busy, calls are misdirected or put on hold or always directed to voice mail.	Frustrations of telephone callers will cost business and injure relationships.	"Audit" your organization's telecommunications; add telephone lines and fax machines as appropriate; train telephone operators. Do not give voice mail numbers to overseas counterparts.	Chapters 8 and 10
Time zones inhibit your telephone communications.	Certain business needs to be discussed by telephone.	Be prepared to be available during nonbusiness hours, and supply valued counterparts with your home numbers. If using theirs, be aware of time zone differences.	Chapter 10
Counterpart often unavailable to speak, despite call reaching his office.	Language differences; cultural discomforts.	Use letters and faxes, or get approval from counterpart to use interpreter.	Chapters 3, 5, 8, 10, and 12

ICD Problem	Possible Cause or Concern	ICD Solution	Reference
Good communications capabilities required during forthcoming overseas trip.	Travel schedule is tight; some appointments still pending; close contact needed with home office; written communications to be prepared and sent during trip.	Before departure, arrange for office services at destinations (hotels, business centers, representatives' offices). Take letterhead, portable computer with modem, and complete address list (including fax and telephone numbers).	Chapter 14
Interpreter required for certain appointments during your trip.	Language differences. Appointments involve important business relationships, proposals, or negotiations.	Bring a colleague who speaks the applicable language or arrange in advance for local interpreters.	Chapter 12
You have the addresses for your business appointments, but not precise locations.	Schedule is tight, and you must not be late for appointments.	Obtain maps and written directions in the local language from hotel or local contact; take a local representative with you. Allow for traffic delays.	Chapter 14

USEFUL CONTACTS AND SOURCES OF INFORMATION

Government Trade Offices and Selected Business Associations

The following government trade offices and business associations can be helpful to Asia-Pacific businesspeople in identifying individuals and organizations with whom to communicate and in arranging introductions. In addition to the trade offices listed, governments often have branch offices in other Asia-Pacific cities. Consult local directories or the country's home trade office. Telephone numbers are given with local dialing codes; for international use, add the prefix given on page 289 and the applicable country code, or consult your local directories. Any 0 quoted before a city code should be deleted when dialing internationally.

AUSTRALIA

Australian Trade Commission
AIDC Tower Maritime Centre
201 Kent Street
Sydney, NSW 2000
AUSTRALIA
Telephone: 02-390-2000
Fax: 02-390-2115

CANADA

Asia Pacific Trade Development
Department of Foreign Affairs and
    International Trade
Lester B. Pearson Building
125 Sussex Drive
Ottawa, ON
CANADA K1A 0G2
Telephone: 613-944-4000
Fax: 613-996-4309

The Canadian Chamber of
    Commerce
55 Metcalfe Street
Ottawa, ON
CANADA K1P 6N4
Telephone: 613-238-4000
Fax: 613-238-7643

The Canadian Manufacturers'
    Association
One Yonge Street
Toronto, ON
CANADA M5E 1J9
Telephone: 416-363-7261
Fax: 416-363-3779

The Asia Pacific Foundation
999 Canada Place
Vancouver, BC
CANADA V6C 3E1
Telephone: 604-684-5986
Fax: 604-681-1370

CHINA

China Council for Promotion of
    International Trade
1 Fu Xing Men Wai Jie
Beijing, 100860
CHINA
Telephone: 1-801-3344
Fax: 1-801-1370

All-China Federation of Industry and
    Commerce
93 Beiheyan Dajie
Beijing, 100006
CHINA
Telephone: 1-513-6677
Fax: 1-512-2631

HONG KONG

Hong Kong Government Trade
    Department
700 Nathan Road
Kowloon, HONG KONG
Telephone: 789-7555
Fax: 789-2491

One-Stop Unit
Hong Kong Government Industry
    Department
Ocean Centre, Canton Road
Kowloon, HONG KONG
Telephone: 737-2573
Fax: 730-4633

Hong Kong Trade Development
    Council
Convention Plaza, 1 Harbour Road
HONG KONG
Telephone: 584-4333
Fax: 824-0249

Hong Kong Customs and Excise
Department
Harbour Building
38 Pier Road, Central
HONG KONG
Telephone: 852-1411
Fax: 398-0145

INDONESIA

National Development Information
Office
Wisma Antara
Jalan Medan Medeka Selatan 17
Jakarta 10110, INDONESIA
Telephone: 21-384-7412
Fax: 21-384-7603

Indonesian Chambers of Commerce
and Industry
Chandra Boulevard
Jalan M. H. Thamrin 20
Jakarta, INDONESIA
Telephone: 21-310-5683
Fax: 21-350-442

Importers' Association of Indonesia
P.O. Box 2244/JKT
Jalan E Pintu Timur Arena PRJ
Jakarta, INDONESIA
Telephone: 21-377-008
Fax: 21-324-422

JAPAN

Japan External Trade Organization
(JETRO)
2-5 Toranomon 2-chome, Minato-ku
Tokyo 105, JAPAN
Telephone: 3-3582-5410
Fax: 3-3582-5027

Japan Foreign Trade Council
Sekai Boeki Centre Building
4-1 Hamamatsu-cho 2-chome,
Minato-ku
Tokyo 105, JAPAN
Telephone: 3-3435-5952
Fax: 3-3435-5969

Tokyo International Trade Fair
Commission
7-24 Harumi 4-chome, Chuo-ku
Tokyo 100-91, JAPAN
Telephone: 3-3531-3371
Fax: 3-3531-1344

The Japan Chamber of Commerce
and Industry
World Trade Center Building
4-1, Hamamatsu-cho, 2-chome,
Minato-ku
Tokyo 105, JAPAN
Telephone: 3-3435-4785
Fax: 3-3578-6622

MALAYSIA

Ministry of International Trade and
Industry
Block 10, Government Office
Complex
Jalan Duta
50622 Kuala Lumpur, MALAYSIA
Telephone: 3-254-0033
Fax: 3-255-0827

Malaysian Industrial Development
Authority
Wisma Damansara
Jalan Semantan
50720 Kuala Lumpur, MALAYSIA
Telephone: 3-255-3633
Fax: 3-255-7970

National Chamber of Commerce
and Industry of Malaysia
The Tower, Plaza Pekeliling
Jalan Tun Razak
50400 Kuala Lumpur, MALAYSIA
Telephone: 3-238-0278
Fax: 3-232-0473

Malaysian International Chamber of
Commerce and Industry
Wisma Damansara
Jalan Semantan
50490 Kuala Lumpur, MALAYSIA
Telephone: 3-254-2117
Fax: 3-255-4946

NEW ZEALAND

New Zealand Trade Development
Board
P.O. Box 10-341
Wellington 6036
NEW ZEALAND
Telephone: 4-499-2244
Fax: 4-473-3193

PHILIPPINES

Department of Trade and Industry
Board of Investments Building
385 Senator Gil J. Puyat Avenue
Makati, Metro Manila,
PHILIPPINES
Telephone: 2-816-0121
Fax: 2-816-0552

One-Stop Action Center
Board of Investments Building
385 Senator Gil J. Puyat Avenue
Makati, Metro Manila,
PHILIPPINES
Telephone: 2-818-1831
Fax: 2-819-1887

Philippine Chamber of Commerce
and Industries
ODC International Plaza Building
219 Salcedo Street, Legaspi Village
Makati, Metro Manila,
PHILIPPINES
Telephone: 2-817-6981
Fax: 3-816-1946

SINGAPORE

Singapore Trade Development
Board
World Trade Centre, No. 10-40
Telok Blangah Road
SINGAPORE 0409
Telephone: 271-9388
Fax: 274-0770

Singapore Economic Development
Board
250 North Bridge Road, No. 24-00
Raffles City Tower
SINGAPORE 0617
Telephone: 336-2288
Fax: 339-6077

Singapore International Chamber of
Commerce
50 Raffles Place, No. 03-02
Shell Tower
SINGAPORE 0104
Telephone: 224-1255
Fax: 224-2785

SOUTH KOREA

Korean Trade Promotion Corpora-
tion
159, Samsung-dong, Kangnam-gu
Trade Center Box 123
Seoul, REPUBLIC OF KOREA
Telephone: 2-551-4181
Fax: 2-551-4477

Korea Foreign Trade Association
Korea World Trade Center
159-1, Samsung-dong, Kangnam-gu
Seoul, REPUBLIC OF KOREA
Telephone: 2-551-5114
Fax: 2-551-5100

Association of Foreign Trading
  Agents of Korea
Dongjin Building, 218, Hangangno
2-ga, Yongsan-gu
Seoul, REPUBLIC OF KOREA
Telephone: 2-792-1581
Fax: 2-785-4373

Korea Chamber of Commerce and
  Industry
45, Namdaemun-no, Chung-ku,
  CPOB 25
Seoul, REPUBLIC OF KOREA
Telephone: 2-757-0757
Fax: 2-757-9475

TAIWAN

China External Trade Development
  Council
333 Keelung Road, Section 1
Taipei 10548, TAIWAN, ROC
Telephone: 2-725-5200
Fax: 2-757-6653

Industrial Development and Invest-
  ment Center
Ministry of Economic Affairs
7 Roosevelt Road, Section 1
Taipei, TAIWAN, ROC
Telephone: 2-394-7213
Fax: 2-392-6835

Government Information Office
3 Chung Hsiao East Road, Section 1
Taipei, TAIWAN, ROC
Telephone: 2-341-9211
Fax: 2-392-8113

Chinese National Association of
  Industry and Commerce
390 Fu Hsin South Road, Section 1
Taipei, TAIWAN, ROC
Telephone: 2-707-0111
Fax: 2-701-7601

General Chamber of Commerce of
  the Republic of China
390 Fu Hsin South Road, Section 1
Taipei, TAIWAN, ROC
Telephone: 2-701-2671
Fax: 2-754-2107

THAILAND

Ministry of Commerce
Foreign Trade Department
Sanamchai Road
Bangkok 10200, THAILAND
Telephone: 2-223-1481
Fax: 2-226-3318

Board of Trade of Thailand
Ministry of Interior
150 Rajbopit Road
Bangkok 10200, THAILAND
Telephone: 2-221-1827
Fax: 2-225-3995

Ministry of Finance
Customs Department
Sunthornkosa Road
Bangkok, THAILAND
Telephone: 2-249-0431
Fax: 2-249-2874

Ministry of Industry
Industrial Promotion Department
Rama VI Road
Bangkok, THAILAND
Telephone: 2-246-1031
Fax: 2-247-8004

Thai Chamber of Commerce
150 Rajbopit Road
Bangkok 10200, THAILAND
Telephone: 2-225-0086
Fax: 2-225-3372

U.S. Department of Commerce
International Trade Administration
Herbert Clark Hoover Building
14th and Constitution Avenue, N.W.
Washington, DC 20230
USA
Telephone: 202-482-3181
Fax: 202-482-5270

Trade Information Center
(a one-stop source of telephone
information on all federal government export assistance programs)
Telephone (from within United
States only): 800-872-8723

Industry Specialists
(providing telephone information
relating to specific industries)
Telephone: 202-482-1461
Fax: 202-482-5697

Country Desk Officers
(providing current telephone information on specific countries)
Telephone: 202-482-3022

Office of Multilateral Affairs
(provides telephone information on
trade policies)
Telephone: 202-482-0603
Fax: 202-482-5939

Department of Industry
101 Hai Ba Trung, District 1
Ho Chi Minh City
SOCIALIST REPUBLIC OF
    VIETNAM
Telephone: 8-98018

Chamber of Commerce and
    Industry of the
Socialist Republic of Vietnam
33 Ba Trieu Street
Hanoi
SOCIALIST REPUBLIC OF
    VIETNAM
Telephone: 2-252961
Fax: 2-56446

DIRECT MARKETING ASSOCIATIONS

The following associations can be helpful in identifying firms that provide direct marketing representation and services. In addition, you can consult local directories.

Australian Direct Marketing
  Association
10F, 52-58 Clarence Street
Sydney, NSW 2000
AUSTRALIA
Telephone: 2-247-7744
Fax: 2-247-4919

Canadian Direct Marketing
  Association
1 Concorde Gate
Don Mills, ON
CANADA M3C 3N6
Telephone: 416-391-236
Fax: 416-441-4062

Hong Kong Direct Mail and Mar-
  keting Association
G.P.O. Box 741
HONG KONG
Telephone: 68-11-77
Fax: 88-41-381

Japan Mail Order Business
  Association
1-15-17 Hiyoshi, Kohoku-ku
Yokohama City 223
JAPAN
Telephone: 3-3813-3966
Fax: 3-3818-2774

Japan Direct Marketing Association
32, Mori Building
3-4-30 Shiba-Koen, Minato-ku
Tokyo 105
JAPAN
Telephone: 3-3434-4700
Fax: 3-3434-4518

Japan Telemarketing Association
1-4-2 Kaminanimon, Taito-ku
Tokyo 111
JAPAN
Fax: 3-3847-9218

New Zealand Direct Marketing
  Association
P.O. Box 33432
Takapuna
Auckland 1332
NEW ZEALAND
Telephone: 9-489-9329
Fax: 9-489-7455

Direct Marketing Association of
  Singapore
100 Beach Road, No. 27-05 Shaw
  Towers
SINGAPORE 0718
Telephone: 748-8449
Fax: 742-4366

Direct Marketing Association, Inc.
11 West 42nd Street
New York, NY 10036-8096
USA
Telephone: 212-768-7277
Fax: 212-768-4546

INTERNATIONAL TELECOMMUNICATIONS COMPANIES

The following are four principal international telecommunications companies and numbers for information and customer service (the 800 numbers are for U.S. access):

AT&T EasyLink Services	800-242-6005
MCI Mail	800-444-6245
Sprint	800-843-6678
Fujitsu Nifty-Serve (Tokyo, Japan)	3-3739-9241

Consult directories in other countries for the local contact numbers of these and other international telecommunications companies.

INTERNATIONAL COURIER SERVICES COMPANIES

The following are the four principal international courier services companies and their United States toll-free 800 numbers for information and customer service:

DHL Worldwide Express	800-225-5345
Federal Express	800-247-4747
TNT Express Worldwide	800-558-5555
UPS Worldwide Express	800-742-5877

Consult directories in other countries for the local contact numbers of these and other international courier services companies.

INTERNET DATABASE SERVICES

The following are the principal on-line Internet database service companies and their United States and Canada 800 numbers for information and customer service:

America Online	800-827-6364
CompuServe	800-848-8199
GEnie	800-638-9636
Prodigy	800-776-3449

Consult directories in other countries for the local contact numbers of these and other on-line Internet database service companies.

TRANSLATION ASSOCIATIONS

The following associations can be helpful in identifying individuals and firms that provide translation and interpreter services. In addition, you can consult local directories.

Australian Institute of Interpreters
and Translators
13 Peacedale Grove
Nunawading, VIC 3002
AUSTRALIA
Telephone: 3-877-4369
Fax: 3-416-0231

Canadian Translators and Inter-
preters Council
1 Nicholas Street, Suite 1402
Ottawa, ON
CANADA K1N 7B
Telephone: 613-562-0379
Fax: None

Translators' Association of China
Wai Wen Building
24 Baiwanzhuang Road
Beijing 10037
CHINA
Telephone: 1-832-3576
Fax: 1-831-2892

Science and Technology Translators'
Association of the Chinese
Academy of Sciences
Bureau of International Coopera-
tion
52 Sanlibe Road
Beijing 100864
CHINA
Telephone: 1-836-1453
Fax: 1-801-1095

Japan Society of Translators
55, 1-chome, Jimbo-cho
Kanda, Chiyoda-ku
Tokyo 101
JAPAN
Telephone: 3-3403-8811
Fax: None

New Zealand Society of Translators
and Interpreters, Inc.
P.O. Box 3461
38 Ireland Street, Ponsonby
Auckland
NEW ZEALAND
Telephone: 9-761-216
Fax: 9-360-1641

Korean Society of Translators
KPO Box 1380
208-30 Bouan-dong
Chongro-ku
Seoul 110
REPUBLIC OF KOREA
Telephone: 2-779-2066
Fax: 2-720-6694

American Translators Association
1735 Jefferson Davis Highway
Arlington, VA 22202
USA
Telephone: 703-412-1500
Fax: 703-412-1501

COUNTRY AND CITY TELEPHONE CODES

The telephone country codes for the countries covered by this book, and the telephone area codes for some of the principal cities of these countries, are listed here. Suburbs of larger cities often have different area codes than those of the central cities. For area codes of suburbs and other cities, consult telephone directories or international telephone operators. If a city code is quoted to you with a "0" before it, always drop this before adding any prefixes when dialing internationally. However, if you are dialing to another city in the same country, the "0" should be dialed.

Before the country code, you will also need to dial the correct code for initiating international calls. From each of the countries covered by this book, these are as follows:

Australia	0011-
Canada	011-
China	00-
Hong Kong	001-
Indonesia	00-
Japan	001-
Malaysia	007-
New Zealand	00-
Philippines	00-
Singapore	005-
South Korea	001-
Taiwan	002-
Thailand	001-
United States	011-
Vietnam	00-

Country	Country Code	City	City Code
Australia	61	Adelaide	8
		Brisbane	7
		Canberra	62
		Darwin	89
		Melbourne	3
		Perth	9
		Sydney	2

Country	Country Code	City	City Code
Canada	1	Calgary	403
		Montreal	514
		Ottawa	613
		Québec	418
		Regina	306
		Toronto	416
		Vancouver	604
		Winnipeg	204
China	86	Beijing	1
		Guangzhou	20
		Shanghai	21
		Shenzhen	755
		Xiamen	592
Hong Kong	852	Hong Kong	None
Indonesia	62	Bandung	22
		Denpasar (Bali)	361
		Jakarta	21
		Medan	61
Japan	81	Hiroshima	82
		Kawasaki	44
		Kobe	78
		Kyoto	75
		Nagoya	52
		Osaka	6
		Sapporo	11
		Tokyo	3
		Yokohama	45
Malaysia	60	Ipoh	5
		Kuala Lumpur	3
		Kuching	82
		Penang	4
New Zealand	64	Auckland	9
		Christchurch	3
		Hamilton	71

Country	Country Code	City	City Code
		Wellington	4
		Whangarei	89
Philippines	63	Bacolod	34
		Cebu	32
		Iloilo	33
		Manila	2
Singapore	65	Singapore	None
South Korea	82	Inchon	32
		Kwangju	62
		Pusan	51
		Seoul	2
		Taegu	53
Taiwan	886	Kaohsiung	7
		Taichung	4
		Tainan	6
		Taipei	2
Thailand	66	Bangkok	2
		Chiang Mai	53
		Phuket	76
United States	1	Boston	617
		Chicago	312
		Denver	303
		Honolulu	808
		Los Angeles	213
		New York	212
		San Francisco	415
		Seattle	206
		Washington, DC	202
Vietnam	84	Hanoi	4
		Ho Chi Minh City (Saigon)	8

ASIA-PACIFIC TIME ZONE TABLE

This table sets forth the time differences in hours between principal Asia-Pacific cities. Standard times are used for the table, and the international date line is ignored. If a time difference is noted, a city located to the east of another has the later time. Conversely, a city located to the west of the other has the earlier time. The only exceptions are Kuala Lumpur and Singapore, which are in a longitude similar to Bangkok, Ho Chi Minh City, and Jakarta but use a time zone to the east.

Examples: Bangkok is five hours earlier than Auckland, and Auckland is five hours later than Bangkok. When it is 9:00 P.M. in Bangkok, it is 2:00 A.M. the next day in Auckland. However, the international date line (between Auckland and Honolulu) takes one day from the calculation if it lies between two points. If it is 9:00 P.M. in Tokyo, it is 4:00 A.M. the same day (not the next day) in San Francisco.

The table must be adjusted for "daylight savings time" by adding or subtracting one hour where applicable. The countries featured in this book that use daylight savings time, by setting clocks ahead one hour in the springtime and back one hour in the fall, are Australia (with the exception of Queensland), Canada, New Zealand, the Philippines, South Korea, and the United States (with the exception of the states of Hawaii, Arizona, and certain local regions). The remaining nine countries remain on standard time throughout the year. The changes of time are normally made on the first Sunday of April and the last Sunday of October. Australia and New Zealand, being in the Southern Hemisphere with their seasons the opposite of those in the Northern Hemisphere, set their clocks back when others are set forward, and vice versa, in March and October. For precise dates, consult your international operator, or better still, a local contact.

	Bangkok	Jakarta	HoChi Minh City	Kuala Lumpur	Singapore	Hong Kong	Beijing	Manila	Taipei	Seoul	Tokyo	Sydney	Auckland	Honolulu	Vancouver	San Francisco	Los Angeles	Chicago	New York
Bangkok	-	-	-	1	1	1	1	1	1	2	2	3	5	7	9	9	9	11	12
Jakarta	-	-	-	1	1	1	1	1	1	2	2	3	5	7	9	9	9	11	12
Ho Chi Minh City	-	-	-	1	1	1	1	1	1	2	2	3	5	7	9	9	9	11	12
Kuala Lumpur	1	1	1	-	-	-	-	-	-	1	1	2	4	6	8	8	8	10	11
Singapore	1	1	1	-	-	-	-	-	-	1	1	2	4	6	8	8	8	10	11
Hong Kong	1	1	1	-	-	-	-	-	-	1	1	2	4	6	8	8	8	10	11
Beijing	1	1	1	-	-	-	-	-	-	1	1	2	4	6	8	8	8	10	11
Manila	1	1	1	-	-	-	-	-	-	1	1	2	4	6	8	8	8	10	11
Taipei	1	1	1	-	-	-	-	-	-	1	1	2	4	6	8	8	8	10	11
Seoul	2	2	2	1	1	1	1	1	1	-	-	1	3	5	7	7	7	9	10
Tokyo	2	2	2	1	1	1	1	1	1	-	-	1	3	5	7	7	7	9	10
Sydney	3	3	3	2	2	2	2	2	2	1	1	-	2	4	6	6	6	8	9
Auckland	5	5	5	4	4	4	4	4	4	3	3	2	-	2	4	4	4	6	7
Honolulu	7	7	7	6	6	6	6	6	6	5	5	4	2	-	2	2	2	4	5
Vancouver	9	9	9	8	8	8	8	8	8	7	7	6	4	2	-	-	-	2	3
San Francisco	9	9	9	8	8	8	8	8	8	7	7	6	4	2	-	-	-	2	3
Los Angeles	9	9	9	8	8	8	8	8	8	7	7	6	4	2	-	-	-	2	3
Chicago	11	11	11	10	10	10	10	10	10	9	9	8	6	4	2	2	2	-	1
New York	12	12	12	11	11	11	11	11	11	10	10	9	7	5	3	3	3	1	-

ASIA-PACIFIC TIME ZONE MAP

Use this map for easy identification of Asia-Pacific time zones. When telephoning toward the west (for example, from San Francisco to Tokyo), times at destination are earlier. When telephoning toward the east (for example, from Bangkok to Los Angeles), times at destination are later. On the map, Tokyo (zone 2) is one hour earlier in a call from Manila (zone 1), and Los Angeles (zone 9) is two hours later in a call from Honolulu (zone 7). However, the international date line (between Auckland and Honolulu) takes one day from the calculation if it lies between two points. (If it is 9:00 P.M. in Tokyo, it is 4:00 A.M. the same day—not the next day— in San Francisco.)

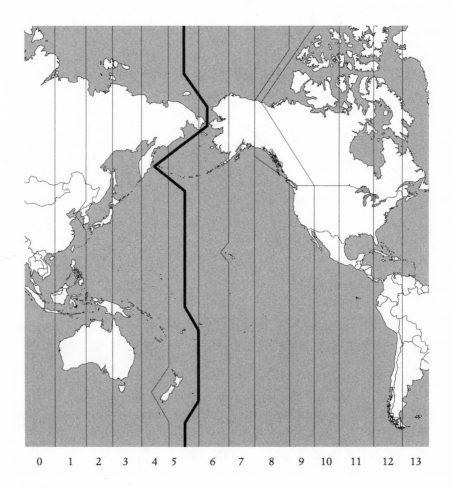

0   1   2   3   4   5   6   7   8   9   10   11   12   13

ASIA-PACIFIC FLIGHT TIME TABLE

Approximate flight times in hours, between principal Asia-Pacific cities, are set forth in the following table. For some long flights, up to two hours are added for stops and connections. Times can vary significantly depending on routes actually flown.

	Bangkok	Jakarta	Ho Chi Minh City	Kuala Lumpur	Singapore	Hong Kong	Beijing	Manila	Taipei	Seoul	Tokyo	Sydney	Auckland	Honolulu	Vancouver	San Francisco	Los Angeles	Chicago	New York
Bangkok	-	3	2	2	2	2	7	4	3	9	6	14	16	14	17	17	17	21	23
Jakarta	3	-	3	2	2	6	7	6	8	12	12	9	13	14	18	18	18	21	23
Ho Chi Minh City	2	3	-	2	2	2	7	4	4	9	6	12	13	14	18	18	18	21	23
Kuala Lumpur	2	2	2	-	1	5	7	6	6	8	9	12	15	14	18	18	18	21	23
Singapore	2	2	2	1	-	5	7	5	7	9	9	13	14	14	18	18	18	21	23
Hong Kong	2	6	2	5	5	-	5	7	4	4	4	13	15	12	16	16	16	19	21
Beijing	7	7	7	7	7	5	-	4	3	3	4	15	17	13	17	17	17	20	22
Manila	4	6	4	6	5	7	4	-	2	5	4	11	13	13	17	17	17	20	22
Taipei	3	8	4	6	7	4	3	2	-	3	3	10	12	9	15	15	15	18	20
Seoul	9	12	9	8	9	4	3	5	3	-	2	12	16	9	15	15	15	18	20
Tokyo	6	12	6	8	9	4	4	4	3	2	-	13	15	7	12	12	12	15	17
Sydney	14	9	12	12	13	13	15	11	10	14	13	-	2	13	17	17	17	20	22
Auckland	16	13	13	15	14	15	17	13	12	16	15	2	-	10	15	15	15	18	20
Honolulu	14	14	14	14	14	12	13	13	9	9	7	13	10	-	4	4	4	8	10
Vancouver	17	18	18	18	18	16	17	17	15	15	12	17	15	4	-	3	4	3	5
San Francisco	17	18	18	18	18	16	17	17	15	15	12	17	15	4	3	-	2	3	5
Los Angeles	17	18	18	18	18	16	17	17	15	15	12	17	15	4	4	2	-	3	5
Chicago	21	21	21	21	21	19	20	20	18	18	15	20	18	8	3	3	3	-	2
New York	23	23	23	23	23	21	22	22	20	20	17	22	20	10	5	5	5	2	-

MEASUREMENT CONVERSION TABLE

When You Know U.S./Imperial Measures

Symbol	Means	Multiply by	To Find	Symbol
in	inch	2.54	centimeter	cm
ft	foot	30.48	centimeter	cm
yd	yard	0.91	meter	m
mi	mile	1.61	kilometer	km
in²	square inch	6.45	square centimeter	cm²
ft²	square foot	0.09	square meter	m²
mi²	square mile	0.84	square kilometer	km²
oz	ounce*	28.35	gram	g
oz (troy)	ounce†	31.10	gram	g
lb	pound	0.45	kilogram	kg
short ton	(2,000 lbs)	0.91	metric ton	t
long ton	(2,240 lbs)	1.12	metric ton	t
fl oz	fluid ounce	29.57	milliliter	mL
c	cup	0.24	liter	L
pt	pint	0.47	liter	L
qt	quart	0.95	liter	L
gal	gallon	3.78	liter	L
ft³	cubic foot	0.03	cubic meter	m³
yd³	cubic yard	0.76	cubic meter	m³
F	degrees Fahrenheit (first subtract 32)	0.55	degrees Celsius	C

[Note: For temperatures above 32° F, an easy conversion from Fahrenheit to Celsius is to subtract 30 from the Fahrenheit temperature and divide by 2. Example: 70° F – 30 = 40 ÷ 2 = 20° C]

---

* For weighing ordinary commodities.

† For weighing precious metals, jewels, etc.

MEASUREMENT CONVERSION TABLE

When You Know Metric Measures

Symbol	Means	Multiply by	To Find	Symbol
cm	centimeter	0.39	inch	in
cm	centimeter	0.033	foot	ft
m	meter	1.09	yard	yd
km	kilometer	0.62	mile	mi
cm^2	square centimeter	0.15	square inch	in^2
m^2	square meter	10.76	square foot	ft^2
m^2	square meter	1.20	square yard	yd^2
km	square kilometer	0.39	square mile	mi^2
ha	hectare	2.47	acre	
g	gram	0.035	ounce*	oz
g	gram	0.032	ounce†	oz (troy)
kg	kilogram	2.21	pounds	lbs
t	metric ton	1.10	short ton (2,000 lbs)	
t	metric ton	0.98	long ton (2,240 lbs)	
mL	milliliter	0.03	fluid ounce	fl oz
L	liter	4.24	cup	c
L	liter	2.13	pint (liquid)	pt
L	liter	1.05	quart (liquid)	qt
L	liter	0.26	gallon	gal
m^3	cubic meter	35.32	cubic foot	ft^3
m^3	cubic meter	1.32	cubic yard	yd^3
C	degrees Celsius	1.80	degrees Fahrenheit (then add 32)	F

[Note: For temperatures above 0° C, an easy conversion from Celsius to Fahrenheit is to double the Celsius temperature and add 30. Example: 22° C x 2 = 44 + 30 = 74° F]

---

* For weighing ordinary commodities.

† For weighing precious metals, jewels, etc.

PRACTICAL AND INTERESTING READINGS

Axtell, Roger E. *Do's and Taboos Around the World* (John Wiley, 1990).

———. *Do's and Taboos of Hosting International Visitors* (John Wiley, 1990).

———. *The Do's and Taboos of International Trade* (John Wiley, 1991).

Besher, Alexander. *The Pacific Rim Almanac* (HarperPerennial, 1991).

Brannen, Christalyn, and Tracey Wilen. *Doing Business with Japanese Men: A Woman's Handbook* (Stone Bridge Press, 1993).

Business Profile Series [guides on doing business in various countries, including those featured in this book] (Hongkong and Shanghai Banking Corporation Limited).

Cronin, Mary J. *Doing Business On the Internet* (Van Nostrand Reinhold, 1994).

De Mente, Boye L. *Chinese Etiquette and Ethics in Business* (NTC Business Books, 1989).

———. *Korean Etiquette and Ethics in Business* (NTC Business Books, 1988).

Dern, Daniel P. *The Internet Guide for New Users* (McGraw-Hill, 1993).

Devine, Elizabeth, and Nancy L. Braganti. *The Travelers' Guide to Asian Customs and Manners* (St. Martin's Press, 1986).

Engholm, Christopher. *When Business East Meets Business West* (John Wiley, 1991).

Fisher, Glen. *International Negotiation* (Intercultural Press, 1980).

Frailey, L. E. *Handbook of Business Letters* (Prentice Hall, 1989).

Gercik, Patricia. *On Track with the Japanese* (Kodansha International, 1992).

Harris, Philip R., and Robert T. Moran. *Managing Cultural Differences* (Gulf Publishing, 1991).

James, David L. *Doing Business in Asia* (Betterway Books, 1993).

Kato, Hiroki, and Joan Kato. *Understanding and Working with the Japanese Business World* (Prentice Hall, 1992).

Leppert, Paul A. *Doing Business in Singapore* (Patton Pacific Press, 1990).

———. *Doing Business with the Koreans* (Patton Pacific Press, 1991).

———. *Doing Business with the Thai* (Patton Pacific Press, 1992).

———. *How to Do Business with Chinese: Taiwan* (Patton Pacific Press, 1990).

Moran, Robert T. *Getting Your Yen's Worth* (Gulf Publishing, 1985).

Moran, Robert T., and William G. Stripp. *Successful International Business Negotiations* (Gulf Publishing, 1991).

Maurer, P. Reed. *Competing in Japan* (Japan Times, 1989).

Musashi, Miyamoto. *A Book of Five Rings*, translated by Victor Harris (Overlook Press, 1974).

Pei, Mario. *The Story of Language* (J. B. Lippincott, 1965).

Poe, Roy W. *The McGraw-Hill Handbook of Business Letters* (McGraw-Hill, 1988).

Price Waterhouse Information Guide Series [guides on doing business in various countries, including many of the countries featured in this book] (Price Waterhouse).

Rearwin, David. *The Asia Business Book* (Intercultural Press, 1991).

Rowland, Diana. *Japanese Business Etiquette* (Warner Books, 1993).

Seglin, Jeffrey L. *The AMA Handbook of Business Letters* (AMACOM, 1989).

Stross, Randall E. *Bulls in the China Shop* (Pantheon, 1990).

The Wall Street Journal Guides to Business Travel: Pacific Rim (Fodor's Travel Publications, 1991).

SURVEY QUESTIONNAIRE

The following questionnaire was sent to over 400 business executives around the Asia-Pacific region during my research for this book.

Users of this book are invited to make a copy of the questionnaire and return it to:

David L. James
The Executive Guide to Asia-Pacific Communications Survey
c/o Kodansha America, Inc.
114 Fifth Avenue
New York, NY 10014
USA

I will review responses periodically, with the intention of incorporating any useful comments or possible omissions in subsequent editions of this book. I regret that I will not be able to respond personally to every survey I receive; however, all feedback will be greatly appreciated.

Confidential International Business Communications Survey

Name:

Company or Affiliation:

Title:

Responsibilities:

Address:

Nationality/Ethnicity:

Note: Anonymous responses are also welcome; however, an indication of your type of company, industry, responsibilities, location, and nationality/ethnicity will greatly help me in best using any information you may provide.

General

1. What is your first language?

What other languages do you write and speak (in order of proficiency)?

---

2. Do you receive and respond to written communications (letters and faxes) in languages other than your first language? If so, what other languages (in order of frequency)?

Most frequent (other than first language)

Second most frequent

Third most frequent

---

3. Do you have overseas telephone conversations in languages other than your first language? If so, what other languages (in order of frequency)?

Most frequent (other than first language)

Second most frequent

Third most frequent

---

4. City and country in which you maintain your office:

---

5. Type of business you are in:

Receiving Communications

1. Do you sometimes respond to a letter or fax from someone you do not know?

☐ Yes (If yes, answer items 2 and 3 below)
☐ No (If no, answer item 4 below)

2. If yes to item 1, are you more likely to respond to a letter or a fax? (Select one.)

☐ Letter
☐ Fax
Comment?

---

3. If yes to item 1, under what conditions do you respond? (Select one or more.)
   ☐ The person is writing at the suggestion of someone I know
   ☐ I know the person's organization
   ☐ There may be a possibility of business gain for my firm
   ☐ Other:

   _____

4. If no to item 1, what are some of the reasons you do not respond? (Select one or more.)
   ☐ The letter or fax is not in my first language
   ☐ The person has not been properly introduced
   ☐ Protocol of customary writing style is not observed
   ☐ The letter or fax appears to be an impersonal form letter
   ☐ It is too long
   ☐ The person uses difficult words, idioms, or slang
   ☐ The person's words and expressions are not polite
   ☐ The person is too informal
   ☐ It is not clear what is requested
   ☐ A positive response would be difficult or impolite
   ☐ Other reasons:

   _____

5. Do you sometimes take international telephone calls from people you do not know?
   ☐ Yes (If yes, answer item 6 below)
   ☐ No (If no, answer item 7 below)

6. If yes to item 5, under what conditions? (Select one or more.)
   ☐ The person is calling at the suggestion of someone I know
   ☐ I know the person's organization
   ☐ There may be a possibility of business gain for my firm
   ☐ Other:

   _____

7. If no to item 5, what are some of the reasons you do not take such calls? (Select one or more.)
   ☐ The caller does not speak my first language
   ☐ The purpose of the call is unknown
   ☐ I do not know the person
   ☐ The person has not been properly introduced
   ☐ Such a call should be preceded by a letter or fax
   ☐ Such calls disrupt other business
   ☐ Other reasons:

   _____

8. In letters and faxes that you receive from people who are writing to you for the first time, how important are the following?

	Very Important	Somewhat Important	Not Important
Quality of stationery	☐	☐	☐
Neat appearance	☐	☐	☐
Colors of stationery and letterhead	☐	☐	☐
Typeface, fonts used	☐	☐	☐
Protocol followed in manner of address, format	☐	☐	☐
Gracious or polite style of writing	☐	☐	☐
Words easy to understand	☐	☐	☐
Other:	☐	☐	☐

Additional observations, if any:

9. What are some of the problems in international written communications received by your firm?

	Common Problem	Occasional Problem	No Problem
Writer uses a language that is not my own first language	☐	☐	☐
Writer uses a language that is not his or her own first language	☐	☐	☐
Writer uses difficult words, idioms, or slang	☐	☐	☐
Too long	☐	☐	☐
Not clear what is requested	☐	☐	☐
A positive response would be difficult or impolite	☐	☐	☐
Poor quality stationery or typing	☐	☐	☐
Protocol is not observed	☐	☐	☐
Writer is too informal, uses first names	☐	☐	☐
Writer's expression is impolite	☐	☐	☐
Someone else signs "for" the writer	☐	☐	☐
The writing says, "Dictated but not read"	☐	☐	☐
Slow mail (letters)	☐	☐	☐
Customs inspections of mail	☐	☐	☐
Other:	☐	☐	☐

Suggestions for better written communications

10. What are some of the problems in international telephone calls received by your firm?

	Common Problem	Occasional Problem	No Problem
Caller does not speak my first language	☐	☐	☐
Caller uses difficult words, idioms, or slang	☐	☐	☐
Caller speaks too rapidly	☐	☐	☐
Caller has difficult accent	☐	☐	☐
Caller does not call at a good time of day	☐	☐	☐
Caller is not on line (caller's secretary has placed call)	☐	☐	☐
Caller is impolite or abrupt	☐	☐	☐
Caller rambles, does not come to point	☐	☐	☐
Caller is not clear about what is requested	☐	☐	☐
Telephone connection is not clear	☐	☐	☐
Lack of privacy	☐	☐	☐
Caller uses a speakerphone	☐	☐	☐
Understanding is difficult without a face-to-face meeting	☐	☐	☐
Other:	☐	☐	☐

Suggestions for better telephone communications

11. What are normally the best times of day, and days of the week, for you to receive telephone calls?

Times of day (local time)

Days of the week

12. If you are not available to take a telephone call, do you prefer that the caller (select one):
☐ State purpose and leave a message for me to return the call
☐ Call back
☐ Speak to someone else
☐ Comment?

13. Suggestions for written communications (letters and faxes) received by you from businesspeople of the following nationalities (things they should do or avoid doing):

Americans

Australians

Canadians

Chinese

Filipinos

Hong Kongese

Indonesians

Japanese

Malaysians

New Zealanders

Singaporeans

South Koreans

Taiwanese

Thai

Vietnamese

Any general comments?

14. Suggestions for international telephone calls received by you from business-people of the following nationalities (things they should do or avoid doing):

Americans

Australians

Canadians

Chinese

Filipinos

_____

Hong Kongese

_____

Indonesians

_____

Japanese

_____

Malaysians

_____

New Zealanders

_____

Singaporeans

_____

South Koreans

_____

Taiwanese

_____

Thai

_____

Vietnamese

_____

Any general comments?

_____

15. In general, does your firm welcome communications from unknown businesspeople?
- ☐ Yes
- ☐ No
- ☐ Comment?

_____

16. If someone is communicating with you from overseas for the first time, do you prefer to receive the communication by (select one):
- ☐ Mail
- ☐ Fax
- ☐ Courier
- ☐ Telephone

17. For ongoing international communications from firms with which you have an active business relationship, do you prefer to receive the communications by (select one or more):
- ☐ Mail
- ☐ Fax
- ☐ Courier
- ☐ Telephone

18. In ongoing communications with firms with which you have an active business relationship, how important is it that there be some "small talk" in letters, faxes, and telephone calls?

☐ Very important ☐ Somewhat important ☐ Not important

If very or somewhat important, what are some good topics for "small talk"?

_____

19. Roughly what percentage of your firm's written communications from overseas are received by:

Mail _____ %
Fax _____ %
Courier _____ %

20. Do you have any further observations about receiving international communications (in writing or by telephone) that you think might be helpful to other businesspeople?

_____

Sending Communications

1. What happens if the communication you receive (letter, fax, phone call) fails to follow accepted protocol or is from an unknown person without an introduction? (Select one or more.)

☐ A response is promptly made anyway
☐ A response might be delayed
☐ It is referred to a lower level of your firm for response
☐ No response is made
☐ Other:

_____

2. Does your firm employ, on a full-time basis, people whose primary responsibility it is to draft or translate written communications and documents:

Into English? Yes ☐ No ☐

Into other languages? (Please list)

_____

3. What are your personal preferences (or those of your secretary or assistant) for the following:

Placement of addressee's address:
   ☐ Top of letter (above salutation)
   ☐ Bottom of letter
☐ Block-style paragraphs
☐ Indented paragraphs
Salutation and close:
   ☐ Typed
   ☐ Handwritten

Salutation style:
- ☐ Formal (invariably use family name)
- ☐ Informal (given name or nickname if well known)
- ☐ Honorific for single woman:
  - ☐ Miss ☐ Ms.

Typical close:
- ☐ Very truly yours
- ☐ Sincerely
- ☐ Other:

Size of stationery:
- ☐ 8½" x 11"5466 ☐ A4 ☐ Other: _____

Color of stationery
  Color of ink used to sign letters: ☐ Black ☐ Blue ☐ Other:

Typefaces, fonts

Other preferences for written communications you send:

---

4. For ongoing international communications to firms with which you have an active business relationship, do you prefer to use (select one or more):
- ☐ Mail
- ☐ Fax
- ☐ Courier
- ☐ Telephone

5. Roughly what percentage of your firm's overseas written communications are sent by:

Mail _____ %
Fax _____ %
Courier _____ %

6. What courier companies do you prefer to use?

---

7. What are some of the problems for your firm in sending international written communications by mail, fax, or courier?

	Common Problem	Occasional Problem	No Problem
Composing communications in languages other than a first language	☐	☐	☐
Being unsure of addressee's protocol, customs	☐	☐	☐
Not knowing when or if communication has been received	☐	☐	☐

	Common Problem	Occasional Problem	No Problem
Slow mail (letters)	☐	☐	☐
Confidentiality (especially faxes)	☐	☐	☐
Expense of faxes	☐	☐	☐
Expense of couriers	☐	☐	☐
Other:	☐	☐	☐

Suggestions for sending written communications

8. What are some of the problems for your firm in making international telephone calls?

	Common Problem	Occasional Problem	No Problem
Time zone makes it inconvenient	☐	☐	☐
Busy signals, circuits busy	☐	☐	☐
Voice mail runaround	☐	☐	☐
Person called is unavailable	☐	☐	☐
Person does not return my call	☐	☐	☐
Person called talks too long	☐	☐	☐
Person called does not speak my first language	☐	☐	☐
Telephone operators and secretaries do not speak my first language	☐	☐	☐
Expense, cost-effectiveness	☐	☐	☐
Teleconferencing not available or does not work well	☐	☐	☐
Other:	☐	☐	☐

Suggestions for making international telephone calls

9. Any further observations about sending international communications (in writing or by telephone) that you think might be helpful to other businesspeople?

Appointments

1. How much notice do you like to have for an appointment with a businessperson visiting from overseas? At least

2. Assuming proper protocol is otherwise followed (for example, having a proper introduction), do you prefer that appointments with businesspeople from overseas be arranged by:

☐ Letter
☐ Fax
☐ Telephone

3.   Who should arrange an introduction of someone whom you do not know? (Select one or more.)
☐ One of my friends or business acquaintances
☐ A bank known to me
☐ A consulting firm known to me
☐ An accounting firm known to me
☐ A law firm known to me
☐ An introduction is not necessary
☐ Other:

_____

4.   Who schedules your appointments? (Select one.)
☐ Only myself
☐ Myself or my secretary or assistant
☐ Only my secretary or assistant
☐ Other arrangement (specify):

_____

Other

1.   Please describe any amusing happenings or unusual occurrences in your experience with international communications.

_____
_____

2.   What does your secretary or assistant do that is especially helpful to you in maintaining effective international business communications?

_____
_____

3.   What suggestions does your secretary or assistant have for the secretaries and assistants of overseas businesspeople?

_____
_____

4.   Any final observations about international business communications that might be helpful to other businesspeople?

_____
_____

5.   What issues, other than those mentioned in this survey, should be covered in a book on international business communications?

_____
_____

HIGHLIGHTS OF SURVEY RESPONSES

Confidential International Business Communications Survey

Here are highlights of the results of my survey of Asia-Pacific business executives, followed by some of the written comments submitted by responding executives (identified only by regional source), including comments by their secretaries and assistants. Not all the written comments listed here are representative of the consensus, but they are set forth as indicative of the diverse attitudes and cultures of the region.

GENERAL ASIA-PACIFIC COMMUNICATIONS

Clear Preferences

Initial contacts are best made with an introduction by a mutual friend or acquaintance.

Initial contacts are best made by letter, with mail or courier delivery, rather than by fax or telephone.

Subsequent business communications by fax are preferred. Sixty-eight percent of respondents indicated that they used the fax 50 percent of the time or more; many indicated that they used the fax more than 80 percent of the time.

"Small talk" and pleasantries in correspondence and conversation are generally considered important.

In written communications, the following are especially important:

▲ Neat appearance
▲ Words easy to understand
▲ Gracious and polite style
▲ Protocol observed

Common Problems

▲ The writer or caller is not clear about what is requested
▲ The writing or conversation is too long
▲ Language differences

SIGNIFICANT AND RECURRING PROBLEMS

Written Communications

▲ Not knowing whether the communication has been received
▲ Slow mail
▲ Concerns over confidentiality
▲ Expense of couriers

Telephone Communications

Overall, there are more problems and frustrations with telephone communications than with written communications

▲ The caller speaks too rapidly or has a difficult accent

▲ The caller often rambles, fails to come to the point

▲ Time zone differences are a problem

▲ The person called is often unavailable

▲ There are often busy signals, or static on the line

▲ Voice mail gives you the "runaround"

SELECTED COMMENTS OF ASIA-PACIFIC EXECUTIVES RESPONDING TO THE SURVEY

Are communications from unknown businesspeople welcome?

From North America:

"Soliciting is not welcome."

"Only if the purpose of the call is stated at the outset."

From Southeast Asia:

"As long as there is common interest."

What are some good "small talk" topics for letters, faxes, and telephone calls?

From Australia/New Zealand:

"Your last or next meeting or conference; family; shared interests."

"Shared experiences, future entertainment or meetings."

"Sports, weather."

From East Asia:

"Anything personal."

"Things shared in common."

"Weather, health, travel plans."

From North America:

"Family."

"Previous meetings, national holidays."

"With Japanese, talk about the weather; with Southeast Asians, talk about family."

"Current events, economy."

"Golf, sports."

From Southeast Asia:

"The other person's well-being."

"Prices, new R&D [research and development]."

"Health, well-being, family, progress of other endeavors."

"Sports, family, common friends, or club."

GENERAL COMMENTS ON COMMUNICATING

From Australia/New Zealand:

"If it can be faxed, that is the best way to go."

"Be short, to the point."

"Be brief, simple, talk money in precise, unambiguous terms."

"Do your 'homework' before involving other people. Correct, careful briefing can make the difference between success or failure."

From East Asia:

"Message must be clear and precise."

"For urgent matters, acknowledge receipt; reply within deadline at all times."

"Think of ways to reduce costs."

"Persons requesting appointments should reconfirm them."

"Don't talk or write too long; state your purpose clearly, but be polite."

From North America:

"Be short and clear; not too many salutations ['social talk']."

"Refer to previous communication and briefly review status."

"Know or find out about the person you are responding to."

"Try to be empathetic."

"Polite, considerate behavior is welcome in any language."

"Good communication is based on mutual trust; every effort should be made to establish and maintain trust through understanding and respect for the other person's cultural ways."

"It's very important to get quickly to the point."

"Use voice mail or e-mail."

From Southeast Asia:

"Pay attention to correct name, rank or position, form of address, relationships to superiors and subordinates."

"Use correct names, addresses, phone numbers."

"Enclose pertinent information."

"Learn English."

"Have empathy for procedures, rules, systems of the host country."

LETTERS

From Australia/New Zealand:

"Content and clarity are more important than 'style.'"

"Do not assume the overseas person has knowledge of the writer's country; keep it simple, state clearly what the writer wants and when."

"Write clearly, concisely, and keep it to the point."

"A letter tends to suggest serious thought or intent instead of a last-minute idea."

From East Asia:

"Write a conclusion at the first."

"Be concise."

"Have clear objectives, use plain language."

"Indicate on the first page the total number of pages."

"Come to the point."

"Use English or Japanese."

"All countries should use either Chinese or English."

"Use English if not my first language [Korean]."

From North America:

"I am interested in the substantive content, not image projection."

"Only the content is important."

"The form of the communication has an immediate impact."

"Do less writing in paragraphs, do more with bullets or numbered items."

"I don't believe that improvement of the nonsubstantive aspects of a letter or fax will significantly enhance the chances of receiving a response."

"Be certain to spell addressee's name correctly."

"Be short and concise."

"Keep to one page."

"Do not write in longhand."

"State request or conclusion at the beginning, then supporting information or data as needed."

From Southeast Asia:

"Use seals and logos, to make your correspondence look official and serious."

"A clear objective should be stated."

"The purpose for writing is the most important point to be made."

"Have exact postage."

"Be specific and clear, don't make 'demands,' and start with pleasantries and an introduction."

"Avoid idioms."

"Be honest and straight."

"Don't drop names in expectation of favors."

"Non-English speakers should use interpreters and translators."

FAXES

From East Asia:

"Sometimes, fax first, then send letter as confirmation."

"Fax is faster; speed is essential."

"Faxes are quick and easy."

"The speed of the fax is important."

"The fax is convenient and fast."

"Take advantage of time zone differences for responses to faxes—get or send an answer overnight."

From North America:

"I will read faxes ahead of letters."

"Often a person's name or fax number is blurred in faxes."

"Use the fax instead of the phone; it cuts down on 'small talk' and is more cost effective."

From Southeast Asia:

"Faxes are more convenient and easier."

"Do not expect a Vietnamese to respond by fax. Too expensive."

"Send by fax with original to follow."

TELEPHONE CALLS

From Australia/New Zealand:

"Execs should speak/call direct (where possible)—otherwise wasted time and irritating transferring between secretaries."

"Plan on paper what to say before calling."

"Speak clearly, state business concisely."

"Work from written notes to ensure clarity."

From East Asia:

"Speak more slowly."

"Getting to the point is most important."

"Send a letter or fax to say when you will call."

"Make points as clear as possible; think before picking up the phone."

"Be available at the other person's convenience."

"Just speak clearly and slowly."

"Come to the point."

"Use English if not my first language [Korean]."

"Voice mail does not work on overseas calls."

"Come to the point—I don't care about the weather in New York."

"Be patient."

"Avoid phone, use fax or letter."

From North America:

"Send fax to advise time and date of call."

"Send a fax first."

"Use a speakerphone only when more than one person is present and announce each person."

"Come to the point quickly."

"Make timely responses, telephone at reasonable hours."

"Plan call with written notes in order of priority."

"Plan what you want to say and say it as simply as possible."

"If the connection is not clear, hang up and place the call again."

"Be sensitive to time zones."

"Calculate time zone differences carefully."

"Do your homework, have your schedule always available."

"Arrange the call beforehand."

From Southeast Asia:

"Don't expect decisions to be made over the phone unless the issue has been debated and agreed previously."

"Be clear."

"Follow up with fax or letter."

"Be respectful and clear."

"Non-English speakers should prepare talking points with help of interpreter/translator prior to call."

"Any pressure from callers turns me off."

"Follow up with fax or letter."

"Jot down important talking points to avoid unnecessarily long calls."

EXECUTIVE SECRETARIES AND ASSISTANTS: APPRECIATIVE COMMENTS FROM ASIA-PACIFIC EXECUTIVES

From Australia/New Zealand:

"Reminds me of appointments and prepares briefing notes on person coming or calling and his/her company."

"If initial telephone connection fails because of nonavailability of person called, persists in arranging further call at convenient time."

"Keeps up with contacts' latest address info, etc., and follows up on all inquiries."

"Maintains schedules and records of communications."

From East Asia:

"My alter ego does as much as possible in handling office business."

"Identifies person with whom communicating (firm name, subject of call), provides a file in advance."

"Pleasant small talk before connecting call, friendly voice, polite."

"Makes certain fax machine has plenty of paper."

"Gives messages for necessary action."

"Handles routine correspondence for me."

"Helps boss use time efficiently."

From North America:

"Determines importance of communication and makes arrangements for disposition."

"Helps in putting through phone calls, maintains good follow-up system."

"Keeps track of incoming communications and responds in a timely manner."

"Keeps a detailed daily file of correspondence."

"Uses the fax to schedule calls."

"They are patient."

"Continually updates fax and phone numbers."

"Speaks excellent, polite, and businesslike English, not too fast."

"My Japanese assistant helps interpret nuances in letters from Japanese, i.e., the real feelings of the sender."

"Has a friendly attitude, promptly responds to requests."

"Opens all correspondence; drafts responses; makes sure all communications are answered."

From Southeast Asia:

"Gets names and references."

"Updates appointments."

"Cordial and friendly in my absence."

"Records and reminds."

"Keeps track of communications, drafts replies."

ADVICE FROM ASIA-PACIFIC EXECUTIVE SECRETARIES AND ASSISTANTS FOR THEIR OVERSEAS COUNTERPARTS

From Australia/New Zealand:

"Keep the boss well informed, in interest of creating and maintaining a happy, successful office."

"Ensure that the boss's message gets through and is answered."

"When contacting overseas people, make sure you are clear in what you are asking for."

From East Asia:

"*Gambatte!* Speak slowly and clearly in English."

"Be prompt in responding."

"Give more than one fax number in case one is busy."

"Be more internationally minded."

From North America:

"Always get and give complete telephone/fax numbers and addresses."

"Be friendly and patient."

"People who answer phones should be able to speak English."

"Keep a sense of humor."

"Speak clearly; make sure boss is *immediately* available when placing a call."

"Communicate in writing rather than orally."

"Keep informed of events that relate to the business."

"Have respect for the ways of others, which might differ from your own."

"Be prepared to take the extra step to assist people, in seeking answers to questions, gathering materials needed by the caller, finding the right people to help the caller if you cannot do this yourself. Be sure to get names, telephone numbers, faxes, addresses, and types of information needed to make a connection. Don't be afraid to be helpful or to get involved. There is a tremendous amount that support staff can do to create a good foundation for future business relationships or to provide valuable information to various businesses and individuals—or to your own supervisors or bosses—re: inquiries etc. or other business."

From Southeast Asia:

"Write in English and include references."

"Speak slowly."

"Be patient and polite (not condescending), be clear and remember the working environment in some countries might be difficult or inefficient."

"Specify purpose of the visit or meeting."

"Learn the communication style of your boss but don't be afraid to be innovative, creative."

Index

Cook, James, 89
Copyright protection, 100
Courier services, 34–35, 207–14, 287
Credit cards, telephone, 222–23, 269–70
Cultural Revolution, 61, 63, 64

Dalsey, Adrian, 212
Death, 26, 45, 46, 47
Decision making, 17–18, 44–45, 270
Defense Department (United States), 230–31
Deng Xiaoping, 144
Deng Ziaoping (Teng Hsiao-p'ing), 143
Dentsu / Young and Rubicam venture, 241
Development Zones, 62
DHL Worldwide Express, 212–13, 287
Dillingham Corporation, 55
Dinners, 39, 46. *See also* Entertaining
Direct Marketing Association, 286
Direct Marketing Association of Singapore, 286
Doi Moi, 129
Dow Jones News / Retrieval, 231

East-West Center, 4
Economic growth, 8–9, 61–62, 79, 85–86, 116–17
EDIs (electronic data interchange messages), 229, 230
Education, 18–19
EEC (European Economic Community), 3, 9, 90
E-mail, 228–30, 232
Embarrassment, avoiding, 41–42, 43, 53, 136–37
Entertaining, 264–68. *See also* Dinners; Luncheons
Erdman, Dave, 36

Ethnic identity, 21–25
Export Hotline, 230

Fax transmissions, 189–206, 233; building mailing lists and, 245; confidential, 191, 202–3; confirming, 192; equipment for, 193–94; examples of, 195–205; fax services and, 213–14, 230; first contacts and, 34; forms / cover sheets for, 195; preceding phone calls, 220; problems with, 190–92; public fax machines and, 270
Federal Express, 212–13, 287
feng shui, 49, 70
Fisher, Bill, 51–52
Flight times, 295
Formality Factor, 29–31, 34, 165–66, 179–80, 182, 184, 186, 200, 243, 250
France, 128
Fujitsu Ltd., 229, 231, 287

GATT (General Agreement on Tariffs and Trade), 3
GEnie, 231, 287
George IV (king), 154
Germany, 22
Gide, André, 57
Gifts, 42, 46–47, 264–68, 273
Government: role of, 20–21; trade offices, listing of, 280–85
Greetings, 271

hangul, 104
Harmony, concept of, 13, 46–49, 94
Hierarchy, 15–16, 94, 110
Hillblom, Larry, 212
Hinduism, 22, 27–28
Ho, Dean T. W., 227, 262
Ho Chi Minh, 128
Hongi Hika, 154

Hong Kong, 5–6, 7, 10, 14; China
and, 62, 65; contacts/information
sources in, 281–82; general information about, 67–71; marketing in,
243, 245, 286; name, title, and
address statements in, 146–47; Singapore and, 98, 99–100; Vietnam
and, 126
Human rights issues, 43, 116, 121
Hung, Frank L., 260
Hutchison Whampoa, 69

ICD (International Communications
Disorder), 5–13, 131; translation
and, 235; troubleshooting guide,
275–78
Identity, ethnic and national, 21–25,
43, 75, 85
India, 7, 27, 74
Individualism, 13–15, 20, 32, 41;
Koreans and, 103–4; language and,
136; religion and, 25, 28; toning
down, 38; in the United States,
121–22
Indonesia, 3, 5–6, 10, 12, 41; con-
tacts/information sources in, 282;
general information about, 72–78;
name, title, and address state-
ments in, 147–48; postal service
and, 210; the role of government
in, 20–21
Information highway, 7, 21, 227–40.
See also Computer(s); E-mail
Intellectual property, 100
International Public Relations, 174,
197
Internet, 7, 230–31, 287
Interpreters, 138, 238–39, 264. *See also*
Translation
Introductions, 16, 20, 31, 250–51
Ireland, 52, 53
Islamic religion, 26–27, 75

Japan, 5–8, 10, 11–12; China and, 64,
79–80; collectivism and, 14, 29;
contacts/information sources in,
282; emphasizing the positive and,
41; ethnic identity issues and, 22,
25; fax communications and, 190,
216; the Formality Factor and,
29–30, 32–33; general information
about, 78–86; gift giving in, 42,
165, 167; greeting rituals in, 271;
impression of Americans in, as
insincere, 37; Indonesia and, 75;
Korea and, 103–4, 106;
lucky/unlucky numbers in, 45–46,
48, 267; marketing in, 241, 244,
246, 247, 286; name, title, and
address statements in, 149–51; personal computer use in, 233; the
Philippines and, 94, 95; Procter &
Gamble ads in, 241; seating
arrangements in, 272; the role of
government in, 20–21; Thailand
and, 116; Vietnam and, 128, 129
Japan Direct Marketing Association,
286
Japan External Trade Organization
(JETRO), 21
Japan Mail Order Business Associa-
tion, 286
Japan Society of Translators, 288
Japan Telemarketing Association, 286
Jardine Matheson, 69
Jet lag, 251–52
Jews, 25
Joint Declaration of China and Great
Britain (1984), 65, 67–68, 70

Keating, Paul, 86
keiretsu, 14
Kelley, Nanci, 232
Kemph Technology & Investment
Company, 206

Kerr, George, 258
Kim Young-sam, 139
King and I, The, 114
Kissinger, Henry, 40
Koo, George P., 259
Korea. *See* Korean War; North Korea
    (Democratic People's Republic of
    Korea); South Korea (Republic of
    Korea)
Korean Society of Translators, 288
Korean War, 104, 105, 109
Kowloon Peninsula, 67–68, 70
Kraprayoon, Suchinda, 115
Kroma International, 206
Kuniyoshi, Ryoji, 261
Kuo Yun, 110

Ladner Downs, 175, 198
Landon, Margaret, 114
Language(s), 9, 131–38; barriers, low-
    ering, 137–38; and cultural tradi-
    tions, 135–37; dialects, 133, 217;
    differences, overview of, 133–35;
    English, troubles with, 131–33;
    ethnic identity and, 22–23; net-
    work communications and,
    233–34; second-language problems
    and, 136–37; telephone usage and,
    216–17. *See also* Interpreters; Trans-
    lation
LANs (local area networks), 227, 229,
    231, 233
Lazarus, Emma, 120
Letterhead, 34, 165–66; color and,
    46–47, 169, 179; examples of,
    171–77; fax transmissions and, 190,
    206; size of, 169; taken on trips,
    262. *See also* Addresses; Letters;
    Logos; Names; Titles
Letters, 11–12, 40, 165–70, 233; Asia-
    Pacific, basic description of,
    166–70; continuing communica-

tions and, 36–49; first contacts and,
    34–35; of introduction, 16, 31;
    sample, 179–82; "thank you," 39,
    273. *See also* Letterhead
Li Peng, 63, 145
Logos, 166, 178, 190, 206, 230, 254
"Loss of face," 41–42
Lucky/unlucky numbers, 45–46, 48,
    70, 267
Luncheons, 39, 43. *See also* Enter-
    taining
Lynn, Robert, 212

Magellan, Ferdinand, 94
Mahathir bin Mohamad, 86
Mailing lists, 211, 244–45. *See also*
    Addresses
MailWorks, 211
mai pen rai, 114
Malaysia, 3, 5–6, 10; China and, 84;
    contacts/information sources in,
    282–83; ethnic identity issues and,
    22–23, 24; general information
    about, 83–89; name, title, and
    address statements in, 151–53;
    postal service and, 210; Singapore
    and, 99, 100
Manchuria, 64
Manson, Peter A., 258
Maoris, 89–90
Mao Ze-dong, 59, 61, 64, 108
Marcos, Ferdinand, 95
Marketing, 165, 241–47; direct,
    244–47, 286; fax transmissions
    and, 192–93; translation and, 235,
    238
MCI Corporation, 229; faxing ser-
    vices, 213; MCI Mail, 231, 287;
    operators, accessing, 263
McNealy, Scott, 227, 229
Measurement conversion tables,
    296–97